PROPOSALS
THAT
WORK

SECOND EDITION

PROPOSALS THAT WORK

A Guide for Planning Dissertations and Grant Proposals

LAWRENCE F. LOCKE
WANEEN WYRICK SPIRDUSO
STEPHEN J. SILVERMAN

SAGE PUBLICATIONS
The Publishers of Professional Social Science
Newbury Park   London   New Delhi

For information address:

SAGE Publications, Inc.
2111 West Hillcrest Drive
Newbury Park, California 91320

SAGE Publications Ltd.
28 Banner Street
London EC1Y 8QE
England

SAGE Publications India Pvt. Ltd.
M-32 Market
Greater Kailash I
New Delhi 110 048 India

Printed in the United States of America

Library of Congress Cataloging-in-Publication Data

Locke, Lawrence F.
    Proposals that work.

    Bibliography: p.
    1. Proposal writing in research--Handbooks,
manuals, etc.   2. Dissertations, Academic--Handbooks,
manuals, etc.   3. Research grants--Handbooks,
manuals, etc.   4. Fund raising--Handbooks, manuals,
etc.   I. Spirduso, Waneen Wyrick.   II. Silverman,
Stephen J.   III. Title.
Q180.55.P7L63   1987   808'.066001   87-28648
ISBN   0-8039-2986-2
ISBN   0-8039-2987-0   (pbk.)

SIXTH PRINTING, 1989

Contents

PART 2 Specimen Proposals

Introduction   144

Specimen Proposals   146

APPENDICES

Preface

This guide contains no direct instruction concerning how to do research. Rather, the material herein deals with the problem of how to write a research proposal. Although the two capacities—skill in conducting research and skill in writing about plans for that research— have a close relationship, they are far from coterminous. Individuals who have acquired considerable information about the mysteries of research methods and data analysis do not necessarily know how to undertake the task of planning and effectively proposing their own investigations.

The importance and, therefore, the perceived difficulty of the proposal task will seem greater under some conditions than under others. Even the novice in research is likely to appreciate fully the significance of the research proposal in preparing a grant application. It is obvious that the probability of funding will rest mostly on the selection of a target for inquiry and the competence displayed in designing and justifying the study. A deceptively large contribution toward funding, however, is made by the clarity and style of writing in the proposal. Many excellent ideas are lost among the multitude of proposals submitted for funding because these ideas were poorly presented and the proposal was difficult to decipher. Conversely, and unhappily, some mediocre research ideas are funded because they are spectacularly presented.

In contrast, few graduate students initially recognize that preparation of the proposal will represent a major hurdle in gaining approval for their thesis or dissertation. No magic formula can make writing such an important document an easy task. When money, academic career, or both are in the balance, a great deal is at stake. Our intention in preparing this guide, however, is to reduce both the perceived and real dimensions of the hurdle.

David Krathwohl's (1966) description of the vision held by many novice researchers seems, in our experience at least, to be quite accurate: "The beginner envisions the researcher as one who dreams up creative ideas, the needed resources miraculously appear, and the hero, in a state of eager anticipation, begins his investigation" (p. 3). The experienced investigator would add a number of less romantic steps to the vision of Krathwohl's novice: the frustrating hours of searching for references that seem always to have been lost from the library, the agonies involved in producing the "miraculous appearance" of needed resources, and ultimately the long, painstaking task of communicating the "creative dream" to an overly busy advisor or a distant and skeptical review committee.

Certainly all researchers would concur in identifying the most critical omission in the novice's vision as the absence of any reference to preparing a plan for research—the proposal. Along with the interpretation of data and preparation of the final report, development of the proposal constitutes the genuinely creative element in the research process.

Conducting research, in the sense of carrying out the plan for investigation, is hard work, but in the end it demands a different type of intellectual ability and may yield less satisfaction than the process of planning the research and developing the proposal. Creating a plan for research is one fountainhead of the essential fascination that keeps talented men and women at a task more often characterized by frustration and tedium than by romance and excitement. The tongue-in-cheek maxim that holds the planning of research and interpretation of data to be the proper business of the scholar, whereas the actual gathering of data is held to be the proper business of graduate students, research assistants, or technicians, may be somewhat overstated, but it reflects a genuine truth about the day-to-day reality of research.

In the context of graduate education the research proposal plays a role that reaches beyond its simple significance as a plan of action. In most instances the decision to permit the student to embark on a thesis or dissertation is made solely on the basis of that first formal document. The quality of writing in the proposal is likely to be used by advisors as a basis for judging the clarity of thought that has preceded the document, the degree of facility with which the study will be implemented if approved, and the adequacy of expository skills the student will bring to reporting the results. In sum, the proposal is the instrument through which faculty must judge whether there is a reasonable hope that the student can conduct any research project at all.

Some readers may feel that the explanatory material contained in this guide places disproportionate emphasis on experimental and quasi-experimental forms of investigation. To the degree that this is true, such a bias reflects generic demands the authors have found likely to be encountered in the requirements for any proposal. Quite simply, our experience has been that writing about the problems of proposing an experimental study represents the most economical method for assisting readers who have a wide variety of research interests.

Proposals for historical or philosophical study must reflect canons unique to those areas of inquiry, and plans for qualitative/ethnographic research will begin with some assumptions (which we present in Chapter 4) that are foreign to the experimental paradigm. Nevertheless, all must begin with questions, must define data sources, must present plans for analysis and must persuade readers of the author's competence. For this guide, then, the value of the experiment rests not in its unique virtues, but in how much it shares in common with all models for inquiry.

Finally, a word of caution for readers who are graduate students. From time to time, it may appear that the authors have attempted to enter into a kind of "collusion" with the student for the purpose of outwitting the research advisor. The realities of university life, with which both students and their advisors are painfully familiar, make such a position difficult to avoid. Nothing, however, could be further from the authors' actual intention. If the student-advisor relationship resembles a contest, there is small chance that reference to a guide for proposal writing will be of any real assistance.

Our purpose from start to finish has been to assist in achieving one end—a fair and useful hearing for your proposed research. If the proposal is rejected, it should be because the investigation lacks sufficient merit or feasibility, not because the document has been inadequately prepared.

Suggestions for Using the Guide

This guide has been divided into two major parts: Part I, Writing the Proposal, and Part II, Specimen Proposals. The chapters that constitute Part I represent the core of the guide, serving both to present generic information that applies to all research proposals, and to discuss some of the problems peculiar to the use of proposals in graduate education and funding agencies. In Chapter 1 we present an introduction to generic elements found in nearly all proposals. In Chapter 2 we address the needs of graduate students facing the task of preparing their first research proposal. Chapters 3 and 5 contain information appropriate to both the graduate student preparing a thesis or dissertation proposal and the novice preparing a first grant proposal. The unique demands of proposing studies using the qualitative paradigm for research are addressed in Chapter 4. The last two chapters, 6 and 7, are directed specifically to those interested in preparing submissions to funding agencies. Finally, in Part II four sample proposals are presented. The sections of the first proposal relate directly to each of the tasks presented in Chapter 1. We have provided a short commentary with each section of this proposal to highlight the key elements. The final three proposals are presented with critical evaluations that illuminate their individual strengths and weaknesses. These proposals represent a wide variety of strategies. The specimens include both successful graduate student proposals and a funded grant proposal.

Readers with different backgrounds will find it useful to employ different methods in using this guide. Those who are completely inexperienced in writing proposals should begin with Chapter 1, which deals with the basic functions of the proposal. Each task is illustrated by a corresponding section in the first proposal in Part II. Readers may wish to continue reading in Part II, which then presents three other examples with different research designs. There they can select an additional proposal to skim quickly, noting how the basic functions are performed. This will make it possible to return to the remaining discussion of content and format with an appreciation of the proposal task based on a concrete illustration.

Readers with some previous experience in research may wish to turn directly to Chapter 2, which deals with specific problems in identifying research topics and initiating the proposal process. Alternately, experienced students or faculty interested in the particular demands and problems presented by the grant proposal should begin with Chapter 6, subsequently turning to other sections of the guide as needed. Readers interested in preparing proposals for qualitative research should read Chapter 4, examine the specimen proposal using a qualitative research design in Part II, and then turn to other parts of the text as needed.

A helpful activity for many readers will be to study the list of general standards for judging the acceptability of a proposal (Appendix A). Although these have been written from the perspective of student thesis and dissertation research, the content standards are equally applicable to grant proposals or plans for investigation at any level. With an understanding of the criteria commonly used in reviewing proposals it should then be possible to form some critical judgments about the adequacy of the specimen proposals in Part II. This exercise will ensure that the reader has grasped the essential elements in preparing a sound proposal.

If particular points of content or style in the specimen proposals present difficulty, it may be helpful to consult the accompanying critique or the corresponding section of general discussion in Chapter 5. In some instances the reader may wish to refer to a more extensive or specialized text selected from Appendix B, which contains an annotated bibliography of supplementary materials having particular relevance to the proposal process.

Finally, before embarking on the construction of a proposal, we urge all readers to review Chapter 3, which deals with special problems in the presentation of proposals. Familiarity with the items in this group of commonly encountered difficulties can both forewarn and forearm the novice researcher, saving time by directing attention to problems that must be confronted in all plans for scientific inquiry.

Acknowledgements

As in many complex writing endeavors, this guide is the product of many persons whose names do not appear on the cover. First, we would like to thank the students in our classes at the University of Texas at Austin and the University of Massachusetts at Amherst who used earlier versions of this text and provided helpful advice for revision. Marv Eisen, John MacDonald, Lance Osborne, and Mary Schatzkamer wrote the excellent specimen proposals used in this guide. We particularly appreciate their willingness to allow us to reprint and critique their work. Professor Claire Weinstein, our good colleague at the University of Texas, provided helpful assistance in locating useful proposals. Professors Patt Dodds, Pat Griffin, and Earl Seidman reviewed an early draft of Chapter 4 and offered many useful suggestions. Special appreciation goes to Kim Graber, whose keen eye and remarkable sense of good order trapped many defects before they could become public embarrassments. Finally, our thanks to Cindy Mills, who typed much of the working manuscript, often from handwritten copy, that we invariably wanted "as soon as possible" and completed that difficult task with precision, punctuality, and good humor.

PART I

Writing the Proposal

Chapter 1

THE FUNCTION OF THE PROPOSAL

A proposal sets forth both the exact nature of the matter to be investigated and a detailed account of the methods to be employed. In addition, the proposal usually contains material supporting the importance of the topic selected and the appropriateness of the research methods to be employed.

Function

A proposal may function in at least three ways: as a means of communication, as a plan, as a contract.

Communication

The proposal serves to communicate the investigator's research plans to those who provide consultation, give consent, or disburse funds. The document is the primary resource on which the graduate student's thesis or dissertation committee must base the functions of review, consultation, and, more important, approval for implementation of the research project. It also serves a similar function for persons holding the purse strings of foundations or governmental funding agencies. The quality of assistance, the economy of consultation, and the probability of financial support will all depend directly on the clarity and thoroughness of the proposal.

Plan

The proposal serves as a plan for action. All empirical research consists of careful, systematic, and pre-planned observations of some restricted set of phenomena. The acceptability of results is judged exclusively in terms of the adequacy of the methods employed in making, recording, and interpreting the planned observations. Accordingly, the plan for observation, with its supporting arguments and explications, is the basis on which the thesis, dissertation or research report will be judged.

The research report can be no better than the plan of investigation. Hence, an adequate proposal sets forth the plan in step-by-step detail. The existence of a detailed plan that incorporates the most careful anticipation of problems to be confronted and contingent courses of action is the most powerful insurance against oversight or ill-considered choices during the execution phase of the investigation. The hallmark of a good proposal is a level of thoroughness and detail sufficient to permit another investigator to replicate the study, that is, to perform the same planned observations with results not substantially different from those the author might obtain.

Contract

A completed proposal, approved for execution and signed by all members of the sponsoring committee, constitutes a bond of agreement between the student and the advisors. An approved grant proposal results in a contract between the investigator (and often the university) and a funding source. The approved proposal describes a study that, if conducted competently and completely, should provide the basis for a report that would meet all standards for acceptability. Accordingly, once the contract has been made, all but minor changes should be supported by arguments for absolute necessity or compelling desirability.

With the single exception of plans for qualitative research (see Chapter 4), proposals for theses and dissertations should be in final form prior to the collection of data. Under most circumstances, substantial revisions should be made only with the explicit consent of the full committee. Once the document is approved in final form, neither the student nor the sponsoring faculty members should be free to alter the fundamental terms of the contract by unilateral decision.

Regulations Governing Proposals

All funding agencies have their own guidelines for submissions and these should be followed exactly. In the university, however, no set of universal rules or guidelines presently exists to govern the form or content of the research proposal. There may be, however, several sources of regulation governing the form and content of the final research report. Because the proposal sets forth a plan of action that must eventuate in a report conforming to these latter regulations, it is important to consider them in writing the proposal.

Although it is evident that particular traditions have evolved within individual university departments, any formal limitation on the selection of either topic or method of investigation is rarely imposed. Normally the planning and execution of student research are circumscribed by existing departmental policy on format for the final report, university regulations concerning theses and dissertation reports, and informal standards exercised by individual advisors or study committees.

Usually departmental and university regulations regarding graduate student proposals are either so explicit as to be perfectly clear (e.g., "The proposal may not exceed 25 typewritten pages" or "The proposal will conform to the style established in W. C. Campbell, *Form and Style in Thesis Writing*"), or so general as to impose no specific or useful standard (e.g., "The research topic must be of suitable proportions" or "The proposal must reflect a thorough knowledge of the problem area"). The student, therefore, should find no serious difficulty in developing a proposal that conforms to departmental and university regulations.

Another potential source of regulation, the individual thesis or dissertation committee, constitutes an important variable in the development of the thesis or dissertation proposal. Sponsoring committee members may have strong personal commitments concerning particular working procedures, writing styles, or proposal format. The student must confront these as a unique constellation of demands that will influence the form of the proposal. It always is wise to anticipate conflicting demands and to attempt their resolution before the collection of data and the preparation of a final report.

Committees are unlikely to make style and format demands that differ substantially from commonly accepted modes of research writing. As a general rule, most advisors subscribe to the broad guidelines outlined in this document. Where differences occur, they are likely to be matters of emphasis or largely mechanical items (e.g., inclusion of particular subheadings within the document).

General Considerations

Most problems in proposal preparation are straightforward and relatively obvious. The common difficulties do not involve the subtle and complex problems of design and data management. They arise instead from the most basic elements of the research process: What is the proper question to ask? Where is the best place to look for the answer? How best to standardize, quantify, and record observations? Determining the answers to these questions remains the most common obstacle to the development of adequate proposals.

Simplicity, clarity, and parsimony are the standards of writing that reflect adequate thinking about the research problem. Complicated matters are best communicated when they are the objects of simple, well-edited prose. In the early stage of development, the only way to obtain prompt and helpful assistance is to provide advisors with a document that is easily and correctly understood. At the final stage, approval of the study will hinge not only on how carefully the plan has been designed, but also on how well that design has been communicated. In the mass of detail that goes into the planning of a research study, the writer must not forget that the proposal's most immediate function is to inform readers quickly and accurately.

The problem in writing a proposal is essentially the same as in writing the final report. When the task of preparing a proposal is well executed, the task of preparing the final report is more than half done (an important consideration for the graduate student with an eye on university deadlines). Under ideal conditions, such minor changes as altering the tense of verbs will convert the proposal into the opening chapters of the thesis or dissertation, or into initial sections of a research report.

Many proposals evolve through a series of steps. Preliminary discussion with colleagues and faculty members may lead to a series of drafts that evolve toward a final document presented at a formal meeting of the full dissertation or thesis committee, or to a proposal submitted through the university hierarchy to a funding source. This process of progressive revision can be accelerated and made more productive by following these simple rules:

(1) Prepare clean, updated copies of the evolving proposal and submit them to advisors or colleagues in advance of scheduled consultations.
(2) Prepare an agenda of questions and problems to be discussed and submit them in advance of scheduled consultations.
(3) Keep a carefully written and dated record of all discussions and decisions that occur with regard to each item on the consultation agenda.

A number of research textbooks and form guides are available to help in developing an adequate proposal. In addition, checklists now exist for reviewing the adequacy of proposals for several specific types of research. Appendix B contains a list of such material.

A useful document for many may be Davitz and Davitz, *Evaluating Research Proposals in the Behavioral Sciences* (1977). This short treatise should be read and reread before actual work on the proposal begins. The checklist of questions provided by Davitz and Davitz should be applied and specific answers noted at each new stage of the proposal's development.

A list of general standards for judging the acceptability of a thesis or dissertation proposal is provided in Appendix A. This list can serve both as a preliminary guide for anticipating problems in development of the proposal and as a checklist to use in revising and refining the final document.

General Format

Guidelines for the format of proposals, even when intended only as general suggestions, often have an unfortunate influence on the writing process. Once committed to paper, such guidelines quickly tend to acquire the status of mandatory prescription. In an attempt to conform to what they perceive as an invariate format, students produce proposal documents that are awkward and illogical as plans for action, as well as stilted and tasteless as prose.

Some universities and many funding agencies make very specific demands for the format of proposals. Others provide general guidelines for form and content. Whatever the particular situation confronting the writer, it is vital to remember that *there is no universally applicable and correct format for the research proposal.* Each research plan requires that certain communication tasks be accomplished, some that are common to all proposals and others that are unique to the specific form of inquiry. Taken together, however, the tasks encompassed by all proposals demand that what is written fit the real topic at hand, not some preconceived ideal. It is flexibility, not rigidity, that makes strong proposal documents.

Specific Tasks

The following paragraphs specify communication tasks that are present in nearly all proposals for empirical research. Each proposal, however, will demand its own unique arrangement of these functions. Within a given proposal the tasks may or may not be identified by such traditional section designations as "Background," "Importance of the Study," "Review of Literature," "Methodology," "Definitions," or "Limitations." Individual proposals are sure to demand changes in the order of presentation, or attention to other tasks not specified below. This particularly will be the case with some of the tasks that are specific to grant proposals (see Chapter 7). Finally, it is important to note that adjacent tasks in the following list often may be merged into single sections.

As you read each of the tasks below, if you want an example you can turn to the first proposal in Part II. In this particular specimen, we have edited the proposal so the sections correspond to the tasks that follow. We have provided a critique preceding each section to summarize the suggestions presented in this chapter. After you have completed this chapter, you may observe the continuity of the specimen proposal by rereading all of the sections in sequence.

Introducing the study

Proposals, like other forms of written communication, are best introduced by a short, meticulously devised statement that establishes the overall area of concern, arouses interest, and communicates information essential to the reader's comprehension of what follows. The standard here is "gentle introduction," which avoids both tedious length and the shock of technical detail or abstruse argument. A careful introduction is the precursor of the next three tasks (statement, rationale, and background) and may, in fact, simply be written as the opening paragraph(s) of an initial section that includes all three.

For most proposals, the easiest and most effective way to introduce the study is to identify and define the central construct(s) involved. In the sense that constructs are concepts that provide an abstract symbolization of some observable attribute or phenomenon, all studies employ constructs. Constructs such as intelligence or teacher enthusiasm are utilized in research by defining them in terms of some observable event, that is, "intelligence" as defined by a test score, or "teacher enthusiasm" as defined by a set of classroom behaviors. When the reader asks, "What is this study about?" the best answer is to present the key constructs and explain how they will be represented in the investigation. The trick in these opening paragraphs of introduction is to sketch the study in the bold strokes of major constructs without usurping the function of more detailed sections that will follow.

Relationships among constructs that will be of particular interest or about which explicit hypotheses will be developed should be briefly noted. Constructs with which the reader probably is familiar may be ignored in the introduction for they are of less interest than the relationships proposed by the author.

The most common error in introducing research is failure to get to the point—usually a consequence of engaging in grand generalizations. For instance, in a proposed study of attributes contributing to balance ability the opening paragraph might contain a sentence such as "The child's capacity to maintain balance is a factor of fundamental importance in the design of elementary school curriculum." The significance of the construct "balance" in accomplishing motor tasks may make it an attribute of some importance in early childhood education, but that point may be far from the heart of a study involving balance. If, for example, the proposed study deals with the relationship of muscle strength to balance, observations about balance as a factor in the design of school curriculum belong, if anywhere, in a later discussion. What belongs up front is a statement that gets to the point: "The task of maintaining static balance requires muscular action to hold the pelvis in a horizontal position. When muscle strength is inadequate to accomplish this, performance is impaired."

Some indication of the importance of the study to theory or practice may be used to help capture the reader's interest, but in the introduction it is not necessary to explain completely all of the study's significance. Present the basic facts first and leave the detail of thorough discussion until a more appropriate point. Use of unnecessary technical language is another impediment to the reader's ability to grasp the main idea. Similarly, the use of quotations and extensive references are intrusions into what should be a clear, simple preliminary statement. Documentation of important points can wait until a full discussion of the problem is launched.

Stating the question

Early in the proposal, often in the introductory paragraph(s), it is wise to set forth an explicit statement of the question to which the investigation will be directed. The statement need not include all subtopics, nor need it be written in the language of formal research questions or hypotheses. It should, however, provide a specific and accurate synopsis of the primary target for the study. An early and specific announcement of this kind satisfies the reader's most pressing need. Such information allows the reader to attend to the author's subsequent exposition and topic development without the nagging sense that the main object of the study has yet to be discovered. Consequently, it is useful to give an opening statement of the question high visibility.

Providing a rationale

Once the reader understands the topic of investigation, the next logical points to be confronted are "Why bother with that question?" and "Is the basic formulation of the question correct?" In explaining why the study is a worthwhile endeavor the author can point to potential utility of results in either or both of two domains: what might be contributed to the evolving structure of knowledge, or what application might be made in a practical setting. The particular form selected for the research question is supported by explanation of why major elements in the study were formulated in a particular way: for example, why particular relationships are proposed, or why particular events or attributes are singled out for observation and description.

Persuasive logic and documentation with factual evidence are what convince readers, but no rationale can be effective until it is clear. To this end it often is helpful to diagram the factors and relationships that support your formulation of the problem. Suppose the proposed hypothesis for an experimental study was that male subjects, aged 60 to 70 years, who exercised daily for six months would have faster reaction time (RT) than a group of unexercised controls. The implication of this complex statement is that there may be a relationship between physical fitness and reactive capacity in older men. The reasons for such a supposition can be diagrammed in simple form.

Assuming that the constructs have been defined. the rationale now can be developed simply by explaining and documenting the information in the boxes.

In most cases this early attention to rationale should be limited to the larger issues of clarifying and justifying major assumptions. The detail of rationale for particular choices in methodology or analysis can be deferred until such matters are discussed in subsequent parts of the proposal.

Formulating questions or hypotheses

All proposals must arrive at a formal statement of questions or hypotheses. These may be set aside as a separate section or simply

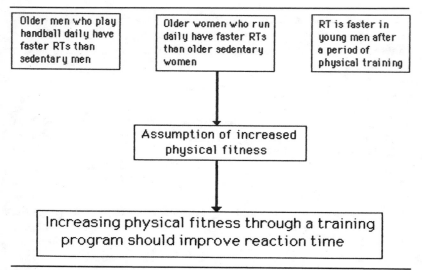

Figure 1.1

included in the course of other discussion. Such statements differ from what was contained in the statement of the question in that (1) they are normally stated in formal terms appropriate to the design and analysis of data to be employed, and (2) they display, in logical order, all subparts of the research topic.

The question form is most appropriate when the research is exploratory. The researcher should indicate by the specificity of questions, however, that the problem has been subject to thorough analysis. By careful formulation of questions, the proposed study should be directed toward suspected alternatives rather than toward a scanning of "interesting" findings.

The hypothesis form is employed when the state of existing knowledge and theory permits formulation of reasonable predictions about the relationship of variables. Hypotheses ordinarily have their origin in theoretical propositions already established in the review of literature. Because the proposal must ensure that the reader grasps how the relationships expressed in theory have been translated into the form of testable hypotheses, it often is useful to provide a succinct restatement of the theoretical framework at a point contiguous to the presentation of formal research hypotheses.

The most common difficulty in formulating a research question is the problem of clarity. Students who have read and studied in the area of their topic for weeks or months often are chagrined to discover how difficult it is to reduce all they want to discover to a single, unambiguous question.

The clarity of a research question hinges on adequate specificity and the correct degree of inclusiveness. The major elements of the investigation must be identified in a way that permits no confusion with other elements. At the same time the statement must maintain simplicity by including nothing beyond what is essential to identify the main variables and any relationships that may be proposed among them. Questions for quantitative studies, for example, must meet three tests of clarity and inclusiveness:

(1) Is the question free of ambiguity?
(2) Is a relationship among variables expressed?
(3) Does the question imply an empirical test?

By applying these standards to the question "Is there a relationship between strength and balance in children?" the study's main elements apparently are identified in reasonably clear fashion. Strength and balance are variables and children are the subject population. A relationship is suggested and correlation of strength and balance scores clearly is implied as an appropriate empirical test of the relationship. The constructs of strength and balance, however, are quite broad and might be taken by some readers to indicate variables different from those intended. These potential sources of ambiguity might be resolved without destroying the simplicity of the question by altering it to ask, "Does a relationship exist between hip abductor strength and static balance in children?" Whether it also might be important to provide more specificity for the generic word "children" would depend on whether the intent was to examine strength and balance in a particular type of child. If not, the generic word would be adequate. If so, the importance of the restriction calls for more careful specification in the question.

Research *hypotheses* differ from research *questions* in that hypotheses both indicate the question in testable form and predict the nature of the answer. A clear question is readily transformed into a hypothesis by casting it in the form of a declarative statement that can be tested so as to show it to be either true or false. Getting exactly the hypothesis that is wanted, however, often is more exacting than it appears.

Unlike a question, the hypothesis exerts a direct influence on each subsequent step of the study, from design to preparation of the final report. By specifying a prediction about outcome, the hypothesis creates a bridge between the theoretical considerations that underlie the question and the ensuing research process designed to produce the answer. The investigator is limited to procedures that will test the truth of the proposed relationship, and any implications to be deduced from the results will rest entirely on the particular test selected. Because it exerts such powerful a priori influence, a hypothesis demands consider-able attention at the start of a study, but makes it easier to preserve objectivity in the later stages of design and execution.

Aside from specific impact on design of the study, the general advantage of the hypothesis over the question is that it permits more powerful and persuasive conclusions. At the end of a study, a research question never permits the investigator to say more than "Here is how the world looked when I observed it." In contrast, hypotheses permit the investigator to say "Based on my particular explanation of how the world works, this is what I expected to observe and behold; that is exactly how it looked! For that reason my explanation of how the world works must be given credibility." When a hypothesis is confirmed, the investigator is empowered to make arguments about knowledge that go far beyond what is available when a question has been asked and answered.

A hypothesis can be written either as a null statement (conveniently called a null hypothesis), "There is no difference between . . .," or as a directional statement indicating the kind of relationship anticipated (called a research or directional hypothesis): "When this, also that" (positive), or "When this, not that" (negative). There are some clear technical advantages to using the null format, particularly when inferential statistics will be used to analyze the data. (See one of the general textbooks on research design reviewed in Appendix B.) Research specialists are not in agreement on the wisdom of writing hypotheses in directional form. Some arguments favor the use of directionality because it permits more persuasive logic and more statistical power. Other arguments, however, favor exclusive use of the null format.

That technical debate is beyond the scope of this guide, but a good rule of thumb for the novice is to employ directional hypotheses when pilot data are available that clearly indicate a direction, or when the theory from which the hypotheses were drawn is sufficiently robust to include some persuasive evidence for directionality. If the investigation is a preliminary exploration in an area for which there is no well-established theory, and if it has been impossible to gather enough pilot data to provide modest confidence in a directional prediction, the format of the null hypothesis is the better choice. Ultimately, as a researcher pursues a line of questioning through several investigations, directional hypotheses become more obvious and the null format less attractive.

Hypotheses can be evaluated by the same criteria used to examine research questions (lack of ambiguity, expression of relationship, and implication of appropriate test). In addition, the statement must be formulated so that the entire prediction can be dealt with in a single test. If the hypothesis is so complex that one portion could be rejected without also rejecting the remainder, it requires rewriting.

Several small, perfectly testable hypotheses always are preferable to one that is larger and amorphous. For example, in the following hypothesis the word "but" signals trouble. "Males are significantly faster in reaction time than females, but male athletes are not significantly faster than nonathletes." The F test for the main effect of sex in the implied analysis of variance (ANOVA) will handily deal with males and females, but a separate test as a part of a factorial ANOVA would be required for athletes and nonathletes. Should the tests yield opposite results, the hypothesis would point in two directions at once.

Similarly, the presence of two discrete dependent variables fore-shadows difficulty in the following example: "Blood pressures on each of 5 days will be significantly lower than the preceding day, whereas heart rate will not decrease significantly after day 3." The implied ANOVA would have to be applied twice. Even a multiple analysis of variance (MANOVA) could not rescue the hypothesis by indicating whether we could accept or reject it. The required follow-up test might reject the blood pressure prediction while accepting that for heart rate. In all such cases division into smaller, unitary hypotheses is the obvious cure.

When there are a number of hypotheses, as a result of interest in interaction effects or as a consequence of employing more than one dependent variable, the primary hypotheses should be stated first. These primary statements may even be separated from hypotheses that are secondary or confirmatory, as a means of giving prominence to the main intent of the study.

Finally, hypotheses should be formulated with an eye to the qualitative characteristics of available measurement tools. If, for example, the hypothesis specifies the magnitude of relationship between two variables, it is essential that this be supportable by the reliability of the proposed instrumentation. Returning to the earlier example of strength and balance, the fact should be considered that the correlation between scores from two tests cannot exceed the square root of the product for reliability in each test. Accordingly, if reliability of the static balance test is .68 and the hip abductor test is .76, then a hypothesis of a positive correlation greater than .80 is doomed to failure ($\sqrt{.76 \times .68} = .72$).

Delimitations and limitations

Often a listing of delimitations and limitations is required to clarify the proposed study. Delimitations describe the populations to which generalizations may be safely made. The generalizability of the study will be a function of the subject sample and the analysis employed. Delimit literally means to define the limits inherent in the use of a particular construct or population.

Limitations, as used in the context of a research proposal, refer to limiting conditions or restrictive weaknesses. There are times when all factors cannot be controlled as a part of study design, or when the optimal number of observations simply cannot be made because of problems involving ethics or feasibility. If the investigator has given careful thought to these problems, and has determined that the information to be gained from the compromised aspect of the study is nevertheless valid and useful, then the investigator proceeds but duly notes the limitation.

All studies have inherent delimitations and limitations. Whether these are listed in a separate section or simply discussed as they arise is an individual decision. If they are few in number and perfectly obvious, the latter is desirable. Whatever format is used, however, it is the investigator's responsibility to understand these constraints and to assure the reader that they have been considered during the formulation of the study.

Providing definitions

All proposals for research use systematic language that may be specific to that field of research or to that proposal. We discuss the use of definitions in greater detail in the section of Chapter 5 titled "Clarity and Precision: Speaking in System Language."

Discussing the background of the problem

Any research problem must show its lineage from the background of existing knowledge, previous investigations, or, in the case of applied research, from contemporary practice. The author must answer three questions:

(1) What do we already know or do? (The purpose here, in one or two sentences, is to support the legitimacy and importance of the question. Major discussions of the importance and significance of the study will come under the "significance of the study" section.)

(2) How does this particular question relate to what we already know or do? (The purpose here is to explain and support the exact form of questions or hypotheses that serve as the focus for the study.)

(3) Why select this particular method of investigation? (The purpose here is to explain and support the selections made from among alternative methods of investigation.)

In reviewing the research literature that often forms the background for the study, the author's task is to indicate the main directions taken by workers in the area and the main issues of methodology and interpretation that have arisen. Particular attention must be given to a critical analysis of previous methodology and the exposition of the advantages and limitations inherent in various alternatives. Close attention must be given to conceptual and theoretical formulations that are explicit or implicit within the selected studies.

By devising, when appropriate, a theoretical basis for the study that emerges from the structure of existing knowledge, by making the questions or hypotheses emerge from the total matrix of answered and unanswered questions, and, by making the selection of method contingent upon previous results, the author inserts the proposed study into a line of inquiry and a developing body of knowledge. Such careful attention to background is the first step in entering the continuing conversation that is science.

The author should select only those studies that provide a foundation for the proposed investigation, discuss these studies in sufficient detail to make their relevance entirely clear, note explicitly the ways in which they contribute to the proposed research, and give some indication of how the proposal is designed to move beyond earlier work. The first section of Chapter 3 provides guidelines for preparing the literature review.

It is important for students and novice proposal writers to resist the impulse to display both the extent of their personal labors in achieving what they know and the volume of interesting but presently irrelevant information accumulated in the process. The rule in selecting studies for review is exactly the same as that used throughout the proposal—limit discussion to what is essential to the main topic. A complete list of all references used in developing the proposal (properly called a bibliography as distinct from the list of references) may be placed in an appendix, thereby providing both a service to the interested reader and some psychological relief to the writer.

Whenever possible, the author should be conceptually or theoretically clear by creating organizing frameworks that encompass both the reviewed studies and the proposed research. This may take the form of something as obvious and practical as grouping studies according to certain methodological features (often for the purpose of examining divergent results), or something as esoteric as identifying and grouping the implicit assumptions made by various researchers in formulating their statement of the problem (often for the purpose of clarifying the problem elected in the present proposal).

In many proposals, creating an organized conceptual framework represents the most important single opportunity for the application of original thought. In one sense, the organizing task is an extension of the need to achieve clarity in communication. A category system that allows division of diverse ideas or recondite events into easily perceived and remembered subsets is an organizational convenience for the author, as well as for the reader. Beyond convenience, however, organizing frameworks identify distinctive threads of thought. The task is to isolate the parallel ways by which researchers, working at different times and in varying degrees of intellectual isolation, have conceived of reality. In creating a schema that deals meaningfully with similarities and dissimilarities in the work of others, the author not only contributes to the body of knowledge, but also deals with the immediate need of communicating this research to others.

Even relatively simple organizing or integrating systems demand the development of underlying conceptual plans and, often, new ways of interpreting old results and presumed relationships. The sequence of variables in the study may provide a simple and generally adequate place to begin arranging the review. Such questions as "What is the relationship between social class and school achievement when ability is held constant?" consist of concepts placed within a convenient sequential diagram. In turn, such conceptual schemata often contain useful assumption about causal relationships and thus can serve as effective precursors to explanatory theory. The most elegant kind of research proposals achieve exactly that kind of linkage, using the framework for organizing the review of literature as a bridge connecting existing knowledge, a proposed theory, and the specific, theory-based hypotheses to be empirically tested.

Explaining procedures

All proposals for empirical research must embody a plan for the careful and systematic observation of events. The methods selected for such observations determine the quality of data obtained. For this reason, the portion of the proposal dealing with procedures the researcher intends to employ will be subject to the closest critical scrutiny. Correspondingly, the presentation of methodology requires great attention to detail. The discussion of method must include sources of data, the collection of data, and the analysis of data. In addition, the discussion must show that the specific techniques selected will not fall short of the claims established in previous sections of the proposal.

The section(s) dealing with methodology must be freely adapted to the purpose of the study. Whatever the format, however, the proposal must provide a step-by-step set of instructions for conducting the investigation. For example, many studies demand explication of the following items:

(1) identification and description of the target population and sampling methods to be used;
(2) presentation of instruments and techniques for measurement;
(3) presentation of a design for the collection of data;
(4) presentation of procedures for collecting and recording data;
(5) explanation of data analysis procedures to be used;
(6) development of plans for contingencies such as subject mortality.

Many justifications for particular method selections will emerge in the development of background for the problem. The rationale for some choices, however, will most conveniently be presented when the method is introduced as part of the investigation plan.

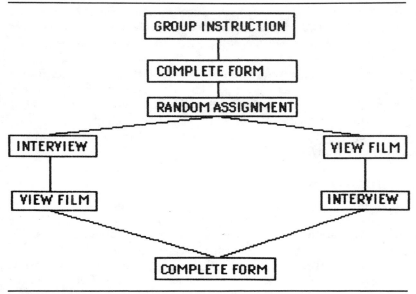

Figure 1.2

In describing such elements, proposals can include pages of description that fatigue and frustrate the reader without yielding a clear picture of the overall pattern. In many cases this problem can be avoided by the use of diagrams. Although the Figure 1.2 displays a counterbalanced treatment design of moderate complexity, it would require no more than a brief paragraph of accompanying text to provide a clear account of the procedure.

When data are to be gathered from multiple subject groups the proposal can consume pages of explanatory text without providing the reader with an adequate sense of how subject variables are related. Figure 1.3, however, shows a subject population divided into 16 subgroups using the four variables of gender, role, education level, and affective state. Given a brief introduction, most readers find further explanation unnecessary.

Providing supplementary material

For the purpose of clarity and economical presentation, many items may be placed in appendices keyed to appropriate references in the main

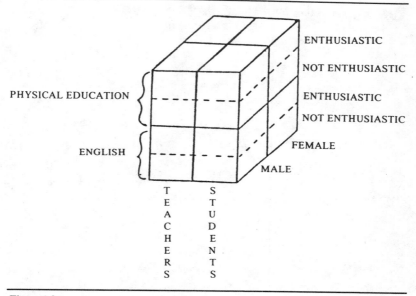

Figure 1.3

text. So placed, such materials become options available to the reader as needed, rather than distractions or impediments to understanding the main themes of the proposal. Included in the appendices may be such items as the following:

(1) specifications for equipment;
(2) instructions to subjects;
(3) letters and other relevant documents;
(4) subject consent forms;
(5) raw data or tabular material from pilot studies;
(6) tabular materials from related research;
(7) copies of paper and pencil instruments;
(8) questions for structured interviews;
(9) credentials of experts, judges, or other special personnel to be employed in the study;
(10) diagrammatic models of the research design;
(11) diagrammatic models of the statistical analysis;
(12) schematics for constructed equipment;

(13) chapter outline for the final report;
(14) proposed time schedule for executing the study; and
(15) supplementary bibliographies.

Chapter 2

DEVELOPING THE THESIS OR DISSERTATION PROPOSAL

Some Common Problems

The general purposes and broad format of the proposal document have now been presented. There remain, however, a number of particular points that cause a disproportionate amount of difficulty in preparing proposals for student-conducted research. In some cases, the problems arise because of real difficulty in the subtle and complex nature of the writing task. In other cases, however, the problems are a consequence of confusion, conflicting opinions, and ambiguous standards among research workers themselves and, more particularly, among university research advisors.

As with many tasks involving an element of art, it is possible to establish a few general rules to which most practitioners subscribe. Success in terms of real mastery, however, lies not in knowing or even following the rules, but in what the student learns to do within the rules.

Each student will discover his or her own set of special problems. Some will be solved only through practice and the accumulation of experience. While wrestling with the frustrations of preparing a proposal, the student should try to remember that the real fascination of research lies in its problematic nature, in the search for serviceable hypotheses, in selecting sensitive means of analyzing data, and in the creative tasks of study design.

Some of the problems graduate students face cannot be solved simply by reading about them. What follows, however, is an effort to alert you to the most common pitfalls, to provide some general suggestions for resolution of the problems, and to sound one encouraging note: Consultation with colleagues and advisors, patience with the often slow process of "figuring out," and scrupulous care in writing will overcome or circumvent most of the problems encountered in preparing a research proposal. In the midst of difficulty, it is useful to remember that problems are better encountered when developing the proposal than when facing a deadline for a final copy of the report.

The problems have been grouped into two broad sections: "Before the Proposal: First Things First," and "The Sequence of Proposing: From Selecting a Topic to Oral Presentation." Each section contains a number of specific issues that may confront the student researcher, and provides some rules of thumb for use in avoiding or resolving the attendant difficulties. Readers should skim through the two sections selectively, since not all of the discussions will be relevant to their needs. Chapter 3 ("Content of the Proposal: Important Considerations") and Chapter 5 ("Style and Form in Writing a Proposal") deal with specific technical problems and should be consulted after Chapter 2.

BEFORE THE PROPOSAL: FIRST THINGS FIRST

Making Your Decision: Do You Really Want to Do It?

An idealized sequence of events leads to a thesis or dissertation proposal.

A. In the process of completing undergraduate or master's level preparation, the student identifies an area of particular interest in which he or she proposes to concentrate advanced study.
B. The student selects a graduate institution that has a strong reputation for research and teaching in the area of interest.
C. The student identifies an advisor who has published extensively and regularly chairs graduate student research in the area of interest.
D. Based on further study and interaction with the advisor, the student selects and formulates a question or hypothesis as the basis for a thesis or dissertation.

As we do not live in the best of all possible worlds, few students are able to pursue the steps of this happy and logical sequence. For a variety of reasons, most students have to take at least one of the steps in reverse. Some even find themselves at the end of several semesters of study just beginning to identify a primary area of interest, in an institution that may be less than perfectly appropriate to their needs, and assigned to an advisor who has little or no experience in that particular domain. For this unfortunate state of affairs, we offer no easy solution. We do believe that one significant decision is, or should be, available to the student— the decision to do, or not to do, a research study. Faced with conditions like those described above, if the option is available, the more rational and educationally profitable course may be to elect not to undertake a research study. You can determine whether this option is available before the school is selected, or at least before the program of study is selected.

There are good and substantial reasons to believe that experience in the conduct of research contributes to graduate education. There also are good and substantial reasons to believe that other kinds of experiences are immeasurably more appropriate and profitable for some students. The question is, "Which experience is right for you?"

If you are, or think you might be, headed for a career in scholarship and higher education, then the decision is clear. The sooner you begin accumulating experience in research activities, the better. If you are genuinely curious about the workings of the research process, interested in combining inquiry with a career of professional service, or fascinated by the problems associated with a particular application of knowledge to practice, again the decision is clear. An experience in research presents at least a viable alternative in your educational plans.

Lacking one of these motives, the decision should swing the other way, toward an option more suited to your needs. Inadequately motivated research tends not to be completed or, worse, is finished in a pedestrian fashion far below the student's real capacity. Even a well-executed thesis or dissertation may exert a powerful negative influence on the graduate experience when it has not been accepted by the student as a reasonable and desirable task.

One problem touches everyone in graduate education, faculty and students alike—the hard constraints of time. Students want to finish their degree programs in a reasonable period of time. The disposition or circumstance of some, however, may define reasonable time as "the shortest possible time." Others find the thought of any extension beyond the standard number of semesters a serious threat to their sense of adequacy. For students such as these, a thesis or dissertation is a risky venture.

Relatively few research studies finish on schedule, and time require-ments invariably are underestimated. Frequent setbacks are almost inevitable. This is one aspect of the research process that is learned during the research experience. Haste in research is lethal to both quality of the product and worth of the experience. If you cannot spend the time, deciding to do research endangers the area of inquiry, your advisor, your institution, your education, your reputation, and any satisfaction you might take in completing the task. In short, if you can't afford the time, then don't do it at all.

Choosing Your Turf: Institutions, Advisors, and Areas

Once a firm decision has been made to write a thesis or dissertation, the choice of an advisor presents a less difficult problem. Here, area of interest dictates selection because it is essential to have an advisor who is knowledgeable. Further, it always is preferable to have one who is actively publishing in the domain of interest.

Competent advisement is so important that a degree of student flexibility may be required. It is far better for students to adjust their interest to accommodate work that is somewhat peripheral to their long-range goals than to attempt research on a topic with which their advisor is completely unfamiliar. It may be necessary for the thesis or dissertation to be part of the advisor's own research program; but so long as the topic remains within the broad areas of student interest, it is possible to gain vital experience in formulating questions, designing studies, and applying the technology and methods of inquiry that are generic to the domain.

It is desirable for student and advisor to interact throughout the development of the proposal, beginning with the initial selection and formulation of the question. On occasion, however, the student may bring an early stage proposal to a prospective advisor as a test of his or her interest or to encourage acceptance of formal appointment as advisor. Experience suggests that this strategy is most likely to produce immediate results if the proposal is in the primary interest area of the advisor. If the proposal involves replication of some aspect of the advisor's previous research, the student may be amazed at the intensity of attention this attracts.

Finding Your Question: What Don't We Know That Matters?

Before launching into the process of identifying a suitable topic for inquiry, we suggest a short course of semantic and conceptual hygiene.

The purpose of this small therapy is to establish a simple and reliable set of terms for thinking through what can sometimes be a difficult and lengthy problem—what do I study?

All research emerges from a perceived problem, some unsatisfactory situation in the world that we want to confront. Sometimes the difficulty rests simply in the fact that we don't understand how things work and have the human itch to know. At other times we are confronted by decisions or the need for action when the alternatives or consequences are unclear. Such perceived problems are experienced as a disequilibrium, a dissonance in our cognition. Notice, however, they do not exist out in the world, but in our minds.

That may sound at first like one of those "nice points" of which academics are sometimes fond, but for the purposes of a novice researcher, locating the problem in the right place and setting up our understanding of exactly what is unsatisfactory may represent much more than an arbitrary exercise. Thinking clearly about problems, questions, hypotheses, and research purposes can prevent mental log jams that sometimes block or delay clear identification of what is to be investigated.

The novice will encounter research reports, proposals, and even some well-regarded textbooks that freely interchange the words "problem" and "question" in ways that create all sorts of logical confusion (as in "The question in this study is to investigate the problem of . . ." or "The problem in this study is to investigate the question of. . ."). The problem is located alternately in the world or in the study, the distinction between problems and questions is unclear, and what is unsatisfactory in the situation is not set up as a clear target for inquiry.

We suggest that you be more careful as you think through the question of what to study. Define your terms from the start and stick with them, at least until they prove not to be helpful. The definitions we prefer are arbitrary, but it has been our experience that making such distinctions is a useful habit of mind. Accordingly, we suggest that you use the following lexicon as you think and begin to write about your problem.

> *Problem*—the experience we have when an unsatisfactory situation is encountered. Once carefully defined, it is that situation, with all of the attendant questions it may raise, that can become the target for a proposed study. Your proposal, then, will not lay out a plan to study the problem but will address one or several of the questions that explicate what you have found "problematic" about the situation. Note that in this

context neither situation nor problem is limited to a pragmatic definition. The observation that two theories contradict each other can be experienced as a problem, and a research question may be posed to address the conflict.

Question—a statement of what you wish to know about some unsatisfactory situation, as in the following: What is the relation between. . .? Which is the better way to. . .? What would happen if. . .? What is the location of. . .? As explained below, when cast in a precise, answerable form, one or several of these questions will become the mainspring for your study—the formal research question.

Purpose—the explicit intention of the investigator to accumulate data in such a way as to answer the research question posed as the focus for the study. The word "objective" is a reasonable synonym here. Although only people can have intentions, it is common to invest our research design with purpose (as in "The purpose of this study is to determine the mechanism through which. . .").

Hypothesis—an affirmation about the nature of some situation in the world. A tentative proposition set up as a convenient target for an investigation, a statement to be confirmed or denied in terms of the evidence.

Given this lexicon, the search for a topic becomes the quest for a situation that is sufficiently unsatisfactory to be experienced as a *problem*. The proposal has as its *purpose* the setting up of a research *question* and the establishing of exactly how (and why) the investigator intends to find the answer, thereby eliminating or reducing the experience of finding something problematic about the world.

Although they use the words "problem" and "question" in a slightly different manner (though one which is entirely consistent), Guba and Lincoln (1981) have devised helpful strategies for logical analysis of three major types of problematic situation (concept, action, and value). If you have a clear sense of some problem, but are encountering difficulty in getting it set up properly as a precise and answerable research question, a review of their discussion and accompanying examples may help untangle your thinking.

The research process, and thus the proposal, begins with a question. Committed to performing a study within a given area of inquiry and allied with an appropriate advisor, students must identify a question that matches their interests as well as the resources and constraints of their situation. Given a theoretically infinite set of possible problems that might be researched, it is small wonder that many students at first are overwhelmed and frozen into indecision. The "I can't find a problem" syndrome is a common malady among graduate students, but fortunately one that can be cured by time and knowledge.

Research questions emerge from three broad sources: logical, practical, and accidental. In some cases the investigator's curiosity is directed to a gap in the logical structure of what already is known in the area. In other cases the investigator responds to the demand for information about the application of knowledge to some practical service. In yet other cases serendipity operates and the investigator is stimulated by an unexpected observation, often in the context of another study. It is common for several of these factors to operate simultaneously to direct attention to a particular question. Personal circumstance and individual style also tend to dictate the most common source of questions for each research worker. Finally, all of the sources depend on a more fundamental and prior factor—thorough knowledge of the area.

It is this latter factor that accounts for the graduate student syndrome. Only as one grasps the general framework and the specific details of a particular area can unknowns be revealed, fortuitous observations raise questions, and possible applications of knowledge become apparent. Traditional library study is the first step toward the maturity that permits confident selection of a research question. Such study, however, is necessary but not sufficient. In any active area of inquiry the current knowledge base is not in the library—it is in the invisible college of informal associations among research workers.

The working knowledge base of an area takes the form of unpublished papers, conference speeches, seminar transcripts, memoranda, dissertations in progress, grant applications, personal correspondence, and telephone calls, as well as conversations in the corridors of conference centers, restaurants, hotel rooms, and bars. To obtain access to this ephemeral resource the student must be where the action is.

The best introduction to the current status of a research area is close association with advisors who know the territory and are busy formulating and pursuing their own questions. Conversing with peers, listening to professorial discussions, assisting in research projects, attending lectures and conferences, exchanging papers, and corresponding with faculty or students at other institutions are all ways of capturing the elusive state of the art. In all of these, however, the benefits derived often depend on knowing enough about the area to join the dialogue by asking questions, offering a tangible point for discussion, or raising a point of criticism. In research, as elsewhere, the more you know, the more you can learn.

While establishing a network of exchange may seem impossible to young students who view themselves as novices and outsiders, it is a happy fact that new recruits generally find a warm welcome within any well-defined area of intensive study. Everyone depends on informal relationships among research colleagues, and this rapport is one source of sustaining excitement and pleasure in the research enterprise. As soon as you can articulate well-formulated ideas about possible problems, your colleagues will be eager to provide comment, critical questions, suggestions, and encouragement.

In the final process of selecting the thesis or dissertation problem there is one exercise that can serve to clarify the relative significance of competing questions. Most questions can be placed within a general model that displays a sequence of related questions—often in an order determined by logic or practical considerations. Smaller questions are seen to lead to larger and more general questions, methodological questions are seen necessarily to precede substantive questions, and theoretical questions may be found interspersed among purely empirical questions. The following is a much simplified but entirely realistic example of such a sequential model. It begins with an everyday observation and leads through a series of specific and interrelated problems to a high-order question of great significance.

OBSERVATION: Older men who are physically active seem to be quicker mentally, especially in tasks that demand speed of response.

(1) What are the characteristics of cognitive function influenced by exercise?
(2) What are the effects of exercise on one type of cognitive function, reactive capacity, throughout the life span?
(3) Is reactive capacity faster in old exercised animals than in old controls?
(4) Is there a sensitive reactive task that can be used with animals as a way of eliminating factors such as intelligence, experience, medication, and the like that would contaminate studies using human subjects?
(5) Are active old men faster on a reactive capacity task than sedentary old men?

QUESTION: What effect does exercise have on cognitive function in older men?

By making the twists and turns of speculation visible in the concrete process of sequential listing, previously unnoticed possibilities may be revealed or tentative impressions confirmed. In the simple example given above, the reader may immediately see other questions that could have been inserted or alternative chains of inquiry that branch off from the main track of logic. Other diagrammatic lists of questions about exercise and cognitive function might be constructed from different but related starting points. One might begin, for example, with the well-established fact that circulation is superior in older individuals who exercise regularly. This might lead through a series of proximal experiments toward the ultimate question, "What is the *mechanism* by which exercise maintains cognitive function?"

Building such diagrams will be useful for the student in several other ways. It is a way of controlling the instinct to grab the first researchable question that becomes apparent in an area. Often such questions are inferior to what might be selected after more careful contemplation of the alternatives. There is a logical sequence to most questions beginning with "What has to be asked first?" Once these serial relationships become clear it is easier to assign priorities.

In addition to identifying the correct ordering and relative importance of questions, such conceptual models also encourage students to think in terms of a series of studies that build cumulatively toward more significant conclusions than can be achieved in a one-shot thesis or dissertation. The faculty member who has clear dedication to a personal research program can be a key factor in attracting students into the long-term commitments that give life to an area of inquiry.

Researchable questions occur daily to the active researcher. The problem is not finding them but maintaining some sense of whether, and where, they might fit into an overall plan. While this condition may seem remote to the novice struggling to define a first research topic, formulating even a modest research agenda can be a helpful process. The guidance of a sequential display of questions can allow the student to settle confidently on the target for a proposal.

THE SEQUENCE OF PROPOSING: FROM SELECTING A TOPIC TO ORAL PRESENTATION

A Plan of Action: What Follows What?

Figure 2.1 can be useful for the novice if one central point is understood. A tidy, linear sequence of steps is not an accurate picture of what happens in the development of most research proposals. The peculiar qualities of human thought processes and the serendipity of retrieving knowledge serve to guarantee that development of a proposal will be anything but tidy. Dizzying leaps, periods of no progress, and agonizing backtracking are more typical than is a continuous, unidirectional flow of events. The diagram may be used to obtain an overview of the task, to establish a rough time schedule, or to check retrospectively for possible omissions, but it is not to be taken as a literal representation of what should or will happen.

To say that development of a proposal is not a perfectly predictable sequence is not to say, however, that it is entirely devoid of order. When the proposal has been completed, a backward glance often indicates that an orderly progression through the steps would have saved time and effort. It is more important to complete some steps in sequence than others. For instance, although the mind may skip ahead and visualize a specific type of measure to be used, Step 11 ("Consider alternative methods of measurement") should not be undertaken until Step 6 ("Surveying relevant literature") is completed. Many methods of measurement may be revealed and noted while perusing the literature. Sometimes suggestions for instrumentation materialize in unlikely places or in studies that have been initially categorized as unlikely to yield information concerning measurement. Additionally, reported reliabilities and validities of alternative procedures will be needed before any final selection can be made. Thus a large commitment of effort to consideration of alternative methods can be a waste of time if it precedes a careful survey of the literature.

For simplicity, many important elements have been omitted from Figure 2.1. No reference is made to such pivotal processes as developing a theoretical framework, categorizing literature, or stating hypotheses. Further, the detailed demands that are intrinsic to the writing process itself, such as establishing a systematic language, receive no mention. What is presented are the obvious steps of logic and procedure—the operations and questions that mark development toward a plan for action. Finally, the reader who begins to make actual use of the diagram will find that the sequence of steps at several junctures leads into what appear to be circular paths. For example, if at question G a single form of inquiry does not present itself as most appropriate, the exit line designated "NO" leads back to the previous procedural step of considering alternative forms of inquiry. The intention in this arrangement is not to indicate a trap in which beginning researchers are doomed forever to chase their tails. In each case the closed loop suggests only that when questions cannot be answered, additional input is required

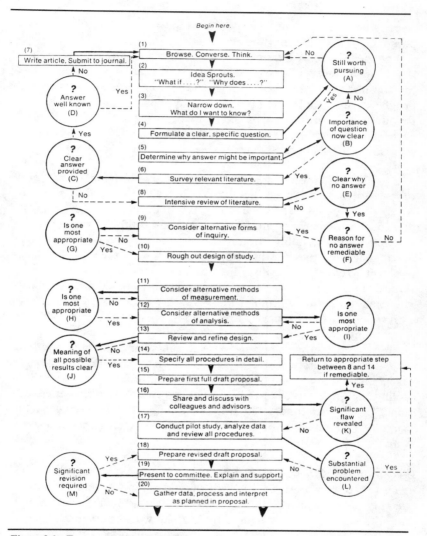

Figure 2.1   Twenty steps to a proposal

NOTE: Boxes represent major procedural steps; unbroken lines trace the main sequence of those steps. Circles represent the major questions to be confronted; the broken lines lead to the procedural consequences of the alternative YES or NO answers.

(more study, thought, or advice), or that the question itself is inappropriate to the case and must be altered.

For the most part Figure 2.1 will be self-explanatory. In the pages that follow, however, we have selected a few of the steps and questions for comment, either because they represent critical junctures in the proposal process or because they have proven particularly troublesome for our own advisees. It will be helpful to locate in the diagram sequence each of the items selected for discussion so that the previous and succeeding steps and questions provide a frame for our comments.

Step 3: Narrow down. What do I want to know? Moving from general to specific is always more difficult for the beginner than is anticipated. It is here that the student first encounters two of the hard facts of scientific life: logistic practicality and the perverse inscrutability of seemingly simple events. Inevitably, the novice must learn to take one small step, one manageable question, at a time. In other words, the proposal must conform in scope to the realistic limitations of the research process itself. At their best, research tools can encompass only limited bits of reality; stretched too far, they produce illusion rather than understanding.

It may be important to think big at first, to puzzle without considering practicality, and to allow speculation to soar beyond the confines of the sure knowledge base. From such creative conceptual exercises, however, the researcher must return to the question, "Where, given my resources and the nature of the problem, can I begin?" Delimiting questions such as "In which people?" "Under what conditions?" "At what time?" "In what location?" "By observing which events?" "By manipulating which variables?" serves the necessary pruning function.

Question A: Still worth pursuing? A question's worth may be viewed from two dimensions: its worth to the individual contemplating the answer, and its worth to the profession, to the academic community, and ultimately to society. Question A, "Still worth pursuing?," is the question that the researcher must answer in terms of personal interests and needs. The world is full of clearly formulated and specific questions that may not, once seen in their formal dress, seem worth the effort of answering. Because researchers are human, perfectly legitimate questions may seem dull, interesting veins of inquiry may peter out into triviality, and well-defined issues may fail to suit for no better reason than a clash with personal style. On the other hand, some questions are supported by the researcher's immediate need to enhance teaching in a vital subject area or to quench curiosity about a long-held hunch.

The basic rule is to be honest before proceeding. If you really don't care about answering the question, it may be better to start again, while the investment still is relatively small.

Step 5: Determine why it might be important to answer. This step places the proposed research in scientific-societal perspective. The study should contribute to the generation or validation of a theoretical structure or subcomponent, or relate to one of the several processes by which knowledge is used to enhance professional practice. The trick here is to justify the question in terms appropriate to the nature of the question. Inquiry that is directed toward filling a gap in the structure of knowledge need not be supported by appeals to practical application (even though later events may yield just such return). Inquiry that arises directly from problems in the world of practice need not be supported by appeals to improve understanding of basic phenomena (even though later events may yield just such return). Each kind of question has its own correct measure of importance. The task of distinguishing the trivial from the substantive is not always easy; do not make it even more difficult by attempting to apply the wrong standard.

Step 6: Survey relevant literature. A preliminary scanning of the most obvious, pertinent resources, particularly reviews of the literature, is a way of husbanding time. It is far better to abandon a line of thought after several weeks of selective skimming than to work one's way via slow, thorough digestion of each document to the same conclusion after several months of effort.

Conscientious students sometimes feel vaguely guilty about such quick surveys. Keeping in mind the real purpose, which is to identify questions that already have satisfactory answers, is one way of easing such discomfort.

Question F: Reason for no answer remediable? In some cases the literature contains an empty area because the state of technology, the available knowledge framework, or the logistic demands peculiar to the question have made it impossible or unreasonable to conduct appropriate forms of inquiry. So long as the gap in knowledge seems to exist because no one has yet defined the question or become interested in pursuing the answer, it is reasonable to proceed. There are other reasons for empty or ambiguous areas in the literature, however, and they signal caution before proceeding.

Question J: Meaning of all possible results clear? The tighter the logic, the more elegant the theoretical framework, the more closely the design is tailored to produce clarity along one dimension—in short, the better the quality of the proposal—the greater the risk that the proposer will be lured into an unfortunate presumption: that the result of the study is known before the data are in hand. That student researchers sometimes are confronted by the stunning news that their treatment produced a reverse effect is in itself neither surprising nor harmful. Being unable to make an intelligent interpretation of such a situation, however, is unfortunate and in many cases unnecessary.

By serious consideration of alternative outcomes at the time of constructing the proposal, it may be possible to include elements in the study that will eliminate ambiguity in some of the most likely results. One method of anticipating the unexpected is to follow through the consequences of rejecting or failing to reject each hypothesis of the study. If the hypothesis was rejected, what is the explanation? How is the explanation justified by the rationale for the study? What findings would support the explanation? Conversely, if the findings of the study fail to provide a basis for rejection, what explanations are to be proposed? What are alternative explanations? At the least, some careful preliminary thought about alternative explanations for each possible result will serve as a shield against the panic that produces such awkward post hoc interpretations as "no significant differences were observed because the instruments employed were inadequate."

Step 16: Share and discuss with colleagues and advisors. There is a well-known syndrome displayed by some who attempt research, symptomized by the inclination to prolong the period of writing the final report—indefinitely. Some people simply cannot face what they perceive to be the personal threat implied in opening their work to challenge in the public arena. These individuals are terribly handicapped and only rarely can become mature, productive scholars. An early sign of this is seen in students who cannot bring themselves to solicit advice and criticism for their proposals.

Sometimes students experience severe criticism because they present their ideas before they have been sufficiently developed into a conceptual framework that represents careful preparation. Many professors avoid speculative conversations about "half-baked" ideas that have just arrived in a blinding flash of revelation to the student. Few professors refuse a request for advice concerning a proposal that has been drafted as the culmination of several weeks of hard thought, research, and development. Even at that, having one's best effort devastated by pointed criticism can be an agonizing experience. The only alternative, however, is to persist in error or ignorance, and that is untenable in research.

If the student is fortunate enough to be in a department that contains a vigorous community of inquiring minds, with the constant give and take of intellectual disputation, the rough and tumble soon will be regarded as a functional part of producing good research. The novice will solicit, if not enjoy, the best criticism that can be found.

The notion that it is vaguely immoral to seek assistance in preparing a proposal is at best a parody of real science and at worst, as in the form of an institutional rule, it is a serious perversion arising from ignorance. Research may have some gamelike qualities, but a system of handicaps is not one of them. The object of every inquiry is to get the best possible answer under the circumstances, and that presumes obtaining the best advice available. It is hoped that the student will not be held to any lesser standard.

It should be obvious that students, after digesting and weighing all the criticism received, must still make their own choices. Not all advice is good and not all criticism is valid. There is only one way to find out, however, and that is to share the proposal with colleagues whose judgments one can respect, if not always accept.

Step 20: Gather data, process, and interpret as in proposal. This is the payoff. A good proposal is more than a guide to action, it is a framework for intelligent interpretation of results and the heart of a sound final report. The proposal cannot guarantee significant results, but it will provide some assurance that, whatever the result, the student can wind up the project with reasonable dispatch and at least a minimum of intellectual grace. If that sounds too small a recompense for all the effort, consider the alternative of having to write a report about an inconsequential question, pursued through inadequate methods of inquiry, and resulting in a heap of unanalyzable data.

Originality and Replication: What Is a Contribution to Knowledge?

Some attention already has been given to considerations that precede the proposal, the critical and difficult steps of identifying and delimiting a research topic, but at least one other preliminary problem—the question of originality—has important ramifications for the proposal.

Some advisors regard student-conducted research primarily as an arena for training, like wood-chopping that is expected to produce muscles in the person who holds the ax, but not much real fuel for the fire. Whatever may be the logic of such an assumption, students generally do not take the same attitude. Their expectations are more likely to resemble the classic dictum for scholarly research, to make an original contribution to the body of knowledge.

An all-too-common problem in selecting topics for research proposals occurs when either the student or an advisor gives literal interpretation to the word "original," defining it as "initial, first, never having existed or occurred before." This is a serious misinterpretation of the word as it is used in science. In research, original clearly includes all studies deliberately employed to test the accuracy of results or the applicability of conclusions developed in previous studies. What is not included under the rubric of "original" are studies that proceed mindlessly to repeat an existing work either in ignorance of its existence or without appropriate attention to its defects or limitations.

One consequence of the confusion surrounding the phrase "original contribution" is that misguided students and advisors are led to ignore one of the most important areas of research activity and one of the most useful forms of training for the novice researcher—replication. That replication sometimes is regarded simply as rote imitation, lacking sufficient opportunity for students to apply and develop their own skills, is an indication of how badly some students misunderstand both the operation of a research enterprise and the concept of a body of knowledge.

The essential role of replication in research has been cogently argued (Bauernfeind, 1968; Borg & Gall, 1983). What has not been made sufficiently clear, however, is that replication can involve challenging problems that demand creative resolution. Further, some advisors do not appreciate the degree to which writing proposals for replicative studies can constitute an ideal learning opportunity for research trainees.

In direct replication, students must not only correctly identify all the critical variables in the original study, but also create equivalent conditions for the conduct of their own study. Anyone who thinks that the critical variables will immediately be apparent from a reading of the original report has not read very widely in the research literature.

Anyone who thinks that truly equivalent conditions can be created simply by "doing it the same way" just has not tried to perform a replicative study. Thorough understanding of the problem and, frequently, a great deal of technical ingenuity are demanded in developing an adequate proposal for direct replication.

As an alternative to direct replication, the student may repeat an interesting study considered to have been defective in sample, method, analysis, or interpretation. Here the student introduces deliberate changes to improve the power of a previous investigation. It would be difficult to imagine a more challenging or useful activity for anyone interested in both learning about research and contributing to the accumulation of reliable knowledge.

In writing a proposal for either kind of replicative study, direct or revised, the student should introduce the original with appropriate citation, make the comments that are needed, and proceed without equivocation or apology to the proposed study. Replicative research is not, as unfortunate tradition has it in some departments, slightly improper or something less than genuine research.

The cross-validation study is another type of study that sometimes is characterized as unoriginal, and even sometimes is confused with replication. An excellent example of a cross-validation study has been provided by Kroll and Peterson (1966). Cross-validation studies most frequently appear in conjunction with or following multiple regression studies, in which the investigator attempts to determine an equation by which to predict a dependent variable or variables. The equations that are derived for the sample used, however, may have been affected by chance correlations and errors of measurement, to the extent that the investigator cannot be sure how predictive the selected set of variables would be for other samples.

Two techniques of cross-validation are used. In one technique the investigator computes a predicted score for each subject—on the basis of the equation derived from the original study—and then correlates predicted scores with the scores that actually were measured in the second sample. If a very high correlation is obtained between those predicted scores and the measured scores in an entirely different sample, the original set of independent variables with their given weights has been validated as being generally predictive of the dependent variable. A second technique is to use the second sample to derive a new set of regression weights and a new multiple R statistic for the originally selected independent variables.

Another situation in which cross-validation is used involves studies in which an investigator selects from a large pool of test items those that significantly discriminate between two or more groups. Again, chance plays a role in the differentiation of the groups—perhaps creating spuriously large differences, or an inflated correlation between the criterion and the sample on which the selection of items was based. In studies of this type, cross-validation on additional groups is required.

Irrespective of the situation in which cross-validation is used, or the technique used to accomplish it, it should be readily apparent that cross-validation does not require a completely original effort. Yet it is a technique sorely needed in the behavioral sciences where the body of knowledge would be expanded and refined much more rapidly if many of the hundreds of theses undertaken each year were careful cross-validations or replications rather than inexperienced and misguided attempts at originality.

Given the limitations of research reports, it often is useful to discuss the source study for the replication or cross-validation with the original author, directly or by mail. Most research workers are happy to provide greater detail and in some instances raw data for inspection or reanalysis. In a healthy science, replication is the most sincere form of flattery. A proposal appendix containing correspondence with the author of the original report, or data not provided in that report, often can serve to interest and reassure a hesitant advisor.

Getting Started: Producing the First Draft

The student who has never written a research proposal commonly sits in front of a desk and stares at a blank piece of paper or an empty video monitor for hours. The mind is brimming with knowledge gleaned from the literature, but how does one actually get started? The concept of "a research proposal" conjures up ideas of accuracy, precision, meticulous form, and the use of a language system that is new and unpracticed by the neophyte researcher. The demands can suddenly seem overwhelming. The student should realize that these feelings of panic are experienced by nearly everyone, not only those who are new to the writing endeavor but those who are skilled as well. Fanger (1985) expressed it beautifully: "I have come to regard panic as the inevitable concomitant of any kind of serious academic writing" (p. 28). For anyone temporarily incapacitated by the "blank page syndrome," the following suggestions may be helpful.

Make an outline that is compatible with the format selected to present the communication task listed in Chapter 1. An initial approval of the outline by the advisor may save revision time later. Gather the resource materials, notes, and references, and organize them into groups that correspond to the outline topics. For instance, notes supporting the rationale for the study would be in one group, and notes relating to the reliability of an instrument to be used would be in another group.

Once the outline is made and the materials gathered, tackle one of the topics in the outline (not necessarily the first) and start writing. If the section to be written is labeled "The Problem," assume someone has asked, "What is the problem of this study?" Your task is to answer that question. Start writing. Do not worry about grammar, syntax, or writing within the language system. Just write. In this way you can avoid one of the greatest inhibitions to creativity—an inward criticism that is so severe that each idea is rejected before it becomes reality. Remember, it is easier to correct than to create. If all the essential parts of a topic are displayed in some fashion, they can later be rearranged, edited, and couched within the language system. With experience, the novice will begin thinking in the language system and forms of the proposal. Until that time, the essential problem is to begin. Awkward or elegant, laborious or swift, there is no substitute for writing the first draft.

If you have access to a microcomputer with word processing capabilities, the same steps hold, but the revisions will be much easier. Put your outline on the word processor and then go back and progressively fill in the detail under each heading. Even if your university requires that the final proposal be typed on a standard machine, word processing offers enormous advantages for early drafts. The effort needed to learn its use will be repaid many times over. The capacity to edit, rearrange text easily, and store manuscript copy for future revision offers great economy. Further, there is a significant psychological advantage in the ease with which revised drafts can be produced. This encourages the author to make revisions that might otherwise be set aside under the press of limited time.

Prologue to Action: The Oral Presentation

Many graduate schools require a formal oral presentation of research plans before the student's committee (or a special seminar group designed for screening proposals). Master's thesis committees vary in number from one professor to a committee of five or six faculty members. A dissertation committee typically consists of four to six members. In some instances, all committee members are from within the department of the student's major. In other instances, the committee is multidisciplinary, with faculty representing other departments on the campus.

If the student has some freedom to exercise choice, committee membership should be designed to maximize the support and assistance available. A student interested in the study of behavioral treatment of drug abuse in young upwardly mobile women could tap the value of different faculty perspectives and skills by blending members from several departments. For this purpose individuals with multiple interests are particularly useful. For example, a faculty member in the Psychology Department might be selected both for statistical competence and interest in behavior modification, someone in the School of Social Work might bring epidemiological expertise regarding drug usage, and a faculty member in the School of Public Health might be a part of the committee because of expertise in both experimental design and therapeutic compliance techniques.

In preparing for the oral presentation, the student should identify in advance the individuals who will hear the presentation, particularly as the presence of scholars from outside the student's discipline may impose special demands on both the presentation and the period of discussion and questions that normally follows. Presence of individuals not on the thesis or dissertation committee, often including an audience of graduate students from other areas of study, certainly makes it imperative to refrain, at least in the oral summary, from technical detail or jargon specific to the area of study.

The type of oral presentation will vary from committee to committee. Some committees will carefully study the proposal and not expect a verbal recitation of what has been written. Rather, they may request a brief review of the student's past experiences that led to selecting the topic of study, some discussion of the skills required for work in the proposed area of research, and some comment about the ultimate purpose in choosing that particular problem. A committee of this type, having broken the ice with such general discussion, may then settle down to question the student on specific points in the proposal.

Other committees may expect the student to summarize orally each part of the proposal, making reference to tables, lists, or diagrams as they occur. Using slides or overhead projections of tables and diagrams as part of such summary usually will enhance the clarity of the presentation. Clear graphics make it easier for the committee to focus its attention on the relevant information. In presentations of this kind, the student should construct an outline of the major headings of the document and be prepared to discuss each of these without reading directly from the proposal. The committee may interject questions as the student progresses through the outline. In special cases where unusual, inventive, or particularly complex equipment is to be used, a model, diagram, or photograph of the item may be helpful.

If a suitable space is conveniently available, a 5- or 10-minute demonstration of data collection may be planned. The student may have a test administrator and subject prepared to undergo data collection as soon as the committee enters the room. These demonstrations serve to bring committee members more quickly within the frame of reference of the student and advisor, and their questions then can be directed exactly to equipment functioning and administrative procedures rather than toward attempts at understanding the nature of the equipment.

A third type of committee may request a 5- or 10-minute summary of the proposal as a whole, the conclusion of which is followed by questions relating to any part of the proposal. It is advisable to discover, either from the chairperson or from conferences with committee members, the type of presentation that is expected.

The major purpose of the oral presentation and discussion with a committee is to bring critical analysis and fresh ideas representing substantial research experience to bear on the student's topic of study. The exposure of major flaws in design or inappropriate analyses may be discussed by the committee and the student, with the result that a solution is identified. The oral presentation should be a cooperative effort toward excellence by faculty and student. Normal apprehensions dictate that few students will look forward to the experience, but it is one that can add substantially to the probability of success.

The oral presentation is the time when the student's general knowledge of the area will become critical. Although much that has been learned about the topic is not appropriate for insertion in the proposal, committee questions and the ensuing discussion will test the extent and depth of the student's knowledge in the area. It will be prudent, therefore, to review working notes prior to the oral presentation and to have the major items of pertinent literature ready for prompt recall. A thorough review of the statistical techniques involved in the proposed study will avoid confusion and possible embarrassment.

The student may be disappointed to be asked questions that reveal a committee member's failure to read the proposal carefully. In these cases it is best to answer the question briefly and then note than an attempt to answer the question can be found in the proposal on a specific page. The student should not reveal impatience with committee members who ask redundant questions; rather it is best to center all attention and skill on the task of achieving complete understanding of the project by the entire committee.

It may happen that a member of the committee will press a general point of view or urge a specific decision that student and advisor do not find compatible with their own understanding of the study. In such cases there is one useful strategy available beyond the exercise of prudence, patience, and ability to contest the matter. If the student tries to give a thorough and lucid statement of the point in a form such as "I believe that I understand what you are suggesting. It is that. . ." the member may become less inclined to impose his or her viewpoint or, at least, less inclined to press for an immediate decision. The reason for this is that most professors are far more concerned with being understood, with being assured that the student has grasped correctly the alternative arguments on which final decisions must be made, than with imposing their personal viewpoint on an unwilling novice.

Another frustrating situation that may occur, although it should not be surprising to the student, is when committee members disagree among themselves on the use of a particular technique, design, or procedure. This happens quite frequently, as faculty members have strong biases regarding such matters as the statement format for hypotheses, the purpose and length of the introductory remarks, or the method of analyzing data. Generally, when serious disagreements arise, the committee eventually will come to some compromise on the issue. The student should take careful notes about the compromises reached and the preferences of each committee member. The student should make certain, before the oral presentation is terminated that each member of the committee understands the nature and extent of the compromise that was accepted.

In preparation for the oral presentation, the student should practice before other graduate students, presenting the proposal just as it will be presented to the committee, and then entertaining a substantial period of questioning. This may be followed by a mock oral presentation in front of students and faculty selected for their interest and competence in the specific area of study. Practice in fielding questions is sound preparation for the oral. It also is wise to hold at least one practice session before the final draft of the proposal is prepared, as questions often point to needed clarifications or revisions in the document.

Chapter 3

CONTENT OF THE PROPOSAL

Important Considerations

The topics covered in this chapter are designed to assist the true beginner. More experienced proposal writers may want to go directly to Chapter 5 or simply skim this chapter for review.

Reviewing the Literature: Writing the Right Stuff

By much deserved reputation, the reviews of literature in student research proposals are regarded as consisting of clumsy and turgid prose, written as *pro forma* response to a purely ceremonial obligation in the planning format. Even when carefully crafted with regard to basic mechanics they make dull reading, and when not so prepared they are excruciating torture for most readers. Much of this problem arises from a misunderstanding of the task served by reviewing the literature, and none of it need be true.

To begin, the common designation used in proposals, "review of the literature," is a misleading if not completely inappropriate title. A research proposal is not the place to review the body of literature that bears on a problematic area, or even the place to examine all the research that relates to the specific question raised in the proposal. Analyses of that kind may be useful documents, publishable in their own right. Indeed, some journals such as the *Review of Educational*

Research are exclusively devoted to such critical retrospectives on scholarship. The task to be performed in the proposal, however, is different. It is not inferior to the true review, it simply is different.

In writing a research proposal, the author is obligated to place the question or hypothesis in the context of previous work in such a way as to explain and justify the decisions made. That alone is required. Nothing more is appropriate and nothing more should be attempted.

Although the author may wish to persuade the reader on many different kinds of points, ranging from the significance of the question to the appropriateness of a particular form of data analysis, sound proposals devote most of the literature review to explaining (1) exactly how and why the research question or hypothesis was formulated in the proposed form and (2) exactly why the proposed research strategy was elected. What is required to accomplish these tasks is a step-by-step explanation of decisions, punctuated by reference to studies that support the ongoing argument. In this, the writer uses previous work, often some critique of previous work, and sometimes some exposition of the broad pattern of knowledge as it exists in the area, to appeal for the reader's acceptance of the logic represented in the proposed study.

Whatever particular arguments must be sustained in the review of the literature, there is no place for the "Smith says this . . ." and "Jones says that . . ." paragraph-by-paragraph recital that makes novice proposals instruments for dulling the senses. This is the place to answer the reader's most immediate questions: What is it the author wants to know, and why has this plan been devised to find the answer? In a good review, the literature is made to serve the reader's query by supporting, explicating, and illuminating the logic now implicit in the proposed investigation.

It follows, then, that where there is little relevant literature, or where decisions are clear-cut and without substantial issues, the review should be brief. In some cases the examination of supporting literature may best be appended or woven into another section of the proposal. To write a review of literature for the sake of having a review in the document is to make it a parody and not a proposal.

Remember, the writer's task is to employ the research literature artfully to support and explain the choices made *for this study,* not to educate the reader concerning the state of science in the problem area. Neither is the purpose of the section to display the energy and thoroughness with which the author has pursued a comprehensive understanding of the literature. If the author can explain and support the question, design, and procedures, with a minimum demand on the reader's time and intellect, then he or she will be more than sufficiently impressed with the applicant's capabilities and serious purpose.

None of this is intended to undervalue the task that every researcher must face, that of locating and thoroughly assimilating what is already known. To do this the student must experience what Fanger (1985) described as "immersion in the subject" by reading extensively in the areas that either are directly or indirectly related to the topic of study. This may lead at first to a sense of frustration and confusion, but perseverance usually leads out of the wilderness to the point at which what is known about the topic can be seen in the light of what is not known. The goals of the proposed study can be projected against that backdrop.

The proposal is the place to display the refined end products of that long and difficult process. It is not uncommon, for example, for the study's best supports to emerge from a sophisticated understanding of gaps in the body of knowledge, limitations in previous formulations of the question, inadequate methods of data collection, or inappropriate interpretation of results. The review of the literature section then becomes a vehicle for illustrating why and how it all can be done better. What readers need, however, is not a full tour retracing each step the author took in arriving at the better mousetrap, but a concise summary of the main arguments properly juxtaposed to the new and better plan for action. Most students will agonize over the many studies discovered that, while fascinating and perhaps even inspiring during the immersion process, in the final stages of writing turn out to fail the test of critical relevance and therefore merit exclusion from the proposal.

It is tempting to see discarded studies and unused note cards as wasted time, but that misses the long view of learning. The knowledge gained through synthesis and evaluation of research results builds a knowledge base for the future. The process of immersion in the literature provides not only the information that will support the proposal, but the intellectual framework for future expertise. What may appear in the crush of deadlines and overload stress to have been pursuit down blind alleys, ultimately may provide insights that will support new lines of thought and future proposals.

Writing the section on related literature often is no more complex than first describing the major concepts that led you to your research question or hypothesis, and then describing the supporting research findings already in the literature. It may be as simple as hypothesizing that A is greater than C. Why do you hypothesize that A is greater than C? Because evidence suggests that A is greater than B, and B is greater than C, therefore it is reasonable to hypothesize that A must be greater than C.

In the review of related literature, you express these conceptual relationships in an organized fashion and then document them with previously reported studies. For example, the first section would include the most important studies indicating that A is greater than B, and the second section would include studies that suggest that B is greater than C. The literature section of your proposal would conclude by showing that, given this information, it is reasonable to hypothesize that A is greater than C.

Look at the example in Table 3.1, which also is represented diagramatically in Figure 3.1. In this table the general research question is posed, followed by the specific hypotheses through which the question will be answered. They are shown here merely to establish the frame of reference for the outline. In this example of the development of the related literature, three major concepts are necessary to support the legitimacy of this hypothesis. In Table 3.1, the question suggests that the way physical fitness and cognitive function are related is through a change in brain aerobic capacity as a result of training. If this is a reasonable question to ask, one would have to show that there have been some prior studies in which physical fitness level has been related to some measure of cognitive function (concept I). Second, some evidence that cognitive function might be altered by aerobic functional capacity of the brain should be shown (concept II). Finally, some evidence should exist that physical movement can alter blood flow shifts in the brain, and that blood flow shifts are related to aerobic capacity (concept III).

Generally the major concepts are supported by two or three major subtopics, all of which lead to the formalization of the general concept. For example, the concept that reaction time and physical fitness level are related (I) can be supported in three different ways, by showing (a) that reaction time is faster in physically fit persons than in sedentary persons, (b) that physical training enhances reaction time, and (c) that reaction time in those on the lowest end of the physical fitness continuum is the slowest of all. Each of these subtopics is supported by the findings from several studies, as shown in the "Outline with References" section of the table.

Writing the related literature section is much easier if an outline is developed in stages of increasingly greater detail, as shown in Table 3.1,

TABLE 3.1

Preparing the Related Literature Section

QUESTION: Is improved or maintained brain aerobic capacity a potential mechanism by which consistent and daily exercise in older humans and animals is related to enhanced function in some aspects of cognitive processing? More specifically, do highly conditioned older animals have a higher brain aerobic capacity and faster reaction time than older sedentary animals?

HYPOTHESES: (1) A measure of cognitive function (mean simple reaction time) and a measure of brain aerobic capacity (glucose uptake) are not related in young experimental (physically trained) and controlled animals that are 3, 6, and 12 months of age; (2) cognitive function will not be significantly different in trained and untrained animals that are 3, 6, and 12 months of age; (3) brain aerobic capacity will not be significantly different in trained and untrained animals that are 3, 6, and 12 months of age; (4) a measure of cognitive function and a measure of brain aerobic capacity will be related for older animals (aged 18, 24, and 30 months); (5) cognitive function will be different in trained and untrained older animals; (6) brain aerobic capacity will be different in trained and untrained older animals.

First Stage Outline: Develop the Concepts that Provide the Rationale for the Study

I.   Reaction time is related to physical fitness level.

II. Maintenance of cognitive function is dependent on maintenance of aerobic capacity in the brain.

III. The aerobic capacity of brain tissue is related to regional blood flow shifts, which are related to physical movement.

Second Stage Outline: Develop the Subtopics for Each Major Concept

I.   Reaction time is related to physical fitness level.

   A.   comparisons to the reaction time of physically active and inactive subjects

TABLE 3.1 Continued

   B. training effects on reaction time
   C. reaction time of those in poor physical condition (cardiovascular disease, hypertension)

II. Maintenance of cognitive function is dependent on maintenance of aerobic capacity in the brain.

   A. relationship of cognitive function and brain aerobic capacity with age
   B. relationship of a neurological measure of brain function, electroencephography (EEG), to cerebral blood flow, and cerebral oxygen uptake in older subjects

III. The aerobic capacity of brain tissue is related to regional blood flow shifts, which are related to physical movement.

   A. increased metabolism in specific regions leads to blood flow shifts to those regions
   B. regional blood flow shifts in motor areas of the brain are related to physical movement

Third Stage Outline: Add the Most Important References That Support Each Subtopic

I. Reaction time is related to physical fitness level.

   A. Physically active individuals have faster reaction times than do sedentary individuals (Botwinick & Storandt, 1974; Clarkson, 1978; Clarkson & Kroll, 1978; Powell & Porndorf, 1971; Spirduso, 1975; Spirduso & Clark, 1977).
   B. Reaction time is faster after a physical training program (Dustman et al., 1984; Gibson, Karpovitch, & Gollnick, 1961; Matsui, 1971; Tweit, Gollnick, & Hearn, 1963).
   C. Cardiovascular diseased patients have slower reaction time than normal individuals (Abrahams & Birren, 1980; Benton, 1977; Hicks & Birren, 1970; Simonson & Enzer, 1941; Speith, 1965).

(continued)

TABLE 3.1 Continued

II.   Maintenance of cognitive function is dependent on maintenance of aerobic capacity in the brain.

    A.   Both cognitive function and aerobic capacity decrease with age (Simonson, 1965).

    B.   EEG, cerebral blood flow, and cerebral oxidative capacity decrease with age (Fitzpatrick et al., 1976; Hevischaft & Junze, 1977; Ingvar, Sjelund, & Ardo, 1976; Obrist, 1975).

III.   The aerobic capacity of brain tissue is related to regional blood flow shifts, which are related to physical movement.

    A.   Increased regional metabolism leads to blood flow shifts (Crossman & Szafran, 1956; Injer, 1978; Szafran, 1965).

    B.   Regional blood flow shifts to motor areas of the brain that are related to physical movements being controlled (Halsey, Blanenstein, Wilson, & Wills, 1979; Ingvar & Skinjk, 1978; Lassen, Ingvar, & Skinhoj, 1978).

prior to the actual writing. Once the outline is developed, this section of the proposal can be written in a straightforward manner, with little backtracking necessary. If meticulous care is taken in selecting each reference, an enormous amount of time will be saved in the long run. The entire process can be summarized in the following 15 steps.

(1)   Determine the major concepts (no more than two or three) that are pertinent to the proposed research question. That is, what are the concepts that must be true in order for your question to be appropriate or hypothesis tenable?

(2)   List concepts either in descending order of importance or in terms of logical presentation. That is, does one concept have to be understood before another can be introduced?

(3)   Prepare an outline with these major concepts as the major headings (Table 3.1, concepts I, II, III).

(4)   Under each major heading list the articles that are most directly related (authors and dates only).

(5)   If the articles under such major heading cluster themselves and suggest a subheading, then arrange the clusters (and their subheadings) under each major heading in logical order. For example, you might note that of nine studies pertaining to the notion of a relationship between reaction time and physical fitness, in five of these animal reaction times

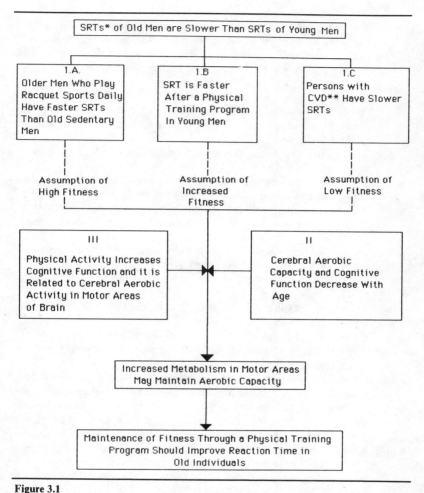

Figure 3.1

*SRT = simple reaction time; **CVD = cardiovascular disease.

were reported, and the other four studies were of human reaction time. The interpretation of these studies, when clustered in terms of type of subject, might be different and have a substantial bearing on the potential outcome of the proposed research.

(6) Without referring to the details in the articles, summarize in one paragraph the combined findings of each cluster of studies. For

example, in concept I.A. of Table 3.1, the summary might be that reaction time of physically active men and women is faster than that of sedentary individuals, as long as the subjects are over 60 years old. The summary of concept I.B. might be that strength training improves reaction time, but aerobic training in older individuals does not improve reaction time. At some point you will have to discuss the interpretation to be made from different results of physical fitness on reaction time, depending on the way physical fitness as an independent variable is measured.

(7) Read the paragraphs and subject them to the "Guidelines for Evaluation of Related Literature Section" (Table 3.2).

(8) Write an introductory paragraph explaining what the two or three major areas are and in what order they will be discussed. Explain why the order used was selected, if that is important. Explain why some literature may be omitted if it might seem logical to the reader that it would be included.

(9) Write a statement at the end of each section summarizing the findings within each cluster of studies. Show how this summary of findings relates to those of the cluster of studies described in the following paragraphs.

(10) Write a paragraph at the end of each major topic that summarizes the major points, supports the cohesiveness of the subtopics, and establishes the relevance of these concepts to the proposed research question.

(11) Write a paragraph at the conclusion that draws together all of the major summarizing paragraphs.

(12) After all of these concepts and subtopics have been carefully introduced, described, and summarized, return to the beginning and insert the documentation for each of the concepts in the proper location. That is, document the statements made in each of the paragraphs by describing the studies leading to them or verifying them.

(13) Each time a reference is inserted, place the complete citation in a special file for eventual compilation of a reference list.

(14) After a week has passed, reread the related literature section and again use the "Guidelines for Evaluating the Related Literature Section" that are provided in Table 3.2. Make whatever revisions seem necessary and wait one more week.

(15) Read the entire related literature section for coherence, continuity, and smoothness of transition from one concept to another. Check carefully for accuracy of all citations and edit for mechanics.

Spadework: The Proper Use of Pilot Studies

The pilot study is an especially useful form of anticipation, and one too often neglected in student proposals. When it comes to convincing

TABLE 3.2

**Guidelines for Evaluating
the Related Literature Section**

After you have written the first draft of the related literature section, answer the questions below. Mark the manuscript where the answers to each of these questions are located.

(1)   Is there a paragraph outlining the organization of the related literature section?

(2)   Does the order of the headings and subheadings represent the relative importance of the topics and subtopics? Is the order of headings rational?

(3)   Is the relation of the proposed study to past and current research clearly shown in the summary paragraphs?

(4)   What new answers (extension of the body of knowledge) will the proposed research provide?

(5)   What is distinctive or different about the proposed research compared with previous research? Is this clearly stated? Is this introduced in the first few paragraphs?

(6)   What are the most relevant articles (no more than five) that bear on this research? Underline these references. Are they in the first topical heading?

(7)   Are these articles presented in a way that denotes their importance? Are some cited so many times they lose power through repetition?

(8)   Has the evaluation of these key articles been presented succinctly in terms of both procedures and interpretation of results?

(9)   Have the results from your own pilot studies been interwoven into the synthesis of the related literature? (In the next section we will discuss pilot studies in some detail.)

the scholarly skeptic (often your own advisor), no argument can be so effective as to write, "I tried it and here is how it worked."

It is difficult to imagine any proposal that could not be improved by the reporting of actual preliminary work. Whether it is to demonstrate instrument reliability, the practicality of procedures, the availability of volunteers, the variability of observed events as a basis for power tests, subjects' capabilities, or the investigator's skills, the modest pilot study is the best possible basis for making wise decisions in designing research.

The pilot study, for example, is an excellent means by which to determine the sample size necessary to discover significant differences among experimental treatments.[1] From the findings of the pilot study, the experimenter may estimate expected group mean differences as well as the error variance per experimental unit. Winer (1971) presents a thorough discussion and presentation of formulas for this technique.

The use of even a few subjects in an informal trial can reveal a fatal flaw before it can destroy months of work. The same trial may even provide a fortunate opportunity to improve the precision of the investigation or to streamline cumbersome methods. For all these reasons, students and advisors should not insist on holding stringent, formal standards for exploratory studies. A pilot study is a *pilot* study; its target is the practicality of proposed operations, not the creation of empirical truth.

Examples of purposes that pilot studies might serve include the following:

(1) to determine the reliability of measurement in your own laboratory;
(2) to ensure that differences that you expect to exist, do in fact exist—that is, if you are studying the different effects of gender on motivation, make sure the sex difference exists;
(3) to "save" a sample that is difficult to obtain until the real research project—that is, test on available subjects until bugs are worked out, before testing world-class athletes;
(4) to determine the best types of skills to use as independent variables; for example, effects of different ankle braces on knee mobility—test jumping vertically, horizontally, and while running, then select one.

The presentation of pilot study results sometimes does create a troublesome problem. Readers may be led inadvertently to expect more of pilot work than it can reasonably deliver. Their concerns with the limitations may distract from its limited use in the main line of the argument being advanced by the author. Accordingly, the best course is to make no more of the pilot study than it honestly is worth—most are no more than a report of limited experience under less than perfectly controlled conditions—and do so only when the report will best illuminate the choices made in the proposal.

Brief reference to pilot work may be made in supporting the broad research strategies selected consequent to the review of research. Some pilot studies may, in fact, be treated as one of the works worthy of review. More commonly, however, the results of exploratory studies are used in supporting specific procedures proposed in the section dealing with methodology.

When the pilot study represents a formal and relatively complete research effort, it is proper to cite the work in some detail, including actual data. When the preliminary work has been informal or limited, it may be introduced as a footnote to the main text. In the latter case, it may be desirable to provide a more detailed account of the work in a section of the appendix, leaving the reader the choice of pursuing the matter further if desired.

Murphy's Law: Anticipating the Unexpected

Murphy's Law dictates that, in the conduct of research, if anything can go wrong, it probably will. This is accepted by experienced researchers and research advisors, but rarely is considered by the novice.

Within reasonable limits, the proposal is the place to provide for confrontation with the inexorable operation of Murphy's Law. Subject attrition cannot be prevented, but its effects can be circumscribed by careful planning. The potentially biasing effects created by nonreturns in questionnaires studies can be examined and, to some degree, mitigated by plans laid carefully in the proposal. The handling of subjects in the event of equipment failure is far better considered at leisure, in writing the proposal, than in the face of an unanticipated emergency. Field research in the public schools can provide a range of surprises, including indisposed teachers, fire drills, and inclement weather, all better managed by anticipation than by snap decisions forged in the heat of sudden necessity.

Equipment failure may interrupt carefully timed data collection sequences, or temporary computer breakdowns may delay data processing and analysis. At best such accidents will do no more than alter the time schedule for the study. At worst they may require substitutions or substantive changes in the procedures. Each step of the research process should be studied with regard to potential difficulty, and plans in the event of a problem should be stated in the appropriate place within the proposal. For instance, if unequal subject attrition occurs across groups, the type of analysis to be used with unequal Ns should be stated in the analysis section of the proposal.

It is impossible to anticipate everything that can happen. A good proposal, however, provides contingency plans for the most important problems that may arise in the course of conducting the study.

Anticipating the Analysis: Do It Now

The proposal is the proper place to reveal the exact nature of the analysis, as well as anticipated plans in the event of emergency. For many students, especially master's candidates, the analysis, if statistical, may represent new knowledge, recently acquired and not fully digested. In addition, the customary time limitation of 12 to 16 months by which the master's candidate is bound adds to the difficulty. The candidate may even be in the middle of a first formal course in techniques of data reduction and analysis during the same period of time used for constructing the proposal. Consequently, students find themselves in the awkward position of having to write lucidly about their analytic tools without yet knowing the entire armamentarium available. As untenable as this position is, and as much sympathy as may be generated by the student's advisor or friends, the omission of a full explanation of the analysis in the proposal may prove to be disastrous. Countless unfortunates have found themselves with shoe boxes full of unanalyzable data, all because the analysis was supposed to take care of itself. A step-by-step anticipation of the analysis to be used is also a double-check on the experimental design.

Descriptive, survey, and normative studies require extensive data reduction to produce meaningful quantitative descriptions and summaries of the phenomena of interest. Techniques for determining sample characteristics may be different from those anticipated on the basis of pilot results, or the study sample may be skewed, resulting in the need to discuss techniques for normalizing the data.

Statistical techniques are founded on assumptions relating to sample characteristics and the relationship between the sample and its respective population. The methods one intends to use to determine whether the sample meets the assumptions implicit in the anticipated analysis should be clearly stated. For example, many statistical techniques must be used only when one or more of the following assumptions are met: (a) normal distribution of the sample; (b) random and independent selection of scores; (c) linear relationships of variables; (d) homogeneity of variance among groups (in regression analysis, this is called homoscedasticity); (e) independence of sample means and variances; and (f) units of measure of the dependent variable on an interval or ratio scale.

How will the student determine which assumptions have been met? What analyses will be used in the event that the assumptions are not met? Will the planned analyses be appropriate in the event subjects are lost so that there are unequal numbers of subjects or trials in the different conditions?

The analysis segment of the proposal should be outlined to correspond with the objectives of the study, so that each analysis will yield evidence relating to a corresponding hypothesis. In addition, the reader should be able to determine how all data collected are to be analyzed. If data are to be presented in tabular or graphic form, an example of one such table, including predicted figures, often will be helpful to the reader. The purpose of a table or figure in a research report is to summarize material and to supplement the text in making it clearly understandable. Tables and graphic presentation may serve the same purpose in a proposal.

Because of their display quality, the inclusion of tables in the proposal may expose errors of research design. For instance, some committee readers may not detect the use of an incorrect error term from a reading of the text, but one glance at the degrees of freedom column in an analysis of variance table will reveal the error. In analysis of variance comparisons, inclusion of several tables may expose the presence of nonindependent variables.

If the analysis activity of the project is studied carefully in advance, many headaches as well as heartaches may be avoided. It may seem to take an inordinate amount of time to plan the analysis, but it is time that will not have to be spent again. As the analyses are completed, the results can immediately be inserted in the prepared tables, and the researcher can complete the project with a feeling of fulfillment rather than a frantic scramble to make sense out of a puzzle for which some of the pieces may prove to be missing.

The Statistical Well: Drinking the Greatest Draught

Students usually can expect help from their advisors with the design of statistical analysis. At minimum, an experienced advisor will have some suggestions about the type of analysis that would be most appropriate for the proposed investigation. Many departments include measurement and evaluation specialists who have statistical consultation with graduate students as a primary part of the professorial responsibility. Other departments work closely with outside statistical and computer consultants who may be in departments of educational psychology, psychology, computer science, or business administration.

The student should not, however, operate under the faulty impression that when the data are collected, they can be turned over to a handy statistical expert who, having an intimate relationship with the local computer, will magically return raw data in the finished form of findings and conclusions. Just as the student cannot expect the analysis of data to take care of itself, neither can the student expect a statistical consultant to take care of it.

The assistance of a statistician or computer consultant, invaluable though it may be, ordinarily is limited to the technology of design and data analysis, and help with using a packaged statistical program on a computer. The conceptual demands of the study and the particular form and characteristics of the data generated are the investigator's province—to be explained to the consultant, not vice versa. Likewise, the interpretation of results is a *logical,* not a technical, operation and thus is a responsibility for which only the investigator is properly prepared.

On finding a friendly computer

There are a variety of interrelated decisions to be addressed as the student contemplates the analysis phase of the study. First, what statistical tool or tools are needed to correctly analyze the data? Then, after the statistical methods are selected, what is the most efficient way to do the analysis? (Note that it is not a good idea to reverse the order of these two questions.) At one time students had few choices with regard to methods of analysis. Either they calculated the statistics themselves on hand or table calculators, or used the university computer to complete the analysis. Today, personal microcomputers have become commonplace and for most a variety of statistical programs are available. In addition, statistical packages for university mainframe computers have become far more versatile. Part of research planning involves making choices among a growing number of attractive options for analysis.

The first step in selecting a computer and program to analyze your data is to find out what computers and packages are available. The student's advisor, other graduate students, and the university computer center can be helpful. Many universities will have both mainframe and microcomputer consultants to help students and faculty. The first step is to eliminate all packages (and computers) that will not allow you to do the desired analysis. This may involve more than checking if the proposed statistical operation is available. For instance, you should be interested in the number of subjects and variables the program or computer can handle, whether data can be stored for reanalysis at a later date and, should data assume an unexpected form, whether other tests that might be needed are available with the same computer and package.

Mainframe computers and the common statistical packages (Biomedical Computer Programs [BMDP], Statistical Analysis System [SAS], and Statistical Package for the Social Sciences [SPSS and SPSS^x]) can accommodate either small or or large data sets for analysis and storage, perform all but the most esoteric of statistical tests, and are available in most computer centers. On the other hand, students may find some mainframe packages difficult to master, and finding a vacant terminal is a persistent problem on some campuses.

An alterantive to using a mainframe is the personal computer that can be used at home, in the office, or even in the student service area of some large computer centers. Packages for microcomputers of this type generally are user- friendly, diskettes for data storage can be purchased at a nominal cost, and many professors or friends will allow the use of personal machines, particularly during off hours. If you have an option, select a computer you will have access to throughout the period of proposal preparation and the subsequent study. Capacity to reaccess the data file from pilot studies, for example, can become vital at a point late in the planning process. Circumstances may even demand that the text of the proposal be altered after data collection has begun.

Microcomputers have some drawbacks. Unless protected with great care they remain painfully vulnerable to electronic accidents. Further, most personal computers cannot handle large data sets, thus limiting their utility for data-rich studies. Finally, despite the large number of statistical programs available for the better known microcomputers, the actual number of sophisticated tools available in any one package remains small.

Whether you choose a microcomputer or a mainframe computer, it is absolutely essential to backup your files by saving an extra copy on the mainframe or on a second microcomputer diskette and having a hard copy (a printout of your data) in more than one place. This applies equally to word processing text for the proposal document. As a matter of practice, have a printout of the data in at least two places. An extra word of caution—pay attention to the computer manual's nagging remainders to save frequently. Remember, data are like eggs, they are most secure when stored in more than one basket.

Selecting the wrong statistical package and computer rarely is fatal in the research process. The selection of a computer or package that does not meet all your needs may require additional time for entering data or may delay completion of the analysis. A little careful planning, however, may eliminate waste and reduce aggravation at a later date.

The care and nurture of consultants

To obtain technical help from an advisor, the student should be prepared to provide basic concepts about the content domain of the investigation, including a concise review of what is to be studied, a clear picture of the form data will take, and a preliminary estimate of alternative designs that might be appropriate to the demands of the proposed research. In addition, whether advice concerning design, statistics, or computer programming is sought from the student's project advisor, from a departmental specialist, or from an expert source external to the department, there are basic rules that must be considered if the student is to glean the most information and help for the smallest cost in valuable consultation time.

Rule 1: Understand the consultant's frame of reference. As with any other situation involving extended communication, it is useful to know enough about the language, predilections, and knowledge base of the consultant to avoid serious misunderstandings and ease the process of initiating the transaction. Research consultants are professionals whose primary interest is in the process of research design, statistical analysis, and the application of computers to research. They use a system language unique to statistics and data management and appreciate those who understand at least the rudiments of this vocabulary. Correspondingly, your consultant will not necessarily understand the system language to be used in the proposal, nor the peculiar characteristics of the data. For example, it cannot be assumed that the consultant knows that some of your data consist of repeated measures. Similarly, it would be unlikely for a statistician to know whether these data are normally distributed across trials.

The consultant cannot be expected to make decisions that relate to the purpose of the study, such as those regarding the balance between internal and external validity. Some designs may maximize the validity of the differences that may be found, but correspondingly trade off external validity, and thus the generalizability of the findings. Decisions concerning the acceptability of such research designs must be made by the proposer of the study. The grounds for such a determination rest in the purpose of the study and thus in conceptual work completed long before the consultation interview.

Consultants can be expected to evaluate a proposed experimental design, assist in selection from a group of alternative designs, suggest more efficient designs that have not been considered, and propose methods for efficiently completing the analysis. Often they can be most helpful, however, if preliminary models for design and statistical analysis have been proposed. This provides a starting place for discussion and may serve as a vehicle for considering characteristics of the data that will impose special demands.

Consultants can provide information about computer programs, the appropriateness of a particular program for the proposed design, and the entry techniques into these programs. Again, some preliminary preparation by the student can make the consultant's advisory task easier and work to guarantee an optimal selection of procedures for processing raw data. This preparation might include talking with other students presently engaged in computer use, reviewing material on computer language and packaged statistical programs, and visiting the computer center for an update on available services.

Normally, the statistics and computer specialists in a university setting are besieged by frantic graduate students and busy faculty colleagues, all in addition to the demands of their own students. Further, they may be responsible for the management of one or more functions in their own administrative unit or in the computer center. Finally, as active scholars they will be conducting their own research. Both the picture and the lesson should be equally clear to the student seeking assistance. Statisticians and computer scientists are busy people. They can provide effective assistance only when investigators come with accurate expectations for the kind of help a consultant can properly provide and come fully prepared to exercise their own responsibilities in the process.

Rule 2: Learn the language. The system languages of measurement, computer science, experimental design, and both inferential and descriptive statistics are used in varying degrees in the process of technical consultation for many research proposals. No one, least of all an experienced consultant, expects fluent mastery in the novice. The student must, however, have a working knowledge of fundamental concepts. These ordinarily include measures of central tendency and variability, distribution models, and the concept of statistical significance. Basic research designs, such as those described in introductory research method books, should be familiar to any novice.

It is, of course, preferable to complete at least one statistics course before attempting any study that will demand the analysis of quantitative data. If, as sometimes is the case, the student is learning basic statistics concurrent with the preparation of the proposal, special effort will have to be concentrated on preparing for consultations concerning design and analysis. The situation will be awkward at best, although many advisors will remain sympathetic and patient if students are honest about their limitations and willing to exert heroic effort once it becomes clear which tools and concepts must be mastered.

Beyond the problem of mastering enough of the language to participate in a useful discussion is the more subtle problem of understanding the particular analysis and techniques selected for the study. The student must not drift into the position of using a statistical tool or a measurement technique that really is not understood—even one endorsed and urged by the most competent of advisors. Ultimately the student will have to make sense out of the results obtained through any analysis. At that point, shallow or incorrect interpretations will quickly betray a failure to understand the nature of the analysis. The student also will have to answer questions about the findings long after the advisor is not around. Expert technical advice can be an invaluable asset in devising a strong proposal, but in the final analysis, such advice cannot substitute for the competence of the investigator.

Rule 3: Understand the proposed study. If the novice researcher does not understand the study sufficiently to identify and ask important and explicit questions, that lack is a major obstacle to a successful consultation. Only when the consultant understands the questions of central interest in the study is it possible to translate them into the steps of statistical analysis and selection of the appropriate computer program. Even if you employ a consultant only to help you with data preparation and analysis, if you cannot communicate exactly what you want, you may get back a printout from an analysis that is not what you had wanted. Further, a host of specific constraints associated with the nature of the study will condition the advisor's decision about which analysis to recommend.

The student should be ready to provide answers to each of the following questions:

(1) What are the independent variables of the study?

(2) What are the dependent variables of the study?

(3) What are the potential confounding variables of the study?

(4) What is the measurement scale of each variable (nominal, ordinal, interval, or ratio)?

(5) Which, if any, of the variables are repeated measures?

(6) What are the reliability and validity of the instruments used to produce the scores for each variable?

(7) What are the population distribution characteristics for each of the variables?

(8) What difference value between dependent variables would be of *practical* significance?

(9) What are the monetary, safety, ethical, or educational risks involved if a Type I error is made?

(10) What is the nature of the loss if a Type II error is made?

In summary, before consulting with a technical specialist the student must be able to express exactly what the study is to be designed to accomplish, identify the help needed in producing such a design, and provide all the explicit details the consultant will need in formulating advice.

Informed Consent: The Protection of Human Subjects

Many universities employ a system of mandatory review for all research proposals involving the use of human subjects. The purpose of such review usually is to protect the subjects' health and welfare or to ensure ethical procedures on the part of the investigator. In addition, many research journals now have specific guidelines that must be followed before a manuscript can be considered for review. Since the student is embarking on a project that is preparing him or her not only to complete the thesis but also for future research activity, it may be helpful to study guidelines from journals to which the research may be submitted before completing the section on the protection of human subjects. A particularly valuable reference is *Ethical Principles in the Conduct of Research with Human Participants*, published by the American Psychological Association (1982).

In recent years the domain of subject health and welfare has expanded, as a greater volume of diverse research activity has necessitated a broader definition of what constitutes ethical behavior for the investigator and reasonable protection for the subject. The point we wish to emphasize here is at once broader and more basic than the traditional concern for the physical and psychological safety of the subject; every human has a right not to be used by other people. Research workers in particular have a special responsibility to act in accord with that basic dictum.

The right not to be used applies with equal force to fifth-graders, college sophomores, and members of professional athletic teams. Subjects who cooperate in scientific investigations have a right to know what they are getting into and a right to give or withhold their cooperation on the basis of that information. The fact that one uses volunteers, or even paid subjects, does not alter their human right not to be treated as chattel. That this rule has so often been ignored in the past accounts in large measure for the difficulties, both obvious and subtle, in obtaining cooperation from prospective subjects.

Social scientists disagree on the degree to which use of psychometric instruments and questionnaires should be circumscribed by the use of procedures to protect the basic rights of subjects. This is an issue to be discussed with advisors during the preparation of the proposal. Our own position on this matter is unequivocal. Concern for the rights of subjects should attend the use of all paper-and-pencil instruments. The procedures employed in taking reasonable account of the subject's right to be informed may be much less elaborate than those used in an experiment involving physical discomfort or some degree of risk, but they should be designed with care and applied with scrupulous uniformity.

It is the ubiquity of questionnaires and the seeming innocuousness of psychometric instruments that present a special danger, a danger made more lethal because it is so much less obvious than the hazards involved in medical, pharmaceutical, or psychiatric research. To employ paper-and-pencil instruments without regard for the rights of subjects produces several unfortunate results. Each time people are involved in a situation in which they are treated as though they have no right to the privacy of their inner thoughts, the implication is that this is indeed the case. In contrast, when the investigator treats entry into the inner thoughts of a subject as a special privilege, granted by a consenting human as an act of informed cooperation, the opposite instruction is given and powerfully reinforced.

Of equal importance for the evolution of knowledge, improper use of paper-and-pencil tests has become an insidious pollution that already has eroded the effectiveness of these valuable instruments. Form questionnaires, pushed under the noses of subjects without explanation, cannot be taken seriously when they are filled out. When the instrument is not made to seem important, when the subject is not treated as though he or she were important, and when this takes place repeatedly over a lifetime, a kind of hardening occurs, which leads to careless, ill-considered responses, and even to deliberately falsified answers. Such data can only produce meaningless and distracting results. Subject populations are a vital resource for the investigator and, like any fragile resource, must be used in ways that preserve them for the future.

At a minimum, you should include the following procedures in any proposal involving human subjects:

(1) Subjects are to be informed of the general nature of the investigation and, within reasonable limits, of their role. A written script may be used in transmitting such information and should be included in an appendix to the proposal.

(2) Subjects are to have the opportunity, after reasonable consideration, to sign a document affirming that they have been informed of the general nature of the investigation and have consented to give their full cooperation. A copy of this form should be included in the appendix to the proposal (see the specimen form for "informed consent" in Appendix C).

(3) Subjects should receive an explanation of all treatment procedures to be used.

(4) Subjects should receive an explanation of any discomforts or risks involved.

(5) Subjects should receive an offer to answer any questions concerning purposes, procedures, discomforts, or risks.

(6) Subjects should be instructed that they are free to withdraw consent, without reprisal, and to discontinue participation in the study at any time.

(7) Subjects should be offered an opportunity to receive feedback on the results of the investigation at an appropriate later date.

Arguments to the effect that such procedures introduce unknown experimental bias effects are, in most cases, spurious. All contacts between investigators and subjects hold the potential for generating unknown effects. The procedure for ensuring the rights of subjects does no more than any other experimenter-subject contact. On the other hand, these procedures, quite aside from their ethical import, can exercise a measure of control over one of the most capricious of all variables—subject cooperation.

If it seems essential to withhold some specific item of information from subjects, then, after careful consideration of alternative courses of action, certainly it must be withheld. In almost all cases, however, there will be some important information that can be given to the subject as a basis for a decision to accept or decline participation. The proposal must present an explicit method for dealing with subjects that clearly indicates the nature of any omission. Further, the proposal must indicate procedures for promptly and thoroughly debriefing subjects whenever information has been withheld.

The basic rule is to treat subjects the way you would like to be treated. Any decision to do otherwise demands both compelling rationale and the most careful scrutiny.

The Scientific State of Mind: Proof, Truth, and Rationalized Choices

Scientific inquiry is not so much a matter of elaborate technology or even rigorous method as it is a particular state of mind. The processes of science rest, in the end, on how scientists regard the world and their work. Although some aspects of scientific thinking are subtle and elusive, others are not. These latter, the basic attitudinal prerequisites for the conduct of scientific inquiry, are reflected in the way a novice speaks and writes about proposed research. More directly, the proposal will reflect the degree to which the author has internalized critical attitudes toward such matters as proof, truth, and publicly rationalized choices.

What matters is not the observance of particular conventions concerning phrasing, but fundamental ways of thinking that are reflected in the selection of words. When, for example, students write, "The purpose of this study is to prove (or, to demonstrate) that . . . ," there always is the dangerous possibility that the intent is to do just that—to prove what they have decided must be true.

Such phrasing cannot be dismissed simply as awkward or naive. Students capable of writing such a sentence without hearing at once its dangerous implications are students with a fundamental defect in preparation. They should be allowed to go no further until they apprehend both the nature of proof and the purpose of research in the scientific enterprise, for clearly neither is understood.

Proof, if it exists at all in any useful sense, is a probabilistic judgment based on an accumulation of observations. Ordinarily, only a series of careful replications can lead to the level of confidence implied by the word "proved." Research is not an attempt to prove or demonstrate, it is an attempt to ask a careful question and to allow the nature of things to dictate the answer. The difference between "attempting to prove" and "seeking proof" is subtle but critical, and a scientist must never confuse the two.

If scientists have no illusions about proof, it is wrong, nonetheless, to believe that they never care about the direction of results obtained from their research. As humans, they often are painfully aware of the distinction between results that will be fortunate or unfortunate for their developing line of thought. As scientists, however, they recognize the irrelevance (and even the danger) of allowing personal convenience or advantage to intrude in the business of seeking knowledge. In the end, researchers must sit down before their facts as children and allow themselves to be instructed. The task lies in arranging the context for instruction, so that the answers to questions will be clear, but the content of the lesson must remain in the facts as revealed by the data.

A second critical sign of the student's ability to adopt the scientific viewpoint is the general way the matter of truth is treated in the proposal. When students write, "The purpose of this study is to discover the actual cause of . . . ," there is danger that they think it is possible to do just that—to discern the ultimate face of reality at a single glance. The most fundamental remediation will be required if such students ever are to understand, much less conduct, scientific inquiry.

Experienced researchers seek and revere veridical knowledge; they may even choose to think of research as the search for truth, but they also understand the elusive, fragile, and probabilistic nature of scientific truth. Knowledge is regarded as a tentative decision about the world, always held contingent on the content of the future.

The business of the researcher is striving to understand. Correspondingly, a high value is placed on hard-won knowledge. Truth is held gently, however, and the experienced investigator speaks and writes accordingly. It is not necessary to lard a proposal with reservations, provisos, and disclaimers such as "it seems." It is necessary to write with respect for the complexity of things and with modesty for what can be accomplished. The researcher's highest expectation for any study is a small but perceptible shift in the scale of evidence. Most scientific inquiry deals not in the heady stuff of truth, "establishing actual causes," but in hard-won increments of probability.

A third sign by which to estimate the student's scientific maturity is the ability (and willingness) to examine alternative interpretations of evidence, plausible rival hypotheses, facts that bid to discomfort the theoretical framework, and considerations that reveal the limitations of the methodology. It is important not only to lay out the alternatives for the reader but to explain the grounds for choice among them. The student who neither acknowledges alternatives nor rationalizes choices simply does not understand research well enough to bother with a proposal.

The mature researcher feels no compulsion to provide perfect interpretations or to make unassailably correct choices. One does the best one can within the limits of existing knowledge and the present situation. The author of a proposal is compelled, however, to make clearly rationalized choices from among carefully defined alternatives; this is one reason readers outside the scientific community find research reports tedious in their attention to detail and explanation. It is the public quality of the researcher's reasoning that makes a community of scientific enterprise possible, not the construction of a facade of uniform certainty and perfection.

Student-conducted research often contains choices that must be rationalized less by the shape of existing knowledge and the dictates of logic and more by the homely facts of logistics: time, costs, skills achieved, and available facilities. The habit of public clarity in describing and rationalizing choices must begin there, with the way things are. An honest accounting of hard and often imperfect choices is a firm step for the student toward achieving the habits of a good researcher—the scientific state of mind.

NOTE

1. Statistical significance, of course, is not synonymous with scientific significance in terms of the evolution of knowledge, or practical significance in terms of solving professional problems. Statistical significance largely depends on sample size and selection of *alpha* level (the level of confidence necessary to reject the null hypothesis). It can be demonstrated between almost any two groups using almost any variable selected, if the sample size is large enough and the power of the test sufficiently high. Such differences between groups may be statistically significant but scientifically trivial and professionally worthless. The pilot study is an excellent device by which the probability of a Type I error may be estimated and an appropriate sample size selected. In this way the investigator can increase the probability that a statistically significant result also will reflect a difference of scientific and practical significance.

Chapter 4

PREPARATION OF PROPOSALS FOR QUALITATIVE RESEARCH

Different Assumptions, Familiar Problems, and New Responses

For readers unfamiliar with qualitative research we will provide a brief definition. First, however, we offer several important caveats. Not all taxonomies for research divide the universe of possible designs into qualitative and quantitative. Indeed, some of the best do not (Burrell & Morgan, 1979; Gage, 1985: Shulman, 1981). It certainly is clear, for example, that the labels themselves are not best understood as simple poles of a dichotomy (Smith, 1983). Further, the work of Eisner (1981) demonstrates that the distance among various forms of qualitative inquiry may at times appear as great as the distance between laboratory experiments and field ethnography.

Given so many provisos, why have we opted for such an obvious oversimplification? The answer is because all forms of qualitative research with which we have had experience make demands on the planning process that are different from those encountered in quantitative designs. For the purpose of this guide, that is sufficient reason to divide research exactly along the practical lines of a simple dichotomy. We leave to others the task of discerning the optimal arrangement and proper understanding of research paradigms.

The purpose of qualitative research is to describe and develop a special kind of understanding for a particular social situation, event, role, group, or interaction. Examples would include a school or classroom, a playground, the process of textbook selection in a particular school district, or the experience of being a first-year teacher, an older adult attending a community college, or a case worker in a social service agency.

This kind of research is descriptive in that text (recorded words rather than numbers) is the most common form of data. Thus interview transcripts, field notes, diaries, and documents are primary sources of information. Qualitative inquiry also is analytic or interpretive in that the investigator must discern and then articulate often subtle regularities within the data. Thus reduction, organization, manipulation, display, and, above all, contemplation of data are primary rather than secondary activities in this form of research.

Most, though not all, qualitative research is naturalistic in that the researcher enters the world of the participant(s) as it exists and obtains data without any deliberate intervention to alter the setting. Even in the case of in-depth phenomenological interviewing, a qualitative technique that does not require the physical presence of the investigator in the subject's home environment, the objective is a reconstruction of experience as it has been experienced in a natural setting.

In all formats for qualitative study, detailed descriptions of context and what people actually say or do form the basis for inductive rather than deductive forms of analysis. That is, theory is created to explain the data rather than being collected to test preestablished hypotheses. The researcher may begin with some preliminary questions in mind or allow some foreshadowing of problems and relationships to direct the initial focus of attention, but otherwise must attempt to bring as few presumptions and as little preconceived structure to the study as possible.

The focus of attention is on the perceptions and experiences of the participants. What individuals say they believe, the feelings they express and explanations they give, are treated as significant realities. In that sense, there is a profoundly relativistic view of the world. The researcher is not seeking the kind of verifiable "truth" that functions in a cause and effect model of reality. The working assumption is that individuals make sense out of their experiences and in doing so create their own reality. In qualitative research, understanding both the content and construction of such multiple and contingent truths is regarded as a valuable task of science.

The purpose of this chapter is *not* to provide advice for those who plan to use interviews, questionnaires, critical incidents, content analysis of documents, or systematic field observation within what are otherwise traditional quantitative study designs. Aside from the technical demands peculiar to each, such methods of data collection and analysis present no special problems for the proposal. References to standard textbook sources, training experiences, and consultant advice will provide all the support needed to make appropriate use of those tools in a proposed study.

The concern here is with the writing of proposals that employ the qualitative paradigm for inquiry.[1] If the researcher begins with assumptions that genuinely reflect the viewpoint of qualitative study, the problems to be surmounted include, but go far beyond, familiarity and facility with data-gathering techniques such as interviewing and participant or nonparticipant observation in a field setting. Analysis of verbal text rather than numeric data is, of itself, a fundamentally different undertaking. In qualitative proposals the investigator/author will be involved in issues not represented in even the most esoteric of quantitative designs. The basic tasks of the proposal remain the same, but here the game must be played by some very different rules.

New Responses to Familiar Problems

Many of the elements of research that concern the quantitative investigator are present in qualitative designs, but they often demand quite different responses. Issues related to framing an appropriate initial question, reliability and validity of data, generalizability of results, replicability, sources of error, management and reduction of data, and interpretation of results are just as much central to an effective qualitative study as they are to a classical laboratory experiment, but the nature of the issues pertaining to each may assume an unfamiliar form.

As an example of how familiar elements of quantitative research take on new meaning in qualitative designs, consider the role of the investigator relative to the process of inquiry. Personal distance from both subjects and data is the key to objectivity in any experiment. Often heroic measures are taken to prevent the introduction of observer bias or subject reactivity. Similar concerns arise in qualitative research, but there the response must assume a quite different form. In a nonparticipant field observation study, for example, the investigator *is* the primary research instrument. Intimate and extended contact with human data sources at the level of direct personal interaction is the only way to make use of the sensitive capacities of that tool.

Direct presence as part of the research process means that the entire biography of the investigator—values, habits of perception, intellectual presumptions, and personal dispositions—becomes potentially relevant to gathering, analyzing, and understanding the data. There is no strategy that can eliminate the routing of data through the perceptual processes of the investigator. All that can be done is to understand enough about the nature of those processes so as to control the most serious threats to capturing an accurate picture of the world as understood by the resident(s) in the setting. At the level of the proposal, this means the task is to assure advisors that the author is both exquisitely aware of what will be brought to the study setting, and reasonably well practiced at the skill of using the self as a research instrument without intruding personal dispositions that distort rather than illuminate the data.

From this it should be clear that the issue of investigator bias as a source of error in qualitative research is a different kind of concern than the problem encountered in more familiar quantitative designs. More to the point here, it requires an entirely different form of control. What has been said in previous chapters about the general functions and uses of the proposal will serve equally well for qualitative designs. What has been said about particular research elements, however, will not apply in many instances. New responses are required for old problems. For that reason it is important to provide the interested reader with resources covering the technical detail required to design and execute a study— matters for which neither the scope of this handbook nor our personal expertise will permit adequate coverage.

Resources for Qualitative Research: Where to Begin?

Because the use of qualitative research in graduate student theses and dissertations outside the social sciences is a relatively recent phenomenon, locating the appropriate background literature without delays and false starts will be a problem for some. Accordingly, we will suggest a starting place for novice researchers who may be interested in considering the qualitative paradigm.

An overview of qualitative literature in the generic area of education can be found in Rogers (1984). More specific applications to the classroom are reviewed in Hamilton (1983), and to the gymnasium in Templin and Griffin (1985). The next step would be to read a beginning-level text, a purpose well served by Bogdan and Biklen (1982) or Patton

(1980). Nearly all of the early uses of qualitative research by graduate students working in educational settings employed one or both of these sources. Finally, Spindler (1982) provides less specific detail about method, but offers a number of excellent examples of what school ethnography can produce, as well as the kinds of questions for which it is appropriate.

If the student has sustained some enthusiasm for the prospect of doing a qualitative study, the next step would be to move on to resources that provide more technical detail on the specific issues to be confronted in a proposal, particularly those dealing with the process of data analysis. Here, Miles and Huberman (1984), Goetz and LeCompte (1984), and Glaser and Strauss (1967) would, taken together, yield sufficient information to support all but exceptional studies.

More specialized references will provide assistance when specific questions must be addressed: Whyte (1984) for the problems and processes of field research; Spradley (1979) for the interview, or participant observation (1980); Cook and Reichardt (1979), Fetterman (1984), Guba and Lincoln (1981), or Patton (1980) for the use of qualitative data in program evaluation; Van Maanen (1983) for applications in organizational analysis; and Bolster (1983), Popkewitz and Tabachnick (1981), Smith and Heshusius (1986) or Lincoln and Guba (1985) for critical analysis of the social and epistemological issues that attend the qualitative study of teaching as a process and schools or classrooms as contexts.

Of particular note as a reference for those writing their first proposal for qualitative research is the recent text by Dobbert (1982). Intended as a handbook for the novice, a section on proposals includes both general discussion and reprints of actual models used in successful grant applications and academic proposals. Although the primary focus is on the design of contracted research to be performed by substantial research teams for social or governmental agencies, there is much advice that will be valuable to anyone preparing a first proposal for qualitative research.

The Decision to Go Qualitative: Questions for the Novice

The decision to undertake a qualitative study brings problems in two broad arenas: those that are external and mostly antecedent to the proposal, and those that are internal as part of content within the proposed design. While some of these difficulties overlap both areas, it will be convenient here to treat them separately.

The external problems that precede the writing of a proposal begin with the author as a person. Every graduate student who is tempted to employ a qualitative design should confront one question, "Why do I want to do a qualitative study?" and then answer it honestly. Some novice researchers, traumatized by a fourth-grade encounter with fractions, see qualitative research as a way of avoiding numbers in general and statistics in particular. So long as question and method are well matched, a choice made on such personal grounds is neither improper nor dysfunctional. Personal biography is a wise consideration in locating questions and methods about which one can be enthusiastic. Unfortunately, having an aversion to math is not the same as having the personal capacities and intellectual interests demanded in the conduct of qualitative research. Avoiding statistics is not so much a *bad* reason for electing to do a field ethnography as it is a motive that is *irrelevant* to locating the kind of research that you will perform well. Having the interest, ability, and patience to acquire qualitative research skills is a far more relevant foundation than discovering you have a bad case of math anxiety.

In the same vein, a student who elects qualitative research because it appears to be either relatively "quick" in terms of time commitment or "easy" in terms of intellectual demands has, in the first instance, simply never talked with anyone who has completed such a study and, in the second instance, not read published reports of qualitative research with much care. Field studies are never quick and rarely are completed within the projected time lines. The analysis of qualitative data demands a sustained level of creative thought rarely required once data are collected in a quantitative study. Qualitative research may be enormously valuable for scientific purposes, and immensely satisfying to the investigator, but quick and easy it is not.

Finally, some individuals find themselves drawn to qualitative forms of inquiry because they are unable to accept the initial assumptions that underlie quantitative research. They simply feel more comfortable, in personal or intellectual terms, with the view of knowledge and reality presumed in qualitative research. Such dispositions may constitute a sound basis for establishing preferences in research style. Close examination of how, whether, and when one "knows" something, is a discipline that might profitably be practiced by all research workers.

Nevertheless, whatever one's predilections concerning such matters as objectivity, truth, and reality, it still is necessary to match method to question. Ideology or personal preference in epistemology do not make it possible to fit round methods into square questions. If you are committed to doing qualitative research, then you are limited to questions that yield best to that scientific paradigm. Determination of the method of inquiry before identification of the question always bears that restriction.

A second pre-proposal problem centers on the investigator's ability to move out of the quantitative mode of thought. For many graduate students the process of becoming comfortable with the qualitative way of thinking about problems requires adopting a view of the world that is alien to the fundamental canons of empirical thought. For most of us, the assumptions of quantitative research have been presented and learned as "science" through at least a dozen years of school and university education. That all things that truly exist must exist in some number, and exist "out there" in some finite form that is knowable as truth, is more than the unspoken premise of quantitative research. It is an assumption that people in Western cultures often accept about what is real and what is not real in the world.

To operate comfortably with the proposition that people *construct* reality, thus allowing truth to reside as much in our heads as "out there," demands a sharp alteration in habitual modes of thought. Even partially accomplished, this is difficult for most and, as experience warns us, is impossible for some. It is important that this be confronted during the early apprenticeship stage, when patient and sympathetic mentors can assist in the difficult transition of habitual perceptions and familiar concepts into a new mode of thought.

Dealing with the researcher as a person leads inevitably to a more immediate and obvious problem; finding sources for training and support. Courses and internships in qualitative research methods are rare at many institutions and unavailable at others. When such opportunities do exist they most commonly occur as upper-level graduate experiences in social science departments. As such they are not always accessible to students with backgrounds in other fields. In sum, both students and professorial advisors may find themselves far more along then they might wish.

While a degree of self-education is possible for both advisors and the solitary student, it is best to have no illusions about how difficult that process might become. Because preparation for qualitative research often is most effective and efficient when it takes the form of apprenticeship, with intensive field experiences and closely supervised data analysis at the heart of the training process, the student without such opportunities must confront some serious questions. In terms of outcomes will such effort be cost-effective? Will the best solution require transfer to a more hospitable department or institution? Is there sufficient time to invest in *both* extensive preparation and a lengthy study? Hard questions, but better raised now than later!

Finally, in some departments (or whole institutions) qualitative research is not yet an acceptable form of inquiry. Individual professors may undertake to enlighten or reeducate their colleagues, or to work for revision of graduate school policies (written or unwritten), but individual graduate students are likely to find themselves overmatched in any such effort. A realistic appraisal of the political territory, including the existence of precedents and the fate of similar efforts, should come before the final commitment to prepare a full-scale proposal. Have potential committee members or needed consultants seen a prospectus or mini-proposal and indicated their willingness to participate? Have qualitative studies actually been accepted by the graduate school? What questions were raised about previous qualitative proposals by review groups at department or school levels? How has the human subject review committee responded to qualitative designs in the past? Those are the practical kind of questions that should be raised.

Given some reassurance that a path might be cleared through the problems of obtaining institutional support and approval, the focus of concern shifts from the external preliminaries of identifying a research question, selecting a mode of inquiry, and developing research skills, to the actual task of writing a proposal. We come here to the concerns that are internal because they are intrinsic to the paradigm. In this second broad arena the problems to be surmounted relate to the special characteristics of qualitative research. The proposal still serves the same functions; but with a new form of inquiry, old problems may require new responses.

The Qualitative Proposal: New Rules for a Familiar Game

For graduate students, many of the problems encountered in preparing a proposal for qualitative research have their origins in the context and expectations of graduate education. The first of these contextual problems is related to the very nature of the document. Ordinarily, the author works to achieve a level of specification and anticipation in the proposal that will bring it as near to a "closed contract" as conditions permit. In contrast, the nature of qualitative research demands an "open contract." Unlike the typical quantitative investigation, the qualitative research worker sometimes must move back and forth between data sources and ongoing data analysis *during the period of data collection.* Initial questions are progressively narrowed or, on occasion, shifted entirely as the nature of the living context becomes apparent through preliminary analysis. While this sort of in-process shift of focus or change in method is less typical of interview-based case studies than of field enthnographies, all subspecies of qualitative research commonly undergo some form of refinement during the period of active investigation.

Accordingly, although all proposals must begin with some clear question or set of questions that can be answered only by describing and understanding a bound slice of the world, neither the specific focus of inquiry nor the exact and final form of method and analysis can be specified in advance for most qualitative studies. In whatever discussion the proposal provides, the initial set of questions and procedures must be established, at least in general or tentative terms. When, however, it is an essential part of the design to develop focus and method that are responsive to the ongoing process of data acquisition, it is difficult to describe precisely what you plan to do in advance. Unfortunately, in many graduate programs that is the expectation that advisors bring to the proposal.

There are two ways to deal with this sensitive problem. The first is to engage in enough careful piloting of method and analysis to permit discussion of the matters that normally concern advisors—initial focus, study site and subjects, obtaining access, number and type of data sources, ethical concerns, forms of data processing and display, and demonstration of needed research skills. Not only can information from a preliminary study help meet the concerns of advisors, pilot work allows the researcher to shape the proposal around concrete experiences rather than speculation. This can yield greater conceptual strength as well as improvements in logistic efficiency.

The second alternative is to create a largely speculative proposal, using the existing literature to foreshadow themes and provide examples of method. At the least, this strategy permits demonstration of the author's familiarity with existing research, ability to think carefully about the problems of field investigation, and capacity to lay out intentions in broad terms. Such theoretical discourse may be sufficient for a committee that is familiar with the qualitative paradigm and confident that the novice's level of preparation will be equal to the demands of the proposed study. Under these conditions, however, it can be anticipated that advisors will be far less helpful in conceptualizing the study or in suggesting useful strategies for data analysis. The concrete products of a good pilot study are a better basis for consultation than even the most elegant of theoretical speculations.

If qualitative proposals deviate from the norm as contracts for future action, they may deviate even more sharply in the specific area of the literature review. Some functions in this section of the proposal will be familiar if not identical replications of those present in the quantitative model. These include seating the study in the foundational literature of the paradigm, citing works that explain and legitimate the particular methods proposed for use, using scholarly works to create a frame of constructs and theory for the particular area of study, and demonstrating how the proposed research would fit into the ongoing dialogue of science.

The unique difference in the use of literature will lie in decisions that may be made concerning use of research reports dealing with the same or closely related questions. There may be sound reasons not to read that literature, at least not until after pilot work is complete, or possibly until a preliminary analysis of the data from the main study is available. The rationale for this departure from expected use of background material is not difficult to appreciate.

Remembering that the investigator *is* the primary instrument on which qualitative research must depend for acquisition of data, it is clear that such an instrument must be fully open to the print of other people's view of their world without imposing the freight of the observer's own perceptions. For that purpose, there are obvious advantages to beginning study without knowledge of conclusions reached by others working in the same context. The necessary critical comparison of results with the published literature may best be left to the final stage of the research process.

Under the best of conditions the problem of what to read often proves to be more complicated than the novice anticipates. In some cases the most helpful information about appropriate methods can only be found embedded in the very reports the student might wish to eschew. In other cases, advisors may argue that whatever contamination might devolve from reviewing previous research presents no more risk than the collection of values and beliefs already present in the novice's head, and thereby urge use of every possible resource in constructing the proposal.

Resolution of these dilemmas will be neither simple nor perfectly satisfying to all parties. The only certain rule applies here as in any other proposal. The author *is* obligated to do a thorough search of the literature so that decisions about the timing and nature of use will relate to the complete body of potentially relevant resources. As with quantitative proposals, whether related research is grouped in a separate review section or is used as needed throughout the proposal is an individual choice.

Another problem encountered in qualitative proposals is the task of "coming clean" about the ways in which personal biography will influence the research process. All researchers, quantitative as much as qualitative, bring significant personal baggage to the tasks of inquiry. It may be possible to pretend that the investigator's person can effectively be isolated from the processes of quantitative research. This pretense, however, is never possible in qualitative research.

Clear threats to accurate perception in terms of previous experience in the research setting, personal values, characteristic assumptions, and obvious bias must be addressed directly in the proposal. This is not done in an attempt to cleanse one's self of personal viewpoint and become neutral relative to the subject of study. Most qualitative researchers hold "objectivity" to be an illusion, a human state that is both impossible and undesirable to achieve. What the investigator brings to the setting can become a positive part of the research process, but only if it is recognized as an inextricable background for every step from question to conclusion. Coming clean thus means the creation of awareness, not the divestiture of self.

While concerns such as observer bias do have analogues in quantitative research, they are here a more pervasive problem, and one for which there are seldom simple solutions. For example, one common example of the problem of investigator biography occurs when graduate students, who themselves are former teachers or school administrators, design a study that requires them to return to the context of public education and play the role of unbiased spectator. Their first attempts to observe often trigger an avalanche of judgments about right or wrong, effective or ineffective, and desirable or undesirable, all based on the observer's past experiences in similar settings. This unbidden flood of evaluation poses a severe impediment to seeing, much less understanding, the world as experienced by the present participants. This particular problem is difficult to overcome and is precisely why it sometimes is best to select problems in a subject area or context with which the investigator has not had extensive previous experience.

The proposal should provide evidence that factors of personal background have been scrupulously examined, understood, and accommodated by clear provisions for self-monitoring at each stage of the study. It often is possible to make plans to control for the influence of biography at the stages of data-gathering and data analysis. It may be desirable, for example, to cross-check the investigator's perceptions and decisions with a colleague wherever it is evident that personal dispositions might interact with bias-sensitive research tasks.

The final problem is not unique to qualitative proposals, but is predictably more complex and troublesome. Issues concerning the ethics of qualitative research continue to stimulate debate and concern, perhaps most so among those who have extensive experience with the paradigm. To resolve these, novices may need lengthy discussion with advisors, and certainly will require long dialogue with their conscience.

The issues here are not all abstract, subtle, gradual, or distant from the person of the investigator. They can be sudden, painful, and fraught with genuine risk. How does the researcher weigh morality and pragmatic concerns when a subject is observed in an illegal action? What does the observer do when an informant suddenly demands access to field notes? What is ethical behavior when circumstances appear to require that the investigator take an active part in the very events for which nonparticipant observation is the desired role? What is the right response when a school principal accuses the program evaluator of collusion with teachers for the purpose of subverting district policy? What action represents ethical behavior when the guarantee of subject anonymity is irretrievably breached after 20 in-depth interviews have already been conducted?

Whenever investigators enter into the daily lives of others at the level of intrusion required for qualitative study, significant problems of ethics are raised. Because the potential for direct harm is less obvious and the issues are more subtle than those typically encountered in quantitative research, ethical problems are easier to overlook in the proposal—and thereby are doubly serious.

The obligation to protect the best interest of subjects has compelling force in the qualitative paradigm. To complete a successful study requires that one or several residents in the study context welcome the investigator as a guest and a trusted confidant. Subjects who, by sharing their intimate version of events, are not exposed to some risk or disadvantage are the exception rather than the rule. This is most commonly the case in terms of possible repercussions on relationships with other people in the setting. It is all too easy for an informant to be regarded as a tattletale. The ideal rule of ethical conduct requires that whenever the researcher has a choice between using or not using material that is valuable to the study but that may make the subject vulnerable, the interest of the subject must be selected over that of the investigation. It is much easier to subscribe to this, however, than it is to carry it out when interesting information must be lost.

At the least, such problems place heavy responsibility on the visitor for sensitive protection of sources. That the novice researcher understands this should be evident in every part of the proposal: the choice of language, the constraints accepted, the security devised to protect data, the establishment of informed consent at entry, the negotiation of subject rights, and the provision of genuine reciprocity with collaborating hosts. The definition of what is right and acceptable conduct may be treated as a matter that is relative to context; for different circumstances there may be different rules of behavior. Determining these definitions with great care, however, is not an optional element in the proposal. Attention to ethical problems is an essential obligation in the planning of all research.

Once the unique problems—the open contract, limited use of the literature, personal biography, and ethical questions—have been considered, the more general tasks of proposal writing can be addressed in the specific forms they assume for qualitative study. Each author will devise a list of tasks based on his or her training and experience, and the particular nature of the proposed study.

The following items seem to rise to the top of many priority lists:

(1) developing a language or set of constructs for talking about the question to be pursued;
(2) identifying an appropriate site, data sources, and methods of gathering information;
(3) setting boundaries for the investigation—what is inside and what is beyond the limits of the study?
(4) determining strategies to ensure reliability and validity in data;
(5) establishing procedures that will leave a clear trail, allowing others to know with reasonable precision how and why decisions were made at each stage of the study;
(6) developing procedures for data management, reduction, and display;
(7) identifying at least the first steps in data analysis; and
(8) laying plans for negotiating entry into the field of study.

At this point it is appropriate to make note of one of the most interesting options available to the scholar who is interested in qualitative techniques. It obviously is possible to gather qualitative and quantitative forms of data within the same study. Whether it also is possible to analyze those data from perspectives that genuinely represent the two distinctive world views, combining results in some truly meaningful fashion, is the subject of continuing and energetic debate (Schofield & Anderson, 1984; Smith & Heshusius, 1986).

Whatever the conclusion of that long dialogue among scientists, it is a fact that a growing number of published studies do include both qualitative and quantitative elements. Further, there is evidence that designs employing such combinations have made important contributions to program evaluation, organizational studies, and policy development (Rossman & Wilson, 1984). Even if quantitative data are not gathered, the investigator may still have to weigh the advantages and disadvantages of the quantification of qualitative information as part of the data reduction process.

The salient question here is whether an attempt to combine qualitative and quantitative paradigms is an appropriate undertaking for a beginner in research. Certainly there are examples in almost every academic and professional literature. Novices can inspect these and form their own conclusions about the complexity of the process and the quality of the result.

Our experience as advisors suggests simply that if doing one kind of research is difficult, doing two kinds at once may be doubly so. The line between what is courageous and what is foolhardy is not always easy to discern. The importance of ending up on the right side of that line, however, is clear and compelling. The work of a novice, like any other, must meet a basic test. It must be done well, with correct use of both the techniques of data acquisition and modes of data analysis common to the scientific paradigm(s) employed. With that in mind, both the power of the design and the capability of the designer become legitimate concerns in planning any study. The resulting rule is clear and simple. Propose only the study you honestly believe you are prepared to execute.

To close on a note of optimism, it is fair to observe that decisions about each of these planning steps are more "forgiving" than they tend to be in quantitative research. The selection of a study site, for example, probably is not as critical as the novice is inclined to believe. There is a strong tendency after reading impressive field studies to believe that the great site produced the fine study. Experienced qualitative research workers, however, are more inclined to credit careful planning, perceptive analysis of data—and luck. None of the decisions made for the proposal is likely to make or break a first effort, even though they are decisions that must be made. Our advice is to plan as carefully as possible, but to keep a healthy respect for the surprises to be encountered and the inevitable adjustments that must be made in the best laid plans.

NOTE

1. A scientific paradigm is a particular way of thinking about meaning in the context of inquiry. Just as each person has a cognitive schema for making sense of the world of daily experience, groups of scientists have particular ways of making sense of their scientific world. The area of paradigmatic epistemology is beyond the scope of this guide, but acquaintance with the concepts and issues therein will be part of the essential preparation of any young scholar. For readers not yet introduced to research paradigms we recommend the work of Tuthill and Ashton (1983) and Smith and Heshusius (1986) as appropriate places to begin, particularly because of their close attention to education and the ways in which research paradigms differ in the physical and social sciences.

Chapter 5

STYLE AND FORM IN WRITING THE PROPOSAL

The writing style of the thesis or grant proposal may be the most important factor in conveying your ideas to graduate advisors or funding agencies. Even experienced researchers must critically evaluate their writing to ensure that the best laid plans are presented in a clear, straightforward fashion. The sections that follow represent primary concerns for proposal writers.

Praising, Exhorting, and Polemicizing: Don't

For a variety of motives arising principally from the reward system governing other writing tasks, many students use their proposal as an opportunity to praise the importance of their discipline or professional field. Some use exhortative language to urge such particular points of view as the supposed importance of empirical research in designing professional practice. Others use the proposed research as the basis for espousing the virtues of particular social or political positions.

There is no need or proper place in a research proposal for such subjective side excursions. The purpose of a proposal is to set forth for a reader the exact nature of the matter to be investigated and a detailed account of the methods to be employed. Anything else distracts and serves as an impediment to clear communication.

As a general rule, it is best to stick to the topic and resist the temptation to sound "properly positive and enthusiastic." Do not attempt to manipulate the opinions of the reader in areas other than those essential to the investigation. The simple test is to ask yourself this question, "Does the reader really need to consider this point in order to judge the adequacy of my thinking?" If the answer is "no," then the decision to delete is clear, if not always easy, for the author.

Quotations: How to Pick Fruit from the Knowledge Tree

Too often, inexperienced writers are inclined to equate the number of citations in a paper with the weight of the argument being presented. This is an error. The proper purposes served by the system of scholarly citation are limited to a few specific tasks (as noted in Appendix B). When a document has all the citations needed to meet the demands of those few tasks, it has enough. When it contains more citations, it has too many and is defective in that regard. Reviewers deem the use of nonselective references as an indication of poor scholarship, an inability to discriminate the central from the peripheral and the important from the trivial in research.

The proper uses of direct quotation are even more stringently limited than the use of general citations for paraphrased material. The practice of liberally sprinkling the proposal with quoted material—particularly lengthy quotations—is more than pointless, it is self-defeating. The first truth is that no one will read them. The second truth is that most readers find the presence of unessential quotations irritating and a distraction from the line of thought being presented for examination. When quotations are introduced at points for which even general citations are unnecessary, the writer has reached the limit of disregard for the reader.

There are two legitimate motives for direct use of another scholar's words: (1) the weight of authoritative judgment, in which "who said it" is of critical importance, and (2) the nature of expression, in which "how it was said" is the important element. In the former instance, when unexpected, unusual, or genuinely pivotal points are to be presented, it is reasonable to show the reader that another competent craftsperson has reached exactly the desired conclusion, or observed exactly the event at issue. In the latter instance, when another writer has hit on the precise, perfect phrasing to express a difficult point, it is proper to employ that talent in behalf of your own argument. The rule to follow is simple. If the substance of a quotation can be conveyed by a careful paraphrase, followed, of course, by the appropriate credit of a citation, with all of the clarity and persuasive impact of the original, *then don't quote*. In almost all instances it is best for the proposer to speak directly to the reader. The intervention of words from a third party should be reserved, like heavy cannon in battle, for those rare instances when the targets are specific and truly critical to the outcome of the contest.

A beneficial technique for students who recognize their own propensity toward excessive quotation is to use the critical summary form of note taking. In this format, after carefully recording a full citation, each article is critically examined and then paraphrased on reference cards in the student's own words. During note-taking, a decision is made on whether the aesthetics of phrasing or the author's importance in terms of authority justify the use of direct quotation. Except in rare instances, quoted material is not transferred to the note cards. Thus direct quoting becomes less tempting during the subsequent writing phase when the student has recourse to notes. This technique also prevents unintentional plagiarism. Obviously, the technique of making photocopies of stacks of articles and then writing with them directly at hand invites excessive quoting.

Clarity and Precision: Speaking in System Language

The language we use in the commerce of our everyday lives is common language. We acquired our common language vocabulary and grammar by a process that was gradual, unsystematic, and mostly unconscious. Our everyday language serves us well, at least as long as the inevitable differences in word meanings assigned by different people do not produce serious failures of communication.

The language of science, specifically the language of research, is uncommon. The ongoing conversation of science, for which a research proposal is a plan of entry, is carried on in system languages in which each word must mean one thing to both writer and reader. Where small differences may matter a great deal, as in research, there must be a minimum of slippage between the referent object, the word used to stand for the object, and the images called forth by the word in the minds of listeners and readers.

The rules of invariate word usage give system languages a high order of precision. Minute or subtle distinctions can be made with relative ease. Evaluative language can be eliminated or clearly segregated from empirical descriptive language. More important, however, the language of research affords the reliability of communication that permits scientists to create a powerful interdependent research enterprise rather than limited independent investigations. When a chemist uses the system language of chemistry to communicate with another chemist, the word "element" has one and only one referent, is assigned to the referent on all occasions, is used for no other purpose within the language system, and consistently evokes the same image in the minds of everyone, everywhere, who has mastered the language.

Various domains of knowledge and various research enterprises are characterized by differing levels of language development. Some disciplines, such as anatomy or entomology, have highly developed and completely regularized language systems whereas others, particularly the behavioral sciences, employ languages still in the process of development. Irrespective of the area of investigation, however, the language of any research proposal must, as a minimum requirement, be systematic within itself. The words used in the proposal must have referents that are clear to the reader and must be used consistently to designate only one referent. When the investigation lies within a subject area with an existing language system, then, of course, the author is bound to the conventions of that system.

Obviously, the researcher should be familiar with the system languages that function in the area of proposed investigation. Reading and writing both the specific language of the subject matter area and the more general languages common to the proposed methodology (statistics, experimental design, psychometrics, computer languages, etc.) are clear requirements for any study. Less obvious, however, is the fact that research proposals, by their exploratory nature, often demand the extension of existing language into new territory. Operations, observations, concepts, and relationships not previously specified within a language system must be assigned invariate word symbols by the investigator. More important, the reader must carefully be drawn into the agreement to make these same assignments.

Advisors and reviewers misunderstand student proposals far more often then they disagree with what is proposed. The failure of communication often occurs precisely at the point where the proposal moves beyond the use of the existing system language. This problem involves a failure of careful invention rather than a failure of mastering technique or subject matter. The following rules may be of some help as the student attempts to translate a personal vision of the unknown into the form of a carefully specified public record.

(1) Never invent new words when the existing system language is adequate. If the referent in established use has a label that excludes what you do not want and includes all that you do want, then it needs no new name.

(2) If there is reasonable doubt as to whether the word is in the system or the common domain, provide early in the proposal the definition that will be used throughout. Readers may give time and attention to deciphering the intended meaning unless you put their minds at ease.

(3) Words that have been assigned system meaning should not be used in their common language form. For example, the word "significant" should not be used to denote its common language meaning of "important" in a proposal involving the use of statistical analysis. The system language of inferential statistics assigns invariant meaning to the word "significant"; any other use invites confusion.

(4) Where a system language word is to be used in either a more limited or a more expanded sense, make this clear when the word first is introduced in the proposal. If the norms for local style requirements permit, this is one of the legitimate uses of footnotes to the text.

(5) Where it is necessary to assign invariant meaning to a common language word in order to communicate about something not already accommodated within the system language, the author should choose with great care. Words with strong evaluative overtones, words with a long history of ambiguity, and words that have well-entrenched usage in common language make poor candidates for elevation to system status. No matter how carefully the author operationalizes the new definition, it is always difficult for the reader to make new responses to familiar stimuli.

(6) A specific definition is the best way to assign invariant meaning to a word. When only one or two words require such treatment, this can be accomplished in the text. A larger number of words may be set aside in a section of the proposal devoted to definitions. The best definition is one that describes the operations that are required to produce or observe the event or object. For example, note how the following words are assigned special meaning for the purpose of a proposal.

(a) Common language word is assigned invariate use:

> *Exclusion* will be deemed to have occurred when both of the following situations occur: The student no longer is eligible to participate in extracurricular activities under any provision of school district policy. The student's name is stricken from the list of students eligible for extracurricular activities.

(b) System language word is employed with limitations not ordinarily assigned:

> *The curriculum* will be limited to those after school activities that the current *School District Manual* lists as approved for secondary school students.

(c) System language word is operationalized by describing criterion:

> *Increased Motivation* will be presumed when, subsequent to any treatment condition, the time spent in any extracurricular activity rises more than 10% of the previous weekly total.

(d) Common language word is operationalized by describing criterion:

> *Dropouts* are defined as all participants who fail to attend three consecutive activity meetings.

(e) System language word is operationalized by describing procedure:

> *Reinforcement* will refer to the procedure of listing all club members in the school newspaper, providing special hall passes for members, and listing club memberships on school transcripts.

(f) Common language word is operationalized by describing procedure:

> *Instruction* will consist of five 10-minute sessions in which the club sponsor may employ any method of teaching so long as it includes no fewer than five attempts for each student to complete the activity.

Editing: The Care and Nurture of a Document

A proposal is a working document. As a primary vehicle for communication with advisors and funding agencies, as a plan for action, and as a contract, the proposal performs functions that are immediate and practical, not symbolic or aesthetic. Precisely because of these important functions, the proposal, in all of its public appearances at least, should be free from distracting mechanical errors and the irritating confusion of shoddy format.

At the privacy of your own desk, it is entirely appropriate to cross out passages and to use scissors, paste (or if using a word processor, adding, deleting, and moving text), and rough drafts as part of the process through which a proposal evolves toward final form. When, however, the proposal is given to an advisor, sent to a funding agency, or presented to a seminar, the occasion is public and calls for an edited, formally prepared document. The document should be easy to read—the proposer should use a good typewriter or printer and, when required, a new ribbon. If using a dot matrix computer printer make certain that extended text can be read without visual strain.

Every sentence must be examined and reexamined in terms of its clarity, grammar, and relationship with surrounding sentences. A mark of the neophyte writer is the tendency to resist changing a sentence once it is written, and even more so when it has been typed. A sentence may be grammatically correct and still be awkward within its surroundings. The tough test is the best test here. If, in reading any sentence, a colleague or reviewer hesitates, stumbles, or has to reread the sentence to understand the content, then the sentence must be examined for possible revision— no matter how elegant, obvious, and precise it seems to the author.

Aside from meticulous care in writing and rewriting, the most helpful procedure in editorial revision is to obtain the assistance of colleagues to read the proposal for mechanical errors, lack of clarity, and inadequacies of content. An author can read the same error over and over without recognizing it, and the probability of discovery declines with each review. The same error may leap at once to the attention of even the most casual reader who is reading the proposal for the first time. One useful trick that may improve the author's ability to spot mechanical errors is to read the sentences in reverse order, thus destroying the strong perceptual set created by the normal sequence of ideas.

Although format will be a matter of individual taste, or departmental or agency regulation, several general rules may be used in designing the layout of the document:

(1) Use double-spacing, substantial margins, and ample separation for major subsections. Crowding makes reading both difficult and unpleasant. *Always* number pages so that readers can quickly refer to a specific location.

(2) Make ample use of graphic illustration. A chart or simple diagram can improve clarity and ease the difficult task of critical appraisal and advisement.

(3) Make careful and systematic use of headings. The system of headings recommended in the *Publication Manual of the American Psychological Association* (1983) is particularly useful for the design of proposals.

(4) Place in an appendix everything that is not immediately essential to the main tasks of the proposal. Allowing readers to decide whether they will read supplementary material is both courtesy and good strategy.

In Search of a Title: First Impressions and the Route to Retrieval

The title of the proposal is the first contact a reader has with the proposed research. First impressions, be they about people, music, food, or potential research topics, generate powerful anticipations about what is to follow. Shocking the reader by implying one content domain in the title and following with a different one in the body of the proposal is certain to evoke a strong negative response. The first rule in composing a title is to achieve reasonable parity between the images evoked by the title and the opening pages of the proposal.

For the graduate student, the proposal title may well become the thesis or dissertation title and therefore calls for careful consideration of all the functions it must serve and the standards by which it will be judged. The first function of the title is to identify content for the purpose of retrieval. Theses and dissertations are much more retrievable than was once the case. In fact, they have become a part of the public domain of the scholar. The increasing use of microfiche and microfilm has made the circulation of unpublished documents many times faster and far broader in geographic scope. Titling research has become, thereby, an important factor in sharing research.

In less sophisticated times, titles could be carelessly constructed and the documents would still be discovered by diligent researchers who could take the time to investigate items that appeared only remotely related to their interests. Today, scholars stagger under the burden of sifting through enormous and constantly increasing quantities of material apparently pertinent to their domain. There is no recourse other than to be increasingly selective in documents actually retrieved and inspected. Hence each title the researcher scans must present at least a moderate probability of being pertinent, on the basis of the title alone, or it will not be included on the reading list for review. In short, the degree to which the title communicates a concise, thorough, and unambiguous picture of the content is the first factor governing whether a given report will enter the ongoing dialogue of the academic community.

Word selection should be governed more by universality of usage than by personal aesthetic judgment or peculiarly local considerations. Computer retrieval systems, such as MEDLINE, DIALOG, and ERIC, on which more and more scholars are depending for leads to related studies in their research field, classify titles according to a limited set of key words. The researcher constructs a search plan that will identify all studies categorized by key words known to be associated with their area of interest. Thus both readers and writers of research reports must describe the research in similar terms or, in too many instances, they will not reach each other.

The title should describe as accurately as possible the exact nature of the main elements in the study. Although such accuracy demands the use of specific language, the title should be free of obscure technical terms or jargon that will be recognized only by small groups of researchers who happen to pursue similar questions within a narrow band of the knowledge domain.

Components appropriate for inclusion in the title

The elements most commonly considered for inclusion in the title are the dependent and independent variables, the performance component represented by the criterion task or tasks, the treatment or treatments to be administered, the model underlying the study, the purpose of the study (predicting, establishing relationships, or determining differences), and any unusual contribution of the study.

Dependent and independent variables ordinarily should be included, although they may be presented under a more general rubric. For instance, the dependent variables of a study might be simple reaction time, discriminatory reaction time, movement time, and reflex time. In the title the four measures might appear as "neuromuscular responses." Similarly, the performance components of the study also may be summarized into a single categorical term.

A clever author can, by careful selection of words, provide information in the title that a theory is being tested by using a word that often is associated with the theory. For instance, the title, "Generalizability of Contingency Management and Reinforcement in Second-Grade Special Education Classes" implies that the investigator is testing the applicability of behavioral theory to a specific population. Much has been communicated by including the single word "generalizability" in the title.

The ultimate purpose of the study in terms of predicting, establishing relationships, or determining differences can be expressed without providing an explicit statement. For example, when variables are expressed in a series, "Anthropometrics, Swimming Speed, and Shoulder-Girdle Strength," relationship generally is implied. If the same study were titled "Anthropometrics and Shoulder-Girdle Strength of Fast and Slow Swimmers," the reader would anticipate a study in which differences were determined.

Any aspect of the study that is particularly unusual in terms of methodology, or that represents a unique contribution to the literature, should be included in the title. A treatment that is unusually long or of great magnitude (e.g., "Longitudinal Analysis of Human Short-Term Memory from Age 20 to 80"), a method of observation that is creative or unusually accurate (e.g., "Hand Preference in Telephone Use as a Measure of Limb Dominance and Laterality"), a sampling technique that is unique (e.g., "Intelligence of Children Whose Parents Purchase Encyclopedias"), and a particular site for measurement that sets the study apart from others (e.g., "Perceptual Judgment in a Weightless Environment: Report from the Space Shuttle") are examples of such aspects.

Components inappropriate for inclusion in the title

Such factors as population, research design, and instrumentation should not be included in the title unless they represent a substantial departure from similar studies. The population, for instance, should not be noted unless it is a population never sampled before, or is in some way an unusual target group. In the title, "Imbedded Figures Acuity in World-Class Chess Masters," the population of the subjects is critical to the rationale for the study. The population in "Running Speed, Leg Strength, and Long Jump Performance of High School Boys" is not important enough to occupy space in the title.

Similarly, research design and instrumentation are not appropriate for inclusion in the title unless they represent an unusual approach to measurement or analysis. The type of research method expressed in "Physiological Analysis of Precompetitive Stress" is common in studies dealing with stress, and surely some other aspect of the study would make a more informative contribution to the title. The approach in "Phenomenological Analysis of Precompetitive Stress," however, represents a unique approach and signals the reader that the report contains information of an unusual kind.

Mechanics of titling

Mechanically, the title should be concise and should provide comfortable reading, free from elaborate or jarring constructions. Excessive length should be avoided because it dilutes the impact of the key elements presented; two lines generally should be adequate. Some retrieval systems place a word limitation on titles, thus enforcing brevity. Redundancies such as "Aspects of," "Comments on," "Study of," "Investigation of," "Inquiry into," and "An Analysis of" are expendable. It is obvious that a careful investigation of a topic will include "aspects of" the topic, whereas the research report has as its entire purpose the communication of "comments on" the findings of a study. It is pointless to state the obvious in a title.

Attempts to include all subtopics of a study in the title sometimes result in elephantine rubrics. The decision to include or exclude mention of a subtopic should be made less in terms of an abstraction, such as complete coverage, and more in terms of whether inclusion actually will facilitate appropriate retrieval. One useful way to construct a title is to list all the elements that seem appropriate for inclusion, and then to weave them into various permutations until a title appears that satisfies both technical and aesthetic standards.

Chapter 6

MONEY FOR RESEARCH

How to Ask for Help

Grant applications, as a generic class of documents, are formal appeals for the award of support, usually in the form of money, for undertakings in which the grantor has special interest. In the strict sense, a grant is an award of funds without a fully defined set of terms and conditions for use, while a contract is a work order from the grantor in which procedures, costs, and funding period have been established in explicit terms. Thus the majority of what are commonly called grant proposals are applications for award of a contract—not a grant.

Further complication is added by the fact that grants may be sought for projects in which the objective is to provide a needed service, or for research studies in which the objective is to produce knowledge, with any service provided being purely incidental. Specialized guides are available for proposals that seek funds for the development of programmatic services. Some of these, such as the excellent text by Lauffer (1983), will be of interest to all novices in the grantsmanship game. The present guide is directed specifically to proposals involving research rather than service to a client population.

The grant request contains two component parts: (1) the application for funding, and (2) the proposal that explains in detail what activities the funds—if granted—will support. Ordinarily, no distinction is made between the application and the proposal, the terms being used nearly interchangeably. Nevertheless, in any application for the support of inquiry, embedded amidst budgets, vitae, descriptions of facilities, and plans for dissemination of results, is a research proposal. To that extent, then, the preparation of a grant application requires the same skills as the preparation of any plan for research.

The differences between the research proposal embedded in the grant application and the dissertation or thesis proposals described earlier in this text rest primarily in the need to (1) conform to the grantor's format, which may be specified in considerable detail, (2) present the study in a way that will have maximum appeal to the granting agency, and (3) master skills required to complete other parts of the application that are not directly part of the research plan itself. In all other respects, a sound research proposal is a sound research proposal, whether mailed to Washington in a grant application or placed on an advisor's desk in the sixth semester of doctoral study.

DECIDING WHERE TO START:
CHOOSING THE RIGHT SOURCE

The Track Record: Are You Ready for a Grant?

Most research projects require financial support, either for equipment, personnel to assist in data collection and management, or for publication and dissemination costs. Because internal sources of support within higher education have declined while research costs have escalated, acquiring external funding for research has become the essential first step for almost all studies. Once underway, a major function for many investigators is to acquire additional funds needed to allow completion of the project.

Departmental budgets, which formerly had small amounts of money allocated to research projects, now are stretched desperately thin just to ensure that classes are taught. Few departments can supply researchers with even minimal funds. Thus a major portion of "research activity" is dedicated to funding the project, and this is no different for beginning researchers. In fact, learning to write proposals for research funding has become an important part of the doctoral education experience. Graduate students who have the opportunity to work in well-funded research projects usually share some of the writing responsibilities so that they can learn the process.

The acquisition of funds must be preceded by a written proposal, so preparation of grant applications has become a skill that often is as important as inquiry skills themselves. Each government agency and independent foundation has a specific form to be completed and a unique process through which the proposal must be evaluated. If the proposer of a research project is skilled, diligent, persistent, patient, and possessed of at least a reasonable share of luck, funds can be obtained. The ratio of proposals presently being funded to those being rejected, however, is about 6:100, so it is obvious that the task of writing a proposal and sending it through the channels cannot be approached in a cavalier manner.

In deciding where to seek support, our first advice is to engage in some serious self-contemplation. Review committees want to feel comfortable in awarding a grant of financial support to an applicant. The committee wants to be assured not only that the proposed study is excellent, but that the researcher is competent to perform excellent work. The best evidence for competence is a series of publications on the topic to be researched. This has come to be known as a track record in the area of the proposed study. What record of accomplishment will you present to attract and reassure those who review your proposal?

An investigator who proposes a research project and includes in the application reprints of research or reports of pilot studies that verify the reliability of the technique proposed or support the directional hypotheses to be employed is more likely to satisfy the review committee that his or her skills are adequate to perform the study. In contrast, when the grant applicant is a complete neophyte, or has not completed a study in the specific area of the proposal, the committee will be forced to depend on less direct evidence of competence and, in the end, mostly on faith and intuition. It is understandable that committees more often avoid investments based mainly on faith and select instead proposals from individuals with a solid track record.

Factors other than track record are weighed by review committees (most notably the quality of the proposal), and novice researchers or veteran investigators entering new areas do sometimes receive grant support. First grant proposals do not automatically encounter a hopeless "Catch 22" that demands that they display previous research. The fact remains, however, that previous performance weighs heavily among those factors that determine success.

The track record has been emphasized here, not to discourage the beginner, but to lend support to a suggestion that the authors of this guide have found particularly useful. A good way to build a track record is to begin with limited aspirations and seek limited funding from local sources, particularly from the institution in which the researcher works.

Almost all universities and colleges have faculty and student research funds available. Most major institutions also have federal funds that are provided in block grants to support work in particular disciplines. Such internal sources ordinarily require only a modest proposal document that is not as lengthy or complex as those required by external agencies. A good strategy for eventually obtaining a larger government or foundation grant is to acquire two or three small ($1,000-$5,000) grants, conduct the investigations, submit the results for publication, and subsequently use those reports as the track record supporting a proposal for more extensive funding. This not only provides the researcher with start-up funds to do the first studies, but it indicates to agency reviewers that your work already has been critically and positively reviewed not only by an editorial board, but by a university funding review committee.

The use of local grant sources also should emphasize how important it is to have envisioned a systematic research program rather than a single study. Each research project can build on the previous one, providing more and more evidence that your ideas are worthy of major funding. In programmatic research it is logical sequence, not the accumulated number of studies, that will impress reviewers. Clearly, a fundable proposal could never be supported by a host of experiments aimlessly conducted on a hodgepodge of tenuously related topics.

Agencies and Foundations: Locating the Money Tree

The first step in preparing a successful proposal is knowing where to apply. Finding the funding source that provides the highest probability for successful application often is a time-consuming process. Given the time that will be expended in preparation of the proposal, however, it is a relatively small investment that can return significant dividends.

If you are so fortunate as to have access to someone who maintains a grant library or monitors information sources concerning agencies and foundations, and who can assist you with identifying a preliminary list of potential sources—your search problem is solved. Many universities house such a library. Sometimes senior professors who have large research programs not only maintain all updated information about sources of funding in their particular area, but know and maintain regular communication with key individuals in granting agencies. Such contacts are invaluable for their knowledge about priorities (and changes in priorities) within the funding agency.

It may be beneficial for a novice to collaborate with a senior researcher on several studies before attempting a proposal on his or her own. A familiar name on a proposal can be very helpful because reviewers have confidence in known quantities and often confer that same confidence on collaborators. Not everyone is in the happy position of association with a senior researcher or research staff. Many young scholars must undertake on their own the unfamiliar task of locating the money tree.

In this process, the first rule is to throw a wide net and keep an open mind about what might constitute a possible source. Do not expect to find an agency with interests exactly matched to your particular research idea. With some creative adaptation it often is possible to adjust the focus of a study sufficiently to interest a funding agency without distorting the primary intent of the investigation. For instance, a proposal involving the role of motor or play behavior in child development might be of interest to sources as widely disparate as the Center for Research for Mothers and Children in the National Institute of Child Health and Human Development, or an early childhood project within the National Institute for Education, all depending on how the study is presented. For this reason, a flexible point of view is helpful in assembling the initial list of potential funding sources.

The search can begin with any of several standard reference works. A comprehensive listing of assistance available from the federal government is contained in the *Catalogue of Federal Domestic Assistance* (*CFDA*). Published annually and updated twice each year, *CFDA* is an invaluable tool in locating agencies with appropriate interests, as well as general information about support programs within those agencies. Some states publish a catalogue that provides similar information for programs of state assistance.

The most useful tool for identifying nongovernmental sources of support is the *Foundation Directory*. This directory categorizes nearly 3,000 of the largest foundations and includes both application information and the number and kind of grants available from each source. Also in the private sector, the Foundation Center operates through its annual publications (*Foundation Grants Index* and *Source Book Profiles*), its three regional reference centers, and its computerized information service to provide extensive coverage of nongovernmental sources. The center is particularly useful for identifying smaller, local organizations with interest in the support of research. Another source available from the Foundation Center, *Foundation News,* contains announcements and articles of interest to foundation administrators and potential applicants.

Many sources in governmental agencies, private foundations, industry and professional organizations are listed in the *Annual Register of Grant Support,* the *Directory of Research Grants,* and the *Grants Register.* Although it covers sources included in *CFDA* and the *Directory,* the *Register* provides much additional information and wider coverage. Included are such esoteric areas as federal equipment use programs and foreign exchange opportunities for research personnel.

The researcher is likely to use these large and expensive compendia in the library or at a research center. Once a more specific list of potential sources has been developed, however, it often is possible to obtain publications from specific agencies that are free or more moderately priced. Most state and federal agencies publish material that describes their research support programs and application procedures. An example is the National Institutes of Health's *Guide for Grants and Contracts* and the National Science Foundation's *Bulletin.* A government document that may be useful to many is the *NIH Public Advisory Groups,* for in this document the Study Section membership lists are provided. It is important to know who will be evaluating your proposal. If you have read the papers of those most likely to review your proposal, you more clearly will understand their perspective on the topic.

Several computer search services are available to the grant seeker. In addition to the retrieval system maintained by the Foundation Center, federal sources are catalogued in the data base of the National Technical Information Service, and both federal and private sources may be searched through the Smithsonian Scientific Information Exchange. Once the research topic can be described with reasonable precision, the modest fees required for computer search and retrieval can circumvent many hours of laborious library work. More important, computer systems provide information about grant sources that is more up-to-date than that provided by annual publications. The most economical way to approach this in terms of time and money is to consult your reference librarian.

Another source of information is to notice the funding agency supporting research that is published or presented at national or regional conferences. The granting agency or foundation always is listed at the bottom of the first page of a research article. Similarly, at the bottom of abstracts printed in conference programs the research grant number and funding sources are given. These can tell an observant reader not only what agencies fund research on a particular topic, but specific interest and funding trends for particular sources. In fact, information in abstracts often is the most current information of this type available.

Finally, a number of commercial publications and services have sprung up in recent years to meet the need for help in searching out sources for research support. Some of these provide valuable information about approaching foundations, new agency priorities, formulating more competitive proposals, and the legislative processes that precede new governmental programs. Used as a supplement to direct contact with funding agencies, information from such publications as *Grantsmanship Center News, Grants Magazine,* and *Foundation News* can help in both correctly targeting proposals and in improving their quality. The familiar series from Peterson's Guides now includes an extensive directory of grants available to graduate students that, if it is updated on a regular basis, should prove to be a standard reference for those seeking support for theses and dissertations (Leskes, 1986).

HOW PROPOSALS ARE REVIEWED

Each funding agency has its own review process, often laid out in the detail of an explicit set of procedures. It is useful for proposal authors to have some general understanding of what may be encountered in the review process. As an example, the process for submitting a proposal to an institute of the National Institutes of Health (NIH) will be described. An overview of the procedure is found in Figure 6.1. Although some aspects of the procedure may vary slightly for different years, the major elements in the review process will be similar for most large government agencies.

The first step in obtaining funds from NIH is to obtain the Public Health Service Grant Application, PHS 398, which provides guidelines, instruction sheets, and application forms. With this, as with other government documents related to the disbursement of funds, be certain that the most recent edition is obtained because there are frequent and sometimes subtle changes in the application format.

In a typical university or college, an application must go through a

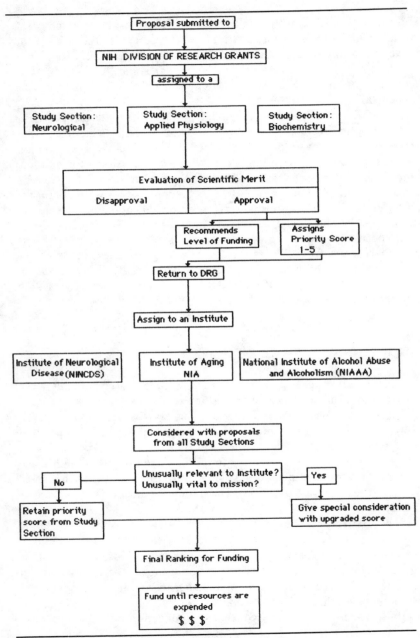

Figure 6.1   Overview of NIH grant proposal process

multitude of steps on its way to NIH, so the target for a final draft should be set one month prior to the NIH submission deadline. At the least, proposal documents will require signatures of officers at a variety of administrative levels. For projects involving a substantial commitment of money, the requirement for review and sign off may extend to the office of the President or, in the case of a public institution, to the Chancellor of the state system. All of these are offices from which prompt response is unlikely.

Once the proposal is ready for submission it is sent to the Division of Research Grants (DRG). The procedure for review after submission to DRG is presented diagrammatically in Figure 6.1. After being received by DRG the proposal is assigned to a Study Section. Each NIH Study Section is composed of 10 to 15 peer reviewers chosen by and reporting directly to the DRG. These reviewers will evaluate the proposal and vote to approve or reject the application. It is wise for the applicant to examine the membership of Study Sections that appear likely to be assigned proposals of the type contemplated.

Some clues may be obtained as to the general orientation of the group and whether any members of the section are published scholars in the particular area of the proposed study. In the latter case, the investigator will want to take special care that the proposal adequately accounts for the work of such members.

Sometimes, especially if the proposal has a large budget, members of the Study Section will determine that a site visit is necessary. Either some or all of the members will visit the campus for the purpose of seeing the laboratories or sites where the intended research will be conducted. The purpose of this visit is to convince Section members that the investigator is competent, that the facilities and equipment are indeed adequate, and that all the support personnel are in fact available. In addition, the members of the site visit team have an opportunity to question the investigator directly about specific issues in the proposal. Site visits usually occur if members of the Study Section feel that the proposal presents a good idea, but that some aspect of it is troublesome. Perhaps the investigator has developed a new measurement technique, the description of which has not fully convinced one or two of the reviewers. Perhaps the investigator plans to measure hundreds of individuals who are over the age of 65, and the committee members wish to discuss sampling problems, availability of subjects, and transportation costs.

Investigators should take the decision for a site visit as a positive sign, · because the Study Section would not invest the time and money into a site visit unless the research idea had been judged to be a good one. Nevertheless, the site visit must be planned in careful detail, all important personnel involved alerted, and preparations made for demonstrations of the key techniques that the site visit team may wish to see. Additionally, the team may wish to hear a brief synopsis of the proposed research project. The investigator should plan this with great care. This presentation, possibly using slides or videotape, will be similar to that made by graduate students at the committee review of their proposed study. The major difference is that this presentation may also include budget and personnel costs.

If the vote of the Study Section is for approval of the proposal, it will be designated "approved but not funded." If rejected, a summary will be made of the primary criticisms. Each reviewer in the Study Section adds a scientific merit priority score to their ballot, varying from 1.0 (highest) to 5.0 (lowest). The average of these scores then becomes the scientific merit priority score attached to the critique of each approved proposal.

At this point the application will be forwarded to the institute that DRG has determined is most appropriate to the nature of the proposed study. The applicant may suggest a specific institute that should be interested and under ordinary circumstances the proposal, if approved, will be sent there. Sometimes an investigator may be responding to what is known as a Request for Proposals (RFP), which is a published request inviting proposals for a particular type of research. In this case the author places the letters "RFP" on the cover sheet with the name of the institute that solicited the proposal.

Next, the proposal is considered by the Advisory Council of the institute to which it was directed. The priority scores for all proposals are rank ordered to form a single list of approved applications. The Advisory Council usually concurs in the recommendations made by the Study Sections. In some cases, however, members of the council will recommend that particular proposals be given special consideration for funding, or they may determine that an application is of questionable relevance to the institute's mission and recommend that it be assigned elsewhere. A reassignment, of course, would require several more weeks to process. This point emphasizes how important it is for the applicant to do everything possible to write the proposal with a specific orientation and to direct it to an institute that would find it attractive.

At the final step, when consideration is given to funding, the approved but unfunded applications are listed in order of their scientific merit priority scores as modified by the institute's Advisory Council, and grants are approved in that order as far as funds permit. If the proposal is approved and funded, notification is sent to the investigator and the sponsoring institution. On occasion, the Study Section will recommend a reduction in budget, or the Advisory Council of the institute may suggest such an alteration. In these cases, an officer of the institute will inform the investigator and provide an explanation. Such recommendations may or may not be negotiable. If the institute is willing to discuss proposed reductions, the investigator will have to confront inquiries about the necessity of specific budget items. Having a clear rationale for each expenditure is the best method for preventing serious erosion of the budget in such bargaining.

While You're Up—Get Me a Grant!

As the competition for grants has grown stiffer over the years, the amount of detail, advanced planning, and preparatory experiments presented by investigators has drastically increased. Shaking the money tree is not quite as easy as it once was when funds were more plentiful. Whereas researchers once spent a week constructing a short proposal, it now may take 3 to 6 months to prepare a sound document. Nevertheless, if your goal is to be an active scholar, particularly if you wish to do so in a university setting, grant writing will be an essential skill—one that you should begin practicing immediately.

When the proper steps are taken in the proper sequence and ample time is allotted to complete each step, proposal writing is at worst challenging and at best enjoyable. It is particularly stimulating when one or more investigators with complementary areas of expertise collaborate on a project. The interaction that occurs during formulation of research questions and planning of the study design is motivating and educational. Furthermore, when the application has been completed, the proposal critiqued by experts, and the project funded, there is a substantial feeling of satisfaction and excitement in knowing that all of the effort will come to fruition in the form of sound research.

Chapter 7

PREPARATION OF THE
GRANT PROPOSAL

Once the funding agency is selected, the first step is to obtain their published guidelines for submitting proposals. These guidelines must be followed meticulously. As a convenient illustration we will discuss here some of the purposes and the considerations to be dealt with in writing the sections required in the "Guidelines for Submitting Public Health Service Grant Applications." The guidelines in the PHS 398 kit provide details and recommend information to include in each section. Many other federal agencies and foundations require similar sections in proposals submitted to them.

About Abstracts

The noun "abstract" normally designates a brief summary of a larger document. Most published research reports are accompanied by such an abstract. Written in the simple past tense, abstracts of this sort are histories of work already accomplished. In contrast, the abstract of a grant proposal is written in the future tense and summarizes work that will be done. When, as sometimes is the case, the abstract is prepared before the full proposal has been developed, it more properly should be called a prospectus or preproposal, but such niceties of language are seldom observed.

Abstracts or preproposals are prepared early in the proposal development process to serve several purposes. First, an abstract may focus the thinking of individuals developing the proposal by establishing a clear and explicit goal to which all subscribe. Second, a concise prospectus can be used for internal purposes to obtain preliminary administrative approval or to solicit support and cooperation from other units. Third, many agencies now require submission of a "letter of intent," which, in essence, is a one- or two-page abstract of the proposed study. These letters are screened by a panel of judges who rank them on preestablished criteria. Authors of the best abstracts are invited to submit full proposals for the second phase of consideration. Under such conditions everything rests on the abstract, and no argument is required to convince the proposer that only the best effort will serve. Finally, whatever its function, an abstract prepared prior to development of the full proposal must be revised to maintain perfect congruence with the evolution of that document. Abstracts that do not match the proposal may receive short shrift from reviewers.

Whether or not a letter of intent is required, the abstract that is submitted with the full proposal bears a disproportionate share of responsibility for success or failure. Often limited to a single page, these few paragraphs are what the reviewer will read first. When the bottom of that page has been reached the reviewer must have a clear impression of the study's objective, method, and justification. If the proposal is to have a fair chance to succeed, however, another impression must have been communicated—that the study contains something of special interest, something that will sustain the reader's attention through the pages that follow. Thus the abstract must accomplish the dual tasks of providing a concise picture of the study while also highlighting its unique characteristics.

In an abstract there is no space for throwaways. Each word and sentence must convey a precise message to the reader. If a point is not essential to an understanding of the study, it is better left to the main body of the proposal. Because the abstract is a one-way, one-shot communication, absolute clarity is essential. No matter how well a point may be explained in the body of the proposal, if the reader is confused by the language of the abstract, the game may have been lost.

For both of the reasons noted above, economy and clarity, the watchword for writing the abstract is *plain language*. Avoid any special constructs that require definition. Don't coin new words in the abstract. Avoid slogans, clichés, and polemical style. Keep adjectives to a minimum and omit flowery descriptions. Finally, remember that the sure sign of an amateur is to apply banalities such as creative, bold, or innovative to one's own ideas. Reviewers, unlike graduate advisors, cannot ask what "that phrase" means at the next conference, may not take the time needed to puzzle through a convoluted sentence, and certainly will not bother to figure out what probably is intended by an imprecise description.

While one can assume that reviewers are both literate and familiar with the research process in broad terms, for the purpose of the abstract it is unwise to assume more. Writing beyond the technical competence of the reviewer can be fatal. The best rule is to imagine that you are explaining your study to an intelligent layperson. By eliminating specialized language and reducing esoteric constructs to their essential components, the abstract can be made intelligible to individuals with a wide range of scientific backgrounds—without appearing to write down to any reader.

The typical format required for a proposal abstract includes the following major elements:

Title
Principal Investigator (Project Director)
Applicant Organization (Institution)
Estimated Cost (Total Funds Requested)
Beginning and Ending Dates
Objective (Purpose of the Study)
Method (Procedures and Design)
Significance (Contribution and Rationale)

Only the last three sections present a challenge to the author's writing skills. The Objective section should begin with a statement of what will be accomplished, presented in the format of a research question or testable hypothesis.

The objective of this study is to determine whether the use of foam cushion inserts in athletic shoes will affect the incidence of heel injuries in runners. Frequency and type of injuries over a 6-month period will be compared for two groups of 100 subjects of varied age, weight, ability, and sex, one group using shoes with cushion inserts, and the other using uncushioned shoes.

Among the most common errors found in this section of the proposal are the following.

Confusion of objectives with procedures. Taking a survey may be a procedure to be employed in the study, but it is not an objective of the study.

Confusion of objectives with the problem. The conditions that make the study important, either in terms of practical application or contribution to knowledge, are better discussed in the section on significance. In the occasional case in which some appreciation of significance is required before it is possible to understand the objective, the best course of action is to create a short subsection titled "The Problem" as a lead into statement of the objective.

Attempting to specify more than one or two major objectives for the study. Save all subobjectives for the body of the proposal. Do everything possible to help the reviewer focus on what is essential.

Failure to be explicit. The best insurance is to start with a conventional phrase that forces you to talk about your intention. "The objective of this study is to . . . "

The clarity and precision with which your objectives are presented may control how carefully the reviewer attends to the subsequent section on procedures, but it is axiomatic that *agencies fund procedures, not objectives.* How research is performed determines its quality, and it is here that the special competence of the reviewer as a research specialist in the area of your proposal will be brought to bear. If the reviewer finishes the one or two paragraphs of this section with a clear, uncluttered idea of what will be done, a full appreciation of how those actions will accomplish the objectives, and a positive impression of what is intriguing or particularly powerful about your approach, your proposal will receive a full hearing.

The significance of the proposed study should be identified in modest but precise terms. Nothing can serve so quickly to make a reviewer suspicious of the merits of a study as to encounter some Chamber of Commerce enthusiasm in the abstract. In plain language, indicate how achieving your objective would be of value to someone, could improve some service, would fill a gap in an evolving body of knowledge, or would permit the correct formulation of a subsequent question. It also is appropriate, and often effective, to indicate a specific example of how a finding from the study might provide human benefit, even at some point subsequent in time or technical development. It is best, however, not to drown the drama of a simple example in needless embellishment. Finally, when deciding which potential consequence should receive emphasis in supporting the significance of the study, it is useful to examine the existing interests and commitments of the funding agency. When the proposed study takes some of its importance from a potential for contribution to ongoing projects of the grantor, there is a powerful argument for special attention to the application.

As the abstract is developed, revised, and given its final review prior to submission, it will be helpful to remember one of the somber facts that has emerged in this age of endemic grantsmanship. Some heavily burdened review committees are so large that it has become necessary to delegate to a subcommittee the task of giving full proposals a complete reading. The remaining reviewers thus may not see more of a given proposal than the cover sheet, the abstract, the author's vita, and, perhaps, the budget. That prospect should be sufficient to encourage attention to producing the best possible abstract.

Impact of Proposed Research

Most funding agencies require a section in the proposal that has a title such as "Significance of the Proposed Research." Funding agencies also are accountable either to the public or to their benefactors for the expenditure of their funds. Reviewers seek the applicant's best forecast as to the usefulness and importance of the results of the proposed project. This prediction assists the review committee in determining the cost-benefit ratio of the proposed study. The significance of the investigation might be explained in terms of synthesizing information from several research areas or by showing how the findings might be applied to human services. It could be impressive to point out that the findings might enable development of other types of research that previously had been impossible. The section needn't be long, but it should be carefully reasoned and should address concerns specific to the mission of the funding agency.

Staffing and Consultant Needs

The staff needed for the research project should be carefully planned and kept as small as possible while maintaining services essential to conduct of the study. The staff budget generally is what drives up the cost of a research project more than any other expense. Along with staff salaries, fringe benefits (medical insurance, retirement) and raises for each year of the grant often must be included. The beginner at this game quickly finds that the costs of a project escalate rapidly as more personnel are involved. When a neophyte is attempting a first grant application, the proposal for staffing should be constructed with a frugality tempered only by feasibility.

The staff requirements should be explained in detail, and if a staff member's function dwindles in the second or third year, then that member should be phased out. Reviewers will note a conscientious effort on the part of the applicant to execute the project at a minimal cost. Positions to be funded for the full term of the study with only global explanation of responsibilities and no indication of compelling necessity also will attract attention—all of it negative. Rumor has it that applicants should pad their budget with some excess and unneeded staff so that the reviewers will have something to cut. This is a foolish notion, because it results in the applicant having items in the budget that are not well justified, which ultimately gives the impression of a casually constructed proposal.

Consultants, too, should be requested sparingly and only when absolutely needed. When they are required, the need should be explicitly stated. If a particular consultant is needed, the applicant should explain exactly why and a letter of agreement from that consultant should be included in the appendix.

The Time Frame

Almost every proposal submitted to government agencies is for funding of a 3- to 5-year project. The application and review process is so time-consuming that the applicant, the institution, and most agencies find the investment of such energy and time best returned if the award is for a substantial period. A time frame, therefore, that states explicitly when specific parts of the project will be completed, has several useful functions.

The first and most obvious use of a projected time sequence is that it keeps the investigator and all personnel on schedule throughout a long period. When all members of the research team have a copy of the time frame, and when it is posted in offices, work rooms, and laboratories, where every member of the team will have daily exposure to its terms, the effect is to encourage steady application of effort.

A second function of the time frame is to forecast for project personnel, reviewers, and the funding agency the probable contents of each progress report that must be filed (usually, annually or bianually over the term of the funding period). Every reader of the time frame can clearly see what events will transpire prior to each progress report, and consequently will expect a full and punctual accounting. This serves also to discourage investigators from procrastinating and later finding themselves having to accomplish an enormous amount in the month or two that precedes a progress report.

A third function that the time frame serves is to document the need for 3 or 5 years of funding for the project. If the reviewers can see in the time frame that every month is filled with work to be done, then it is clear that a project of the length proposed is necessary.

Fourth, if the time frame is well described, it will enhance the reviewer's understanding of the entire project and will further document the applicant's organizational skills. A well-conceived time frame, in which each part of the project is estimated in terms of its onset and duration, goes a long way toward convincing the reader that the applicant knows the area, the methodologies to be used, and all other aspects of the project. If it is well written, it also will preclude at least one possible criticism—that the project cannot be completed in the amount of time proposed, or conversely, that it does not require funding for the full period of time requested.

The time frame should include the schedule for hiring personnel, ordering equipment and supplies, putting equipment and facilities into operation, meeting with personnel from other institutes or agencies, acquiring subjects for the investigation, data accumulation, data analysis, and report write-up. In preparing the time frame, the applicant should try to think through and record every step that will be taken in the project. Then how long each step will take must be estimated. The more people who are involved in a step, the longer it probably will take. The applicant may even find, after working out the time schedule, that the project will take longer than anticipated and the funding period must be extended. If such extension makes the project too expensive, it may be necessary to consider a more economical design. For all of these reasons, the time frame should be carefully worked out before the budget is made final.

Support Services

Any large project will require an extensive array of support services from the university and any other agency or unit of the community that is involved with the project. Insofar as possible, the need for support services should be anticipated, both by providing money for them in the budget and by ensuring that what must be purchased exists and can be delivered. If a computer graphics person is needed, one should be located to ensure that such a person is available. Specialized computer services may be required from the computer center, or unusual transportation capacity may be needed, such as the need to move video equipment into the community. These types of research support must be located and confirmed as part of preparation for the proposed study.

All space needs such as laboratories, offices, or work areas for technicians should be anticipated. If the research project is going to tax any unit of the university, the people involved should be consulted prior to the final draft of the proposal. Examples include proposed projects in which a large number of telephone calls will be imposed on the departmental switchboard, frequent mass mailings that will be planned for the postal pickup, or dozens of students who are to wait in lines in a hallway immediately outside classrooms. The applicant should try to anticipate any hardship that the project may create for anyone. This will prevent, insofar as possible, logistic problems that create ill will among support service staff, and frustration on the part of the researcher.

When support from other sources is critical to the research project, the researcher should obtain a written agreement from the appropriate officials specifying that the needed service will be available. This letter of agreement may be included in the appendix of the proposal. For example, if a specific school classroom is essential to the project, a letter reserving that facility for the specified period of time should be obtained. It would be an unpleasant surprise, for instance, to begin use of another researcher's environmentally controlled laboratory for a year-long study, and then discover it will not be available for the final 2 months of the project. Every precaution must be taken to prevent such disastrous accidents.

Vitae: Presenting Yourself

It would be easy to underestimate the importance of this section in a grant application. For many readers, vitae represent one more instance of the paperwork syndrome that infects higher education. Personal resumes are required, accumulated, and ignored in a host of bureaucratic functions. In consequence, unlike people in the business world, academics often pay relatively little attention to the construction and maintenance of attractive and utilitarian vitae. Like McGee's closet, they simply are allowed to accumulate the residues of scholarly and professional life without much thought to order, economy, or impact.

There are two common misapprehensions about the vitae section of a grant proposal: (1) that they are not read by reviewers, and (2) that as a pro forma section, vitae have little influence on the success of a proposal. Both notions are untrue. Vitae are read. Many reviewers read vitae before they read the body of the proposal. Not only do vitae influence the judgments of reviewers, they are the one part of the proposal in which the applicant can be aggressive by taking the argument for competence directly to the reviewer's attention.

The resumes of individuals to be associated with the proposed study are the primary vehicles for arguing that the interests, training, and experience of the investigator(s) make support of the study reasonable. The techniques for mounting this offensive are not difficult to imagine.

(1) If a format is provided, follow it exactly by revising and retyping every resume. If a format is not provided, invent one that will best serve the strategies noted below.

(2) Keep vitae reasonably short by being selective about content. Reviewers will be looking for the obvious items and these should be given prominence:

> publications in the area of the study
> publications in areas related to the study
> receipt of previous grants in the area of the proposal
> receipt of research grants in any area
> involvement in a similar study whether funded or not
> evidence of relevant training completed (e.g., postdoctoral study in the area)
> unpublished papers or conference presentations in the area of the study
> completed pilot studies in the area of the proposal

Take care to give emphasis to current items. Items older than five years should not be included unless they help to establish a track record that is directly related to the study. Don't burden the reviewer with irrelevant clutter.

(3) Use a uniform format that is divided into subsections with prominent headings. The idea is that the format should make it impossible for a hurried reader to miss material that supports the competence of the investigator. Preferably provide only research publications. When there are few, cite relevant presentations or abstracts. Be certain, however, that the research publications are listed first, and that abstracts and presentations are categorized as such. It is not wise to list all of these in a mixture, leaving the reviewer to assume that you do not know the difference

between an abstract and a publication, or that you are trying to give the impression of a great deal of scholarly activity by intermingling these three types of activity.

(4) Use short sections of highlighted text to provide detail about the exact nature of previous research experiences relevant to conduct of the proposed study. You are not limited just to the citation of dates, project titles and publications. Tell the reviewers exactly what they need to know, in a form that makes the task as easy as possible.

Where a team of investigators is to be involved, it will not always be easy to prepare an effective vitae section. Individualism in personal matters is a common trait among productive scholars, and the vitae is correctly regarded as a personal matter. Nevertheless, this is a place where flexibility and some cooperative effort will improve the chances that all participants will improve their vitae—by winning a grant to support their scholarship.

Dissemination of Results

The final step that transforms the personal act of inquiry into research is dissemination of a report into the public domain. Peers must review procedures if results are to be treated as reliable knowledge, and if knowledge is to be useful it must reach those who can make application. For those two reasons, many funding sources stipulate that plans for dissemination of results must be included as part of the proposal.

The rules here are reasonably simple.

(1) Tell which results will be reported.
(2) Indicate which audiences you intend to reach.
(3) Specify how you plan to disseminate the final report.
(4) Be specific, citing particular conferences, development projects, local, state or federal agencies, publications, or colleagues working on related research projects.
(5) Think carefully about how to reach appropriate audiences and go beyond the requisite printed report and ubiquitous paper at a national conference. Consider such strategies as summaries directed to interested scholars in other institutions, use of computer-based retrieval services, and releases through news media.

Typically, costs for dissemination can be built into the budget. Expenditures for everything from travel to conferences to printing and mailing of reports are legitimate. Be sure, however, to base each item on careful estimates of actual costs. For example, obtain actual quotations for proposed air travel in support of dissemination.

The Budget

Although not a part of the plan for research, the budget is a central element in a grant application. It will be examined in detail by almost all members of a typical review committee, even those who may not be as intensely interested in the details of the proposed study as members who are primarily responsible for evaluating the adequacy of design and methodology. Most application formats require that the budget be presented in brief form with no more than a page or two of appended explanation. Experience suggests that such explanation should be provided even if it is not specifically required.

Personnel for which funds are requested must be essential to the study. The most effective way to demonstrate such need is to specify responsibilities for each position. If project personnel must have special certification or advanced degrees, it is important to tell why a less qualified person could not be used. Enough information should be provided to support the level of commitment required in each position, whether for full-time or fractional employment.

Supplies and equipment must be documented with care. Review committees will appreciate efforts to give exact and realistic estimates of supplies needed, rather than the use of speculative round numbers. For instance, if video tape is to be used, rather than simply requesting $1,125 for the purchase of tapes, the applicant should explain that 15 minutes will be required for 100 subjects on three occasions without possibility of reusing tapes. That will require one tape per four subjects, or 25 tapes at $15 each, or a budget item of $1,125.

If funds for the purchase of large equipment are requested, the budget justification section might explain what attempts have been made to obtain the items by other means, and why alternative plans such as rental or sharing won't suffice. Generally, funding agencies are not well disposed to requests for extensive equipment purchases, particularly large and expensive items. The position of many agencies is that the university or college should supply all of the basic and less specialized equipment, as well as most large items that represent expensive and permanent investments in research capability. Young researchers may be dismayed to discover that their university takes the opposite position, holding that the investigator should obtain all expensive equipment through extramural funding, but that is the way things often work in a complex society.

Funding agency officers understandably would rather award money to applicants who already have the necessary equipment. In that manner, the agency's funds go directly into research activities rather than into building the capacity to perform research. The only counter to this logic is to make the best possible case for why the applicant's facility is ideally, if not uniquely, positioned for the conduct of the particular study—given the addition of the needed equipment. Another helpful strategy here is to point out any substantial ways the applicant's institution is contributing to the proposed study in terms of equipment, facilities, or personnel assigned to the project. Agency and foundation personnel like to feel that research projects, especially large ones, are a joint university/agency enterprise, and they tend to resent any implication that they constitute a goose that lays golden eggs.

Budget lines for ancillary items such as analysis of data, preparation of manuscripts, and communication with consultants may be permitted under the rules for application, but should be explained with great care. Consultants, for example, must be justified in detail. In the golden days of research when grants were plentiful, consultants sometimes were included in proposals simply because they were good professional friends who had an interest in the study. Today, a consultant must be demonstrably necessary to completion of the study. Even when such need exists, caution is required in preparing the explanation. If the consultant is needed because the investigator has not mastered a technique that is central to execution of the study, a reviewer may wonder why the grant should be awarded to someone who is deficient in skills commonly used by workers in the area.

Travel costs also require careful explanation. Only travel that is necessary to complete the research and, perhaps, to disseminate the findings should be included in the budget. If travel to specific conferences for the purpose of presenting reports from the study are included, the nature of the audience should be indicated and the relevance of the conference to the study demonstrated.

Another major item in a proposed budget will be indirect costs (overhead) that the funding agency will pay directly to the institution. Such costs vary widely and are negotiated by the agency and the university or college. Many large institutions have a standing policy on overhead for all grant contracts. Indirect charges presumably reimburse the university for the cost of building maintenance, processing of paper work, utilities, and so on—all items that would have to be purchased by the grantor if the study were conducted at a facility owned by the agency. Other budget items dictated by the institution are insurance, retirement, and medical benefits for project personnel.

It is wise to take an early draft of the budget to the university officer in charge of grant negotiations and obtain assistance on all items not directly dictated by the nature of the research process itself. After several projected budgets have been written, the mysteries associated with indirect costs and employee benefits may become understandable to the researcher, but a substantial amount of grief can be avoided on the first effort if competent help is solicited and advice faithfully followed.

As a corollary to budget making, if a significant amount of support is to be provided by the institution in the form of new inputs of equipment, facilities, supplies, or personnel, the researcher must be sure to obtain formal approval from appropriate officers before proceeding too far into development of the proposal. In many institutions, agreement of the chairperson, dean, and a vice president (at minimum) is required for such expenditures. It is best to have the needed commitments in hand well in advance of the point at which the proposal will be submitted for review.

It may be useful to demonstrate that respected scholars with expertise in the area of the proposed research regard the project as worthy, and the investigator(s) as competent. For this purpose, letters containing such endorsements may be included in the proposal (usually in an appendix).

Letters of Endorsement and Confirmation

A second type of letter includes those that confirm the cooperation, support, or participation of organizations or individuals essential to the study. If, for example, schools and teachers or students are to be involved in any way, it is essential to have evidence that the appropriate authorities have reviewed the proposal and are prepared to participate if the grant is awarded. Similar brief notes may be required from the directors of service units such as the computer center, university health services, or laboratory facilities in other departments.

The documentation provided in such cases need not be elaborate or extend beyond what seems essential. The goal is simple. The applicant must provide some assurance that the staff, facilities, support service, and subject populations envisioned in the proposal will, in fact, be available.

Using Planning Models and Flowcharts

Preparation of a grant proposal often involves dealing with a number of individuals in administrative units external to the author's home base. Institutional review and approval, soliciting peer reviews, obtaining letters of support, accumulating budget information, gathering commitments from personnel, assembling vitae, and obtaining multiple signatures all serve to complicate the process. A series of subdeadlines emerge that must be met in serial order. For these reasons, even a relatively straightforward grant proposal may quickly exceed managerial habits that are entirely adequate for the limited scope of theses or dissertations.

In response to the complicated network of steps that are demanded in developing many grant proposals, myriad management models, flowcharts, checklists, and step-by-step guides have been devised to assist the author (see Appendix B). Some of these, such as the PERT (Program Evaluation and Review Technique) system (Borg & Gall, 1983; Taha, 1982), lend themselves primarily to larger research or development undertakings. Some management systems designed for action projects in education rather than research convert readily to serve studies of curriculum or instruction, but are awkward to adapt to the needs of investigations in biological or behavioral science. Others can be quite helpful, but also are expensive to obtain.

The best option for the novice who is attempting to stay organized may be to devise a do-it-yourself flowchart, complete with assigned responsibilities and deadlines. An example is shown below. Once a problem has been defined and an appropriate funding agency has been identified, the following items can be supplemented as required by local circumstance and displayed with boxes and arrows to form a flowchart of sequenced events with appropriate time frame warnings.

Time Frame
>   First response to the request for proposals
>   Preproposal or letter of intent deadline
>   Deadline for submission to Human Subject Review Committee
>   Deadline for obtaining administrative signatures
>>   Chairperson
>>   Dean
>>   Office of Sponsored Research
>>   Director of Computer Services
>   Deadline for submission to typist
>   Deadline for submission of proposal
>   Award announcement date

Major Development Steps
    Obtain guidelines
    Contact program officer at funding agency
    Select primary authors of proposal
    Prepare abstract or prospectus and submit letter of intent
    Contact units for support or collaboration
    Obtain initial administrative approval
    Complete review of the literature
    Determine study design
    Prepare first draft of proposal
    Prepare abstract of proposal
    Initiate human subjects review
    Initiate internal peer review
    Prepare budget
    Revise proposal based on feedback
    Collect vitae
    Obtain letters of endorsement
    Obtain written assurances from support sources
    Complete institutional forms
    Type final document
    Obtain administrative signatures
    Duplicate proposal
    Submit proposal

The novice will do well to remember the corollary of Murphy's Law that states, "Everything takes longer than you expect." Where one must depend on the voluntary cooperation of busy individuals in other parts of the university, several weeks of cushion are wise when establishing any set of target deadlines. This particularly is true of the typing and collation of the proposal. Even when produced on a word processor, the typing alone may take several weeks. It invariably will take longer than you anticipate. Since a proposal is a large project often involving 50 to 100 typed pages, all of which must have no errors at all, it will take the office staff away from other duties for unacceptable periods of time if typing is left to the last minute. Further, each draft must be checked and double-checked. The end result is a process that makes Murphy's corollary look positively optimistic.

Common Reasons for Rejection

Grant competitions are mediated through review processes that, whatever their unique characteristics, involve individual, human readers. This fact produces an implacable rule. *What is not noticed is not funded.* Amidst the sometimes formidable stack of proposals, the document that does not catch the eye—and thus the reward of closer attention and deeper consideration—cannot compete on the more formal criteria associated with quality of design and congruence with the agency's priorities. It is for that reason that we have given such close attention to the abstract and introduction that must project whatever attractive elements are contained in the research question or proposed methodology.

Reasons for rejection may be phrased in diplomatic terms, but the most common reasons for unsuccessful applications boil down to a surprisingly small set of simple and familiar failures.

(1) Deadline for submission was not met.

(2) Guidelines for proposal content, format, and length were not followed *exactly.*

(3) The proposed question, design, and method were completely traditional, with nothing that could strike a reviewer as unusual, intriguing, or clever.

(4) The proposed study was not an agency priority for *this* year.

(5) The proposal was not *absolutely clear* in describing one or several elements of the study.

(6) The proposal was not *absolutely complete* in describing one or several elements of the study.

(7) The author(s) simply did not know the territory as revealed in the review of literature.

(8) The proposed study appeared to be beyond the capacity of the author(s) in terms of training, experience, and available resources.

(9) The proposed method of study was unsuited to the purpose of the research.

(10) The budget was unrealistic in terms of estimated requirements for equipment, supplies, and personnel.

(11) The cost of the proposed project appeared to be greater than any possible benefit to be derived from its completion.

(12) The authors(s) took highly partisan positions on issues and thus became vulnerable to the prejudices of the reviewers.

(13) The quality of writing was poor—for example, sweeping and grandiose claims, convoluted reasoning, excessive repetition, or unreasonable length.

(14) The proposal document contained an unreasonable number of mechanical defects that reflected carelessness and the author's unwillingness to attend to detail. The risk that the same attitude might attend execution of the proposed study was not acceptable to the reviewers.

Because the probability of rejection for any given proposal is high, it is important for the beginner to keep this final point in mind.

Perfectly sound proposals are rejected. Research of considerable value may remain unsupported for no reason that can be associated with the quality of the proposal. Rejection must not be taken, by itself, as evidence of a fundamental defect. At a given point in time, a given proposal may simply not appeal to a given reviewer who must make difficult choices among equally strong contenders. Under such circumstances subjective factors determine decisions and provide no wholly logical explanation for rejection. The section of this guide dealing with resubmission will provide some assistance for researchers who find themselves in such an unhappy position.

Rejection, Feedback, and Resubmission

A rejection, especially of the first proposal submitted, should not be unexpected and must be considered simply a fact of life. Just as it takes practice to learn how to perform any complex task truly well, it takes practice to write successful proposals. So long as the applicant has opportunity to profit from evaluative feedback, each attempt should produce significant improvement.

Most review procedures will provide some form of summary review as part of the rejection process. This statement will list the main criticisms of the proposal and may even suggest changes. The applicant should consider each criticism or suggestion and, if resubmission is contemplated, respond to as many of them as possible with changes, clarifications, or strengthened rationale in a revised proposal. In addition, since several months pass between the submission time and the notification of results, it is probable that the researcher can add new data or new publications that will strengthen the revised proposal.

Sometimes criticisms center on the way the proposal was written, or at least the summary review may suggest that the proposal did not communicate to reviewers what the applicant intended. In these cases, the proposal can be rewritten for clarity and resubmitted. In other cases, the reviewers may have understood the proposal correctly, but have encountered problems with the general idea of the research or with the importance of the question relative to the cost required to obtain the answer. When the latter occurs, the applicant's only recourse is to strengthen the rationale of the study to support its importance more effectively. Finally, when reviewers raise serious questions about design or methodology, the decision is simple—either provide better substantiation for the choices made, or change them.

An extensive revision of the proposal may include data from new pilot investigations designed to answer some of the earlier criticisms of the reviewers. Not only does this directly confront their concerns, but it also may convince the reviewers that the applicant is engaged in ongoing work within the area of the proposal. Sometimes a proposal's author will be able to use critical feedback from a rejection to convince an in-house committee to fund a small study that responds to some of the points raised.

Once criticisms have been answered or revisions executed, the rejected proposal may be resubmitted. An accompanying letter should state that the new document is a resubmission and should be returned to the same review group. This is important because sometimes a new set of reviewers will find a new set of criticisms based on their own particular set of scientific biases. Proposals can be resubmitted several times, provided there is no indication from the agency that the question is inappropriate or unimportant.

A telephone conversation with the individual who coordinates the review process (usually an executive secretary) often can clear up any ambiguities that exist in the summary statement that accompanies most rejections. Such assistance is particularly useful in the event that it is not clear whether the primary reason for rejection rests in the proposal as a written document, or in the substance of the research question itself. Sometimes the responsible officer of the agency or foundation will give the applicant some estimate of the probability for success in a resubmission and even may be willing to provide some suggestions for improvement.

After the first shock, a rejection should not inhibit anyone. Often a rejection only serves to reveal how a next and much superior draft can be prepared. While it doubtless is better to have the desired funds, an unsuccessful application can provide something of substantial value: the opportunity to learn how to write a more effective proposal.

Summary

If you have read this far, we hope you are not immobilized by the thought of undertaking the tasks described. Difficult and demanding as proposal writing can be, the rewards are clear and attractive—a well-planned study and money to make it go. In addition, each time a proposal is written the process becomes easier. Many of the proposal sections, when written on a word processor, simply can be updated and reused in subsequent documents. For example, each time a proposal is submitted, the basic description of a university research facility simply is updated and reprinted. The same process can occur with a particular methodology used in a line of research. Once the description has been written, it need only be updated and then recycled. Grant gathering, like any other intellectual skill, improves with practice. You may never find yourself regarding the process as enjoyable, but the challenges are always fresh and the sense of satisfaction in completing a good presentation can be a significant reward. Better still, of course, is obtaining the money!

REFERENCES

American Psychological Association. (1982). *Ethical principles in the conduct or research with human participants.* Washington, DC: Author.

American Psychological Association. (1983). *Publication manual of the American Psychological Association* (3rd ed.). Washington, DC: Author.

Bauernfeind, R. H. (1968). Research notes. *Phi Delta Kappan, 50,* 126-128.

Bogdan, R., & Biklen, S. K. (1982). *Qualitative research for education: An introduction to theory and methods.* Boston: Allyn & Bacon.

Bolster, A. S. (1983). Toward a more effective model of research on teaching. *Harvard Educational Review, 53*(3), 294-308.

Borg, W. R., & Gall, M. D. (1983). *Educational research: An introduction* (4th ed.). New York: Longman.

Burrell, G., & Morgan, G. (1979). *Sociological paradigms and organizational analysis.* Exeter, NH: Heinemann.

Campbell, W. C. (1969). *Form and style in thesis writing.* Boston: Houghton Mifflin.

Cook, T. D., & Reichardt, C. S. (Eds.). (1979). *Qualitative and quantitative methods in evaluation.* Newbury Park, CA: Sage.

Davitz, J. R., & Davitz, L. J. (1977). *Evaluating research proposals in the behavioral sciences: A guide* (2nd ed.). New York: Teachers College Press.

Dobbert, M. L. (1982). *Ethnographic research: Theory and application for modern schools and societies.* New York: Praeger.

Eisner, E. W. (1981). On the difference between scientific and artistic approaches to qualitative research. *Educational Researcher, 10*(4), 5-9.

Fanger, D. (1985, May). The dissertation, from conception to delivery. *On Teaching and Learning: The Journal of the Harvard-Danforth Center, 1,* 26-33.

Fetterman, D. M. (1984). *Ethnography in educational evaluation.* Newbury Park, CA: Sage.

The Foundation Center. (periodically). *Foundation News* New York: Author.

The Foundation Center. (revised quarterly). *Source book profiles.* New York: Author.

Gage, N. L. (1985). *Hard gains in the soft sciences: The case of pedagogy.* Bloomington, IN: Phi Delta Kappa.

Garonzik, E. (Ed.). (1985). *The foundation grants index* (13th ed.). New York: Foundation Center.

Glaser, B., & Strauss, A. L. (1967). *The discovery of grounded theory: Strategies for qualitative research.* Chicago: Aldine.

Goetz, J. P., & LeCompte, M. D. (1984). *Ethnography and qualitative design in educational research.* Orlando, FL: Academic Press.

The Grantsmanship Center. (bimonthly). *The Grantsmanship Center News*. Los Angeles: Author.

Guba, E., & Lincoln, Y. S. (1981). *Effective evaluation*. San Francisco: Jossey-Bass.

Hamilton, S. F. (1983). The social side of schooling: Ecological studies of classrooms and schools. *Elementary School Journal, 83*(4), 313-334.

Kroll, W. P., & Peterson, K. H. (1966). Cross validation of the Booth Scale. *Research Quarterly, 37,* 66-70.

Lauffer, A. (1983). *Grantsmanship*. Newbury Park, CA: Sage.

Lerner, C. A., & Turner, R. (Eds.) (biennial). *The grants register*. London: Macmillan.

Leskes, A. (Ed.). (1986). *Grants for graduate students 1986-88*. Princeton, NJ: Peterson's Guides.

Lincoln, Y. S., & Guba, E. G. (1985). *Naturalistic inquiry*. Newbury Park, CA: Sage.

Marquis Professional Publications. (1984). *Annual register of grant support* (18th ed.) Chicago: Author.

Miles, M. B., & Huberman, A. M. (1984). *Qualitative data analysis: A sourcebook of new methods*. Newbury Park, CA: Sage

National Science Foundation. (monthly). *NSF Bulletin*. Washington, DC: Author.

Oryx Press. (yearly). *Directory of research grants*. Scottsdale, AZ: Author.

Patton, M. Q. (1980). *Qualitative evaluation methods*. Newbury Park, CA: Sage.

Plenum Publishing. (quarterly). *Grants Magazine*. New York: Author.

Popkewitz, T. S., & Tabachnick, B. R. (Eds.). (1981). *The study of schooling: Field based methodologies in educational research and evaluation*. New York: Praeger.

Renz, L. (Ed.). (1986). *The foundation directory* (10th ed.). New York: Foundation Center.

Rogers, V. R. (1984). Qualitative research—another way of knowing. In P. L. Hosford (Ed.), *Using what we know about teaching* (pp. 85-106). Alexandria, VA: Association for Supervision and Curriculum Development.

Rossman, G. B., & Wilson, B. L. (1984). *Numbers and words: Combining quantitative and qualitative methods in a single large-scale study*. Paper presented at the annual meeting of the American Educational Research Association, New Orleans, LA. (ERIC Document Reproduction Service, No. ED 246-123)

Schofield, J. W., & Anderson, K. (1984). *Integrating quantitative components into qualitative studies: Problems and possibilities for research on intergroup relations in educational settings*. Paper presented at the annual meeting of the American Educational Research Association, New Orleans, LA. (ERIC Document Reproduction Service, No. ED 248-250)

Shulman, L. S. (1981). Disciplines of inquiry in education: An overview. *Educational Researcher, 10*(6), 5-12, 23.

Smith, J. K. (1983). Quantitative versus qualitative research: An attempt to clarify the issue. *Educational Researcher, 12*(3), 6-13.

Smith, J. K., & Heshusius, L. (1986). Closing down the conversation: The end of the quantitative-qualitative debate among educational inquirers. *Educational Researcher, 15*(1), 4-12.

Spindler, G. (1982). *Doing the ethnography of schooling*. New York: Holt, Rinehart & Winston.

Spradley, J. P. (1979). *The ethnographic interview*. New York: Holt, Rinehart & Winston.

Spradley, J. P. (1980). *Participant observation*. New York: Holt, Rinehart & Winston.

Taha, H. A. (1982). *Operations research: An introduction* (3rd ed.). New York: Macmillan.

Templin, T. J., & Griffin, P. (1985). Ethnography: A qualitative approach to examining life in physical education. In C. L. Vendien & J. E. Nixon (Eds.), *Physical education teacher education* (pp. 140-146). New York: John Wiley.

Tuthill, D., & Ashton, P. (1983). Improving educational research through development of educational paradigms. *Educational Researcher, 12*(10), 6-14.

United States Department of Health and Human Services. (periodically). *NIH guide for grants and contracts.* Washington, DC: Government Printing Office.

United States Department of Health and Human Services. (semiyearly). *NIH public advisory groups: Authority, structure, functions, members.* Washington, DC: Government Printing Office.

United States Office of Management and Budget. (1985). *Catalog of federal domestic assistance.* Washington, DC: Government Printing Office.

Van Maanen, J. (Ed.). (1983). *Qualitative methodology.* Newbury Park, CA: Sage.

Whyte, W. F. (1984). *Learning from the field.* Newbury Park, CA: Sage.

Winer, B. J. (1971). *Statistical principles in experimental design* (2nd ed.). New York: McGraw-Hill.

PART II

Specimen Proposals

Introduction

The specimen proposals presented here were selected with several intentions. First, we wanted to display proposals using different designs and paradigms for research. Second, we wanted the proposals to involve research topics drawn from different areas. Third, we wanted to illustrate typical proposals for both theses and dissertations as well as for grant funding. All four proposals presented in this guide have accomplished the goals of their respective authors—successful acceptance by a graduate committee or, in the case of the grant proposal, the award of funding for research.

The reader may wish to examine more than one of these proposals. Since different designs and styles are used, each proposal illustrates a different way to implement our suggestions. You may gain valuable ideas for proposal writing from reading the proposals in which the research designs are different from the one you plan to use. In the specimen proposal presented first we have provided an experimental laboratory study focusing on adult subjects of different ages. This proposal has been edited so each section corresponds to a task presented in Chapter 1. We provide comments to help you focus attention on the important aspects of each task. The second proposal presented here is a dissertation proposal employing qualitative methodology to examine women returning to a community college after an extended absence from schooling. The third example presented in this part of the book employs a quasi-experimental design for a study to be conducted in the field setting of elementary school classrooms. The final proposal involves the field test of an intervention to reduce pregnancy rates in teenage subjects.

Each of the proposals in this guide has been edited for the present use and is accompanied by our comments. The documents were not selected for perfection, but for general excellence and demonstrated success. Our accompanying analyses are not intended to be critical of the authors. It is easy to play the role of "Monday morning quarterback" with ample time and little of the pressure associated with preparing a proposal. It also is likely that each of the authors, having implemented the proposed study, would now make some changes in the original document. Hindsight always is 20/20. Our comments, then, are intended to draw the reader's attention to parts that we feel are particularly well executed, to raise needed questions, and to make apparent alternative courses of action.

PROPOSAL 1: EXPERIMENTAL DESIGN

The Effects of Age, Modality and Complexity of Response, and Practice on Reaction Time

INTRODUCTION

In the introduction the author moves from an artificial introduction to a specific focus on the important constructs for this proposal. In the first paragraph a brief vignette from history effectively captures the reader's attention. In the second paragraph, the author further piques the reader's interest by suggesting that recent findings are challenging 75 years of dogma concerning the topic. The next three paragraphs introduce primary constructs; the mechanisms that may control motor responses with aging. In paragraphs six and seven the author introduces special aspects of design that will be incorporated into the study. The introduction is concluded by a sentence that summarizes the major topics of the previous paragraphs and leads into the rationale to follow. Note that the introduction immediately acquaints the reader with the topic, and leaves extensive detail for later sections of the proposal.

Eighty-six years ago, visitors to an international health exhibition had the opportunity, after paying a small fee, to "try their powers." Men and women of various ages, from the teens to the seventies, were timed to see how quickly they could press a key in response to a light [their reaction time, (RT)]. The results of this "study" (Galton, 1899) reflected exactly what one might intuitively expect: the older subjects were slower than the younger ones. In the years since, the research techniques have steadily grown

This proposal was prepared by Lance Osborne as part of the thesis research requirement in the Department of Physical and Health Education at the University of Texas at Austin. The thesis was supervised by Waneen Wyrick Spirduso. Mr. Osborne currently is a Teaching Specialist at the University of Texas at Austin.

more rigorous and the paradigms have varied considerably, yet, the findings continue to support the notion that as individuals grow older they become slower.

The long history of reports indicating that older individuals are generally slower than young ones in reaction time suggests that any exception would be quite a surprise. Yet, in the last ten years, data supporting an exception to the age-related slowing of response speed have surfaced. Nebes (1978), Salthouse and Somberg (1982), and Thomas, Waugh, and Fozard (1978) using simple reaction time paradigms incorporating vocal responses found no significant differences between the response latencies of old and young subjects. These findings have raised the questions, "Is the motor act of vocalization really immune to the age-related decrement in response speed typically found for other types of motor responses, and if so, why?"

Because of its apparent resistance to aging, vocalization may be a very important phenomenon to study in order to understand more clearly the mechanisms responsible for age-related slowing. The control of limb movement is independent of the motor control of speech, even though the same central nervous system structures are involved in its planning and control (Heilman et al., 1973; De Renzi, Mottle, & Nichelli, 1980). A better understanding of how age differentially affects control of manual or vocal responses to an external stimulus also might elucidate the extent to which the two motor systems share similar information processing mechanisms.

In the search for the mechanism(s) to which age-related changes might be attributed, certain peripheral changes can be safely eliminated. First, although an age-related muscle atrophy occurs throughout most of the body, the duration of muscle contraction does not contribute a very high proportion of the total delay from stimulus to the onset of the movement. Thus delay in this component of the response would not result in a large delay in SRT (Clarkson, 1978; Weiss, 1965). Thus the lack of age-related atrophy in muscles involved in vocalization cannot account for the apparent lack of decrement in vocal response speed. Second, since the peripheral nerve conduction velocity is slower in older individuals, and the path from the brain to the finger is longer than the path from the brain to the thoracic, laryngeal, and superlaryngeal structures, it might be inferred that the effect of age would be less with speech motor acts. However, it has been shown that, although foot and finger movements are slower than jaw reaction times, the difference in response speed between old and young is similar for each of these responses despite the difference in peripheral nerve conduction velocity (Hugin, Norris, & Shock, 1960).

It is reasonable, therefore, to propose that a mechanism of aging is located centrally, and that it is possible that differential aging effects on the central control are response specific, e.g., the control of manual responses may deteriorate more rapidly with aging than the control of vocal responses. The general slowing of response speed with age may, however, be related to a change that is more generalizable to one or more stages of information processing, such as the programming of motor responses (Haaland & Bracy, 1982). If this were the case, vocal responses to a stimulus may not be affected by age because they involve motor control of a multiple-joint action. These actions may be more flexibly controlled due to motor equivalence/compensatory patterns than manual responses which may be, due to the constraint of operating around one or two joints, actually more complex due to fewer degrees of freedom (Abbs et al., 1984). In addition, vocal responses to a stimulus may be more ethologically relevant and more highly practiced than manual responses such as depression of a key.

Haaland and Bracy (1982) suggest that by methodologically varying both manual and vocal skills along the dimension of motoric complexity, more may be learned about differences that exist among motor systems in the aging person. To isolate the effects of response complexity on response programming, it is important that conditions are held constant across the two earlier stages of information processing: the stimulus identification stage and the response selection stage (Kerr, 1978).

Finally, most investigators reporting age differences in performance of psychomotor tasks have failed to provide enough practice at those tasks. To obtain a valid measure of any differences, should they exist, requires the control (through substantial practice) of confounding factors such as task unfamiliarity or high anxiety. Practice will be used in this experiment in an effort to reduce the novelty of the tasks and to stabilize the scores. In addition, the effects of practice on age differences in performance for all of the reaction time tasks will be examined. The analysis of practice effects, should they exist, and the manipulation of both response mode and complexity, may clarify knowledge concerning the interactions of age, response mode and complexity.

PURPOSE

In the statement of purpose the four experimental factors of the study are introduced: age, mode of response, complexity, and practice. The general question of interest in the study (see Chapter 2 for a discussion of the difference between a question and a purpose) is implicit in the purpose stated in the first sentence (Are there *age* differences in response *speed* in two *different motor* systems?). In the second sentence the factor of complexity is added. A secondary purpose, to control for practice effects, is described in the last sentence. Each of the purposes grows out of the introduction, and the statement here prepares the reader for the rationale that follows.

In this investigation, an age difference in response speed will be tested in comparable vocal and manual tasks. Two motor systems (vocal and manual) will be varied in terms of response programming complexity (simple and complex) in parallel fashion in both motor systems. The level of complexity in this study will be varied according to whether the response requires a limited or relatively larger number of coordinated muscles in the response. To ensure that the question raised pertains to manual or vocal capacities and not to learning, the tests will be administered over a period of three days.

RATIONALE

In this rationale, the theoretical logic of the relationships assumed and postulated are clarified. Following a simple pattern of argument (see Chapter 3), *if* (a) old individuals respond slower than young individuals with their hands, *and* (b) motor task complexity exaggerates age differences, *but* (c) old respond as quickly as young with their voice, *then* (d) old manual response is slower because it is more complex. The final statement shows how the answer to this question will provide information that not only accurately describes the source of differences between the reaction latencies of the young and old, but also contributes insights as to the nature and mechanisms of motor control.

The central control of manual reaction responses is slower in older individuals, particularly those responses that may be more complex than others (Welford, 1982). Vocal reaction responses, however, appear to be spared by aging. Inasmuch as the manual and vocal motor systems are independent, and older individuals are relatively more affected by complexity, the failure to find age differences in vocal reaction time paradigms might be attributed to the fact that vocal and manual tasks differ not only on the dimension of motor system used, but on complexity as well. The results of this study should provide information that will determine whether aging affects a central motor processing stage that is general to all motor systems, or whether the prime aging effect is specific to a particular motor system.

HYPOTHESES

Note that the hypotheses are specific to a particular relationship that is being tested statistically. For example, in hypothesis 1 the relationship between the type of motor response and speed of response is tested by the analysis of variance main effect for motor system. This is a very clear and unambiguous test.

When the literature provides the investigator with information suggesting the direction of differences (in this example several of the cited reports suggest that the manual responses will be longer than the vocal), the directional hypothesis provides a more powerful test. No similar information is available to suggest whether complexity of response would interact with a specific type of motor system; thus hypothesis 3 is written in the null form. The reader may wish to submit each of these hypotheses to the tests suggested in Chapter 1: Is the hypothesis unambiguous? Does it express a relationship? Is the appropriate statistical test implied?

In order to fulfill the purposes of this study, several hypotheses are formulated. These hypotheses are expressed directionally where the results from past experiments suggest directionality. When direction is unpredictable, they are written in the null form.

Hypothesis 1. The mean reaction time for manual responses is significantly faster than that for vocal responses.

Hypothesis 2. The mean reaction time for simple responses is significantly less than that for complex responses.

Hypothesis 3. The difference between mean reaction time for response type (simple or complex) is not significantly interactive with mode of response (manual or vocal).

Hypothesis 4. The mean reaction time of young subjects is significantly faster than that of old subjects.

Hypothesis 5. The mean reaction time of old subjects is not significantly different from that of young subjects when using vocal responses.

Hypothesis 6. The mean reaction time of old subjects is significantly greater than of young subjects when using manual responses.

Hypothesis 7. The difference between the mean reaction time of the old subjects and of the young subjects using the simple response type is not significantly different from the difference using the complex response type (regardless of response mode).

Hypothesis 8. The mean reaction time for old subjects is not significantly different from that for young subjects using simple-voice or complex-voice responses.

Hypothesis 9. The mean reaction time for old subjects is significantly greater than that for young subjects when using simple-manual or complex-manual responses.

Hypothesis 10. The mean reaction time, averaged over all conditions, is significantly improved from day one to day two, and from day two to day three.

Hypothesis 11. The improvement, with practice, in mean reaction time for the old subjects is not significantly different from that for the young subjects.

DELIMITATIONS

The delimitations expressed below specify that inferences from this study may only be made to the sex, age, and educational level of the sample used. Other restrictions relate to the specific type of response investigated, and the amount of practice provided. Those who would replicate the proposed study are cautioned that results will pertain only to samples matching the description given. By describing the delimitations, the author also is promising the committee that, when the analyses are complete and the results are known, inferences will not be made that extend beyond what is appropriate.

Because of the age grouping and sex of the subjects chosen for this study, it is not possible to generalize the results to females or to other age levels. The results also cannot be completely generalized from this university-drawn sample to the general population. Any conclusions concerning motor-system-specific, dependent age differences will have to be limited to the two response modes (finder and voice) used in this experiment; these results cannot be generalized to other modes of response. Conclusions concerning the response-complexity issue must be limited to the degree and types of complexity provided in the responses in this experiment; the results cannot be generalized to other levels of complexity. Because the amount of practice provided in this experiment was limited to three days, the results cannot be generalized to include the performance of tasks where more than three days of practice are provided.

LIMITATIONS

Inasmuch as older people are more variable in their responses, the results from this study would be more reliable if older individuals could be administered many trials over several days, dependent on when the subjects' performance plateaued. Also, direct measurement of important control variables, such as blood pressure, are always better than self-report or indirect assessments. However, the same variable that contributes to greater variability, the age factor, also dictates that these direct measures and practices are not possible. The author has determined that the information to be gained from these measures is nevertheless valuable and will contribute a reliable answer to the questions proposed.

Older individuals tire quickly and become disenchanted with testing after several blocks of trials. They have reached the age where they may not be motivated and certainly do not feel compelled to tolerate a long, arduous battery of testing for many consecutive days. Devoting extended periods of time to being tested is inconvenient and difficult for most subjects; consequently, the practice/testing time in this study will be conducted only for three days. Pilot work has provided evidence to suggest that reaction times are close to baseline levels by three days. The screening of subjects for health problems such as high blood pressure or the use of response-slowing drugs will be limited to self report. Formal methods of screening are costly, inconvenient, and unavailable to the investigator. However, by excluding all subjects with self-reported medications and health problems, errors that might occur should be minimized and should be an error on the conservative side.

DEFINITIONS

Below the author has provided definitions for those terms that are system language words used within the domain of motor control research. Most of the words to be defined (e.g., response programming) are words that either singly or in phrases have an invariant meaning for researchers in this field. In the case of the term "complexity," the investigator operationally assigns an invariant meaning to a common language word. This makes it available for systematic use throughout the proposal. Note that source citations are provided where possible.

Complexity. In this study, a level of complexity is operationally defined as more complex if the response latency is significantly slower. The motor responses were selected because of differences in the relative nature and number of coordinated muscles involved in producing the immediate response and, significant differences in the response latencies observed in pilot work.

Fractionated Reaction Time. Reaction time can be partitioned into "central" and "peripheral" components by using electromyography (EMG) to record the electrical activity from the muscles (Weiss, 1965). During a portion of the RT, the EMG is silent, indicating that the signal to move has yet to reach the muscle. Later in the RT, electrical activity is recorded from the activated muscle but no movement occurs for a time. The interval from the stimulus signal to the first EMG activity is termed *premotor RT* and is thought to represent time spent in central processes; while the interval from the first sign of change in EMG to actual movement is termed *motor time* (MT) and represents processes associated with the muscles and their actions in initiation of the response (Schmidt, 1982, p. 75).

Response Programming. Response programming occurs in the final stage of the information processing model. Once a stimulus has been identified and the proper response has been selected, the response programming stage is responsible for the preparation of the motor apparatus and the initiation of the action (see Schmidt, 1982, p. 93; Figure 2.1).

Variable Error. The variable error used in this study is a measure of inconsistency in responding. It is the variability of a subject's response latencies about the mean response latency (Schmidt, 1982, p. 66).

REVIEW OF LITERATURE

This review of literature section provides the background for the selection of hypotheses and method. Note that in paragraph three an overview of the review section is provided. This is an important step in helping the reader understand what is to follow. The review may or may not have a short introduction (as provided here in the first two paragraphs) before the overview paragraph. In Chapter 3 we provide an extended discussion of how to prepare a literature review. As you read this, however, notice how the author often summarizes the literature in conceptual categories rather than undertaking a study-by-study discussion. Summaries provided at the end of the two longer sections help the reader identify the important generalizations to be made.

Throughout its history, the behavioral study of aging has revealed at least one consistent finding: that older adults are slower than young adults in response speed. Reportedly, this phenomenon can be observed regardless of the mode of response

(Birren & Botwinick, 1955; Welford, 1977) and regardless of the type of stimuli (Talland, 1965; Welford, 1977) involved in the response task.

Efforts to isolate possible mechanisms responsible for this age-related slowing have been largely successful only in revealing mechanisms that are probably not causes: the slowing is not the result solely of sensory diminution (Botwinick, 1972, 1978), not muscle atrophy (Weiss, 1965), nor a reduction of nerve conduction velocity (Hugin, Norris, & Shock, 1960). Possible compound effects of all of these changes have not been tested. Through default, most investigators agree that an alteration in the central nervous system is presently the best candidate for the mechanism responsible for the age-related slowing (Botwinick & Thompson, 1966; Clarkson, 1978; Weiss, 1965). In addition, lack of sufficient practice with a particular task has been suggested as a possible cause for at least some of the age differences observed (Grant, Storandt, & Botwinick, 1978; Murrell, 1970; Salthouse & Somberg, 1982a).

In this study the focus will be on age related changes in RT in performing simple and complex tasks. The review of literature section has three sections related to this topic: (1) response-specific aging effects; (2) motor responses and an information processing model; and (3) vocal reaction time paradigms (without age as a factor).

Response-Specific Aging Effects

Vocal responses

Surprisingly, an exception to this general slowing in older individuals has been reported. In studies of simple reaction time using vocal responses, Nebes (1978), Thomas, Waugh, and Fozard (1978), and Salthouse and Somberg (1982) found no significant age differences. These findings were somewhat incidental: they were reported in investigations in which other response tasks were of central interest, or where the vocal RT measures were used as controls. These results were obtained only from simple response tasks and when (except in Salthouse & Somberg, 1982) a limited amount of practice was provided. Nebes

(1978) is the only investigator among these who discussed a possible explanation for the vocal RT findings. He suggested that perhaps the neural substrate for speech is less susceptible than that of manual movements to the loss of brain cells which has been shown to occur with increasing age. However, Nebes (1978) added that explanations along those lines must remain speculative.

Voice onset time

Another recent study in speech research was conducted to determine the effect of aging on voice onset time (VOT). VOT was defined as a delay in the onset of vocal fold vibration for the vowel that follows release of the consonant; this reflects supralaryngeal and laryngeal coordination speed. Neiman, Klich, and Shuey (1983) measured VOT from spectrograms for 10 women between 20 and 30 years old and 10 women between 70 and 80 years old. Their findings, contrary to their expectations, revealed that VOT was generally the same in older and younger subjects. The only explanation that was offered was that changes due to aging may have little effect on glottal adjustments and/or articulatory adjustments used to control VOT.

Summary

Together, the results from these various studies lend support to the notion that the act of vocalization, unlike other behavioral acts, may be affected differently or not at all by age. Furthermore, the mechanism that is responsible apparently involves the central control processes. Haaland and Bracy (1982) have proposed that the general slowing of response speed with age may be related to the response programming stage in an information processing model. The motor programming of manual and vocal responses, rather than using a centralized, general control mechanism, may be specific to the motor system used. Motor response specificity has been demonstrated with simple reaction time (Nebes, 1978; Thomas et al., 1978). Thus, different mechanisms of response programming for different modalities might respond differently to aging.

Motor Responses and an Information Processing Model

Stages of information processing

At least three stages have been proprosed that intervene between the presentation of a stimulus and the evocation of a response (Figure 1). First the subject must identify the stimulus and acknowledge that it has occurred. This is commonly known as the stimulus-identification stage. Second, after a stimulus is identified the subject must decide what response to make. This occurs in the response selection stage. Finally after the response has been selected, the system must be readied for the correct action and must initiate that action. This final stage is frequently called the response-initiation (Kerr, 1978) or response-programming stage (Schmidt, 1982). It is the final stage that, when isolated, may reflect response-specific programming changes with aging.

The author provided in Figure 1 a box diagram of a currently accepted model of information processing. In the interest of space we have deleted the diagram, but it was a clever technique as it allowed the author to organize the description of each stage of the model, and commonly used methods of identifying the stage, around the boxes in the figure.

Kerr (1978) outlines the appropriate steps for focusing on the response programming stage:

The time for encoding and identifying stimuli and for associating stimuli with task-appropriate responses must remain constant across conditions so that differences in initiation time can be identified with movement programming stages rather than processes that occur before programming (e.g. remembering that red means right). The most straightforward approach standardizes the number of task alternatives across conditions. Other variables known to affect reaction time (e.g. signal intensity, warning interval duration) must also be controlled. Only when one is comfortable with the assumption that initial processing times remain equal across conditions should differences in initiation time be attributed to programming stages.

Response programming and response complexity

While information about the first two stages of processing was obtained very early in the history of motor behavior research, information about the response programming stage was, until recently, undeveloped. It was not until the early studies by Henry and Rogers, that thinking about a response-programming stage began. In 1960, Henry and Rogers studied the nature of the movement to be made in a simple-RT paradigm, in which subjects knew on any given trial which response was to be made. The three responses ranged from the simplest (merely lifting the finger from a key) to the most complex which involved lifting the finger from a key, moving forward and upward to strike one ball with the back of the hand, moving forward and downward to push a button, and then forward and upward again to strike a second ball. For each level of complexity, the stimulus and response alternatives were the same; therefore, the processing time in the stimulus-identification and response-selection stages should have been constant. These levels of increasing complexity involved additional *accuracy* requirements and increased movement *duration,* and for each level there was a significant increase in the reaction time. Since the publication of the Henry and Rogers study many investigators have found similar results (see Kerr, 1978, or Klapp, 1977, 1980, for reviews). In one modification of the original paradigm, Sternberg, Monsell, Knoll, and Wright (1978) found that RT was directly related to the number of elements in a sequence of action by studying response speeds for spoken words and typed letters. In a review of several of these studies, Schmidt (1982, p. 112) observed that: "Regardless of the variations in method and movements, the effect of movement complexity on RT has been interpreted as relating to the time necessary to prepare the movement during the response-programming stage of RT." Like that of Henry and Rogers (1960), and the others that followed, this investigation involved the isolation of changes that occurred in the response-programming stage due to changes in the complexity of the motor response; but, in the effort to find the locus of aging differences between vocal and manual tasks, the manipulations of complexity were along somewhat different lines.

Complexity differences between manual and vocal tasks

Even at its simplest level, the act of vocalization involves the coordinated effort of several muscles in the respiratory system, while a manual act, such as pressing a button with the index finger, simply requires the flexion of two adjacent, co-agonist muscles. Perhaps the aging differences found between vocal and manual response speeds are not based on the obvious motor system differences, but are instead the result of differences in the motoric complexity of the two skills. Other investigators have suggested theories along these lines.

Abbs, Gracco, and Cole (1984) have suggested that movements constrained around a single joint may present a more difficult programming/control problem to the nervous system than their apparently "more complex" multijoint counterparts, i.e., speech. Based on speech perturbation studies of their own, and consideration of other recent experiments on speech and manual movement coordination, Abbs et al. (1984) summarize some of their findings: " . . . multiple degrees of freedom in natural motor behaviors may facilitate rather than burden the processes of motor learning and neural control. . . . The learning and neural programming of skilled motor behaviors would be significantly more demanding if the criterion for successful performance is restricted to a single stereotyped pattern of muscle contraction and movement."

Summary

These observations, when coupled with those of Haaland and Bracy (1982) suggest the possibility of a response-specific programming difference involved between vocal and manual activities that lends itself to a greater or lesser aging effect; and that perhaps that difference, rather than being just modality-specific, is a function of the differential complexity in *initiating* the two acts. Motor response specificity can be tested directly, but specific programming differences such as these are more difficult to isolate. Haaland and Bracy (1982) suggest that investigators who directly manipulate the complexity of (only) the motor response would be more directly determining whether motor programming capabilities change with aging. This would require circumventing the earlier stages of information processing in order to isolate any response programming differences and, as discussed in the previous section, is not a novel idea (for a review, see Kerr, 1978; Klapp, 1977, 1980; Schmidt, 1982, chap. 4; Sternberg et al., 1978); but, in this investigation, the accuracy and duration of the response movements were not factors. In fact, after the initial response, there was no additional movement; it was simply the number of coordinated muscles involved in the direct initiation of the response that provided the levels of complexity. It was assumed that if the response-programming stage was properly isolated, and latency differences (between the levels of complexity in this study) were observed, that those latency differences would be the result of different processing speeds in the response-programming stage. If age differences interacted with these complexity differences, it would support the notion that the modality differences were actually the result of differences in complexity.

Vocal RT Paradigms (Without Age as a Factor)

Other researchers studying speech have focused on vocal reaction time, but not age effects. However, several of these studies described results and methodologies that were helpful in pursuing the present investigation. Izdebski and Shipp (1978) measured the difference between voluntary vocal and digital (finger) response speeds in young adults using simple RT methodology. The vocal RT's were studied as a function of sex, stimulus type (auditory and somesthetic), and subject lung volume. Among these variables, only lung volume produced significant differences, suggesting a need to standardize lung volume in any future vocal reaction time paradigms. More relevant to this investigation, Izdebski and Shipp (1978), Nebes (1978), Thomas et al. (1978), and Salthouse and Somberg (1982) found that the average digital RT's were significantly shorter than the times for vocal reactions; a finding that may be a result of the measurement used in the vocal tasks. Results from pilot work for this investigation indicated that hidden, highly variable latencies may characterize reaction times that are measured with a vocally triggered relay such as that used by these investigators. Latency measurements made directly from voice patterns reproduced on a storage oscilloscope are more reliable and accurate.

Summary

If the results from previous studies involving vocal response are valid, it may be inferred that the act of vocalization is an exception to the general slowing of response speed observed in the aged: that age-related slowing is response specific. It is important that such an exception be validated through replication; taking care to avoid possible confounding with insufficient practice and unreliable measurements. Furthermore, it may be possible—by manipulating certain variables and isolating the response-programming stage—to search for the mechanism(s) responsible for such an exception. Once possible mechanisms are isolated, theories that explain a response-specific age difference can be generated and tested more readily.

METHOD

The method section that is presented here begins with an overview paragraph and a diagram of the steps in collecting the data. For most proposals an overview paragraph should come first and, if supplemented with an appropriate diagram, few readers will have difficulty in understanding how the parts of the method section mesh into the overall plan. All the major components of method are identified by side headings. The author makes good use of pilot data in this section and, appropriately, puts complex detail into an appendix.

In this study age differences in reaction time will be examined in the performance of simple and complex manual and vocal tasks. The reaction time of a group of older (60 years and over) and younger men (18-30 years old) will be tested on 3 days on four tasks: (1) a manual task that is simple; (2) a manual task that is complex; (3) a vocal task that is simple; and, (4) a vocal task that is complex. A diagrammatic overview is presented in Figure 2.

Subjects

The subjects will be 40 males obtained from a university population. Sampling males of different ages from this population

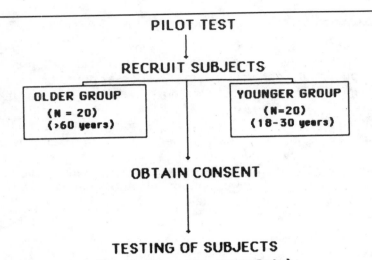

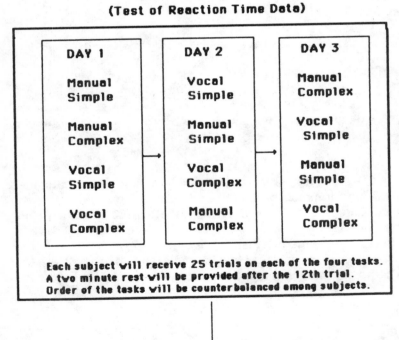

Figure 2

will provide some university-related homogeneity in the variation in cognitive abilities and types ordinarily found in the general population. Results from previous studies involving reaction time indicate a need to control for variations in cognitive ability and type. Twenty, composing the older group, will be volunteers from the faculty population and will be 60 years of age or older. Since many of these individuals will be close to or beyond the age of retirement, only those who remain actively involved with the university (retired faculty organization, alumni association, part- or full-time lecturer, instructor, or researcher) will be accepted. Twenty, composing the young group, will be volunteers from the student population and will range from 18 to 30 years of age. All subjects will be screened to insure that they are non-smokers and not currently taking any medication that might alter response speed. All subjects will be right handed, in good health and, according to self report, without any neurological disorder.

Design

Reaction times of the two age groups (old and young) will be compared with regard to the complexity of the reaction task (simple or more complex, hereafter called complexity), the response modality (vocal or manual), and the number of days of practice (1-3 days). The design will be a between (age) and within (complexity, mode, and practice) model analyzed by a $2 \times 2 \times 2 \times 3$ factorial analysis of variance.

Apparatus

Measurement of simple manual reaction time will be accomplished using an index-finger-activated microswitch connected to a Standard Electric Time digital timer (Model ABC-11) (see Appendix A for an instrumentation diagram). The timer has a manufacturer reported accuracy of +/-.00016 seconds. Measurement of the complex manual reaction time will be accomplished using index-finger- and thumb-activated microswitches connected in series to the same timer. The speech acoustic signals from vocal reactions will be recorded through an Ebel XY89A microphone, on a Packer Dck 1234 tape deck at a speed of 3 3/4 inches per second. The signals will be reproduced on the same tape deck and channeled into a Brand Name Storage Oscilloscope

(Model XXYY) to produce voice patterns from which reaction times will be obtained (see appendix B for an instrumentation diagram).

The red stimulus light for all reaction time tasks will be a 120 VAC neon lamp, measuring two centimeters across, and set in a flat-black background. The occurrence of a warning bell will be manually controlled via a French millisecond timer (Model 00033). The same timer will control the activation of the stimulus light. The inter-trial interval of five seconds will be controlled by a French interval timer (Model 00112). Both the millisecond and interval timer have a manufacturer reported accuracy rating of 0.1% +/-1 LSD and a repeatability measure of 0.1% +/-1 LSD.

Pilot Testing of Instrumentation

Manual instrumentation

Because RT's on several different instruments will be compared, it is important to establish that differences observed will not be attributed to instrument-related mechanical or bio-mechanical differences rather than central processing differences. In the manual tasks, RT's on one microswitch were to be compared in a pilot study with RT's on two additional micro-switches, set in series. If these switches were mechanically different or caused biomechanical inconsistencies that would bring about latency differences, it would confound interpretations of the manual results.

Since this investigation will center on changes in latency due to changes in the central processes (only), it has to be established that the speed in the peripheral components of RT (motor time; pressure, throw times, and spring tensions of the switches) is constant across each task (see Figure 3). The construct validity of this investigation would be suspect if any differences in this peripheral component existed from task to task, e.g., if RT on the simple task was significantly shorter than that for the complex task, the results would be confounded if the motor time for the simple task also was significantly shorter.

Equipment was not available to test the throw times and spring tensions of the switches *mechanically*, nor the muscle-exerted pressure, but (behavioral) RT tests were conducted with each

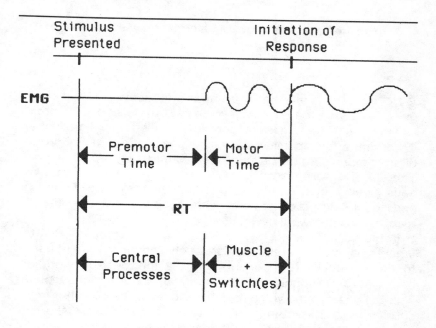

Critical events involved in the reaction time paradigm. The trace is a hypothetical EMG record. (Adapted from Schmidt, 1982, p.75)

Figure 3

individual switch: a well practiced subject, who had just completed three days of testing, completed 10 warm-up trials and 25 test trials of RT with each *individual* switch (see Table C-1, Appendix C). In addition, in a separate test, the EMG of the muscles involved in the responses was recorded during several trials on both the simple and complex apparatus. The motor time for these trials was compared and analyzed for differences between tasks (Table C-2, Appendix C). The behavioral RT test revealed very little difference between the means from each switch. However, in the EMG testing, the motor time for the simple (index finger only) task was 41% longer than the motor time for the complex (finger/thumb) task. Therefore, since in the investigation, RT on the simple task was significantly shorter than RT on the complex task, the difference was probably a conservative estimate of the differences that existed.

Vocal instrumentation

In order to make valid comparisons between vocal RT (measured from the onset of a voice pattern on an oscilloscope) and manual RT, which was recorded directly from a digital timer, it was important to make certain that measures of RT on the digital timer would be the same if measured on the oscilloscope. Therefore, RT for several trials of the manual tasks were simultaneously viewed on the timer and on the oscilloscope (see Figure 4), and absolutely no differences were observed between the RT recorded on the two instruments.

In the vocal tasks, it also was important to establish that no inherent latency differences existed between the instrumentation for the two different consonants, e.g., that the vocal fold vibration necessary for producing the "zz" sound occurred simultaneously with the onset of the voice pattern, and not before or after (thus shortening or extending the apparent latency). To make this particular comparison the production of the consonant sounds was recorded simultaneously at the vocal cords and at the mouth. Vocal fold vibrations were recorded via a phonometer (a device for measuring the intensity of sounds) and the onset of the voice pattern was, via the microphone previously described viewed on the same phonometric readout (see Appendix D for instrumentation diagram). As expected, no vocal fold vibrations occurred in the production of the "ss" sound, and in addition, there were no latency differences between the onset of the voice pattern and the onset of vocal fold vibration in the production of the "zz" sound.

Procedures

General

Each subject will be administered a consent form (Appendix E) to read and sign. He will be seated at a table where the microphone, manual apparatus, and stimulus lights are positioned. Before trials for either vocal or manual reaction time begin, each subject will receive standardized instructions (Appen-

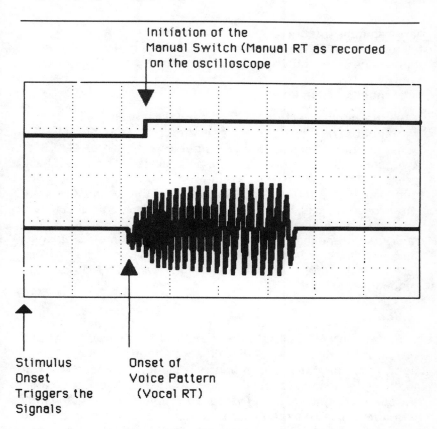

Initiation of the
Manual Switch (Manual RT as recorded
on the oscilloscope

Stimulus
Onset
Triggers the
Signals

Onset of
Voice Pattern
(Vocal RT)

A schematic diagram of manual and vocal response
signals as seen on a storage oscilloscope.

Figure 4

dix F) for that task. The order (Appendix G) in which the two
response types (vocal and manual) and in which either a simple or
complex version of the two tasks will be administered will be
counter-balanced across all subjects. Each subject will complete
25 trials of both the simple and complex versions of the manual
and vocal tasks on three consecutive days. Based on pilot data, 25
trials will be enough to provide sufficient practice and a sufficiently

large sample, but not so many as to fatigue the subjects. A two-minute rest was given after the first 12 trials of each task on all three days of testing.

Manual reaction time

In the simple version of the manual task, upon hearing a warning buzzer, the subject will direct his attention to the stimulus light. After a randomly assigned warning interval (2, 3, or 4 seconds), the stimulus light will be activated. The subject will press the microswitch with the index finger as quickly as possible upon seeing the stimulus light activated. In the complex version, the procedure will be the same except that, upon seeing the stimulus light activated, the subject will engage the index-finger microswitch and the thumb microswitch on the complex reaction-time apparatus (see Appendix H) (for a diagram of the manual tasks; see Appendix I for the muscles involved in the production of the manual tasks).

Vocal reaction time

In the vocal RT tasks, the protocol will be similar. A warning buzzer will sound to direct the subject's attention to the stimulus light, place his tongue in a neutral position against the lower teeth, and, after a randomly assigned interval (2, 3, or 4 seconds), the stimulus light will be activated. The subject will be constantly monitored, by the experimenter, to insure that his mouth is the proper distance from the microphone. In the simple version, upon seeing the light activated, the subject will say the consonant, "ss" (producing a hissing sound) into the microphone as quickly as possible. In the complex version, upon seeing the light activated, the subject will say the consonant, "zz" (producing a buzzing sound as in the beginning of the word, xylophone) into the microphone as quickly as possible. The initial enunciation of the consonant will form the onset of the voice pattern, from which reaction times will be measured. Pilot data were not obtained for these particular sounds, but for a variety of others. The results reflected a low level of within subject variability for the various vocal sounds tested (see Table J-1, Appendix J). These sounds—"ss" and "zz"—were chosen because the muscle activity involved in the production of each is relatively simple, and because the enunciation of each yield clear and reliable voice patterns (Figure 4) from which to measure RT. The pilot data provided a basis for complete confidence that no significant difference in variability will occur between (and therefore confound) the measures from the vocal and manual tasks (see Table J-1, Appendix J).

Analysis

The mean RT and standard deviation for each set of trials will be computed. Scores that were two standard deviations above or below the mean will be discarded and new means and standard deviations computed. These data will be averaged across subjects in each age group for each of the three days: a 2×2×2×3 (age: young/old × modality: vocal/manual × complexity: simple/complex × practice: days 1, 2, and 3). ANOVA factorial analysis with repeated measures on the last three factors then will be computed twice: once for reaction time and once for the standard deviation data. Tukey's-HSD post hoc comparisons will be made between means in the interactions.

In the proposal the author used appendices to include the following:

Appendix A. Instrumentation Diagram for the Manual Apparatus
Appendix B. Instrumentation Diagram for the Vocal Apparatus
Appendix C. Pilot Testing of Instrumentation
Appendix D. Instrumentation Diagram for the Testing of the Vocal Tasks
Appendix E. Subject Consent Form
Appendix F. Task Instructions
Appendix G. Testing Order
Appendix H. Switch Diagram
Appendix I. Muscles Used in the Manual Tasks
Appendix J. Pilot Data

Appendix J, Pilot Data, contained descriptive data for each group, subgroup, and interaction, sample Analysis of Variance tables, and figures plotting the pilot data. As indicated in Chapter 3, sample tables are a valuable and often neglected component of the proposal. When included, they may reveal problems that are not easily identified from a reading of the text.

PROPOSAL 2: QUALITATIVE STUDY

Returning Women Students in the Community College

Note to the Reader

The proposal which follows involves use of the qualitative paradigm for research. If you are unfamiliar with this kind of inquiry, reading Chapter 4 will help in understanding the unique planning problems that must be confronted. If you are familiar only with experimental and quasi-experimental designs, Chapter 4 will explain what otherwise will seem unusual or inappropriate ways of handling some elements in the proposal.

Not only may this be your first encounter with some of the methods used here, but the author's assumptions about such basic matters as the nature of reality, the definition of truth, and the meaning of reliability, generalizability, and replicability, may seem sharply different from those ordinarily made. The test of a qualitative proposal, for example, is not whether it is so carefully explicit and thorough as to allow replication with similar findings. Details of research focus, method, and analysis often are not established in the proposal, because they only can be fully determined once the investigation is in process. Further, if replication were attempted (most qualitative specialists would argue that it is impossible) the product of identical findings would constitute more of a surprise than an expected outcome.

There must, of course, be rules of thought and procedure which insure that qualitative designs represent systematic inquiry. Research must always be distinct from reportage, reflective

---

The original of this proposal was prepared by Mary Bray Schatzkammer under the direction of Professor Earl Siedman, in partial fulfillment of the requirements for the Ed.D. in the Division of Instructional Leadership of the School of Education at the University of Massachusetts, Amherst. The ensuing dissertation was completed and accepted by the Graduate School on May 15, 1986.

observation, or connoisseurship. The research traditions of qualitative study are sufficiently different from the more familiar canons of quantitative science to require some investment of study before attempting to read a proposal or study report.

It is in those very differences, however, that rest the special powers of the qualitative paradigm. In the following proposal, the author examines the problems encountered by women returning to college after absence from formal schooling. The research question, however, does not focus only on a reconstruction of what happened to them. The author asks as well, "What did it feel like to be there?"

A method of inquiry designed to help us discover and share the experience of other individuals, produces consequences for both the investigator and the reader. No longer the detached, dispassionate outside observers, they are led toward the center of things—toward life as it is lived. That is a different vantage point for understanding the world, one which can yield results of exceptional utility as well as dramatic persuasiveness.

The title clearly identifies the subjects (women students), the setting (community college), and a key variable in the study (returning to school). It has the virtue of being both brief and easy to read. As in-depth phenomenological interviewing is a relatively infrequent and recently developed tool for qualitative research, the method of investigation also might have been named in the title. What is lost in brevity might be more than returned in improved retrieval. At this particular time in the history of educational research, with so much interest in new paradigms for inquiry, both graduate students and established scholars will be using key words for both research paradigms (such as "qualitative") and particular methods (such as "in-depth interviewing") as the basis for retrieving studies of interest from database systems (such as *Dissertation Abstracts International*).

INTRODUCTION

Question and Overview

In the dissertation I will explore, through in-depth interviews, the meaning of the experience of older women students who return to school after some years of absence from traditional education and who choose a community college as their first point of re-entry. What is it like to be a returning woman student? What are the aspirations, expectations, and concerns of returning women students? How does the community college experience fit into the context of their everyday lives? Given where they have been and where they hope to be, what meaning does the community college experience have for them? In a time when women are returning to school in record numbers, when the press for equal rights for women is a dominant political issue, and when, among institutions of higher education, the community college proclaims most strongly an egalitarian mission—do these returning women students find their educational experience adequate and equitable?

> The opening sentence is a model of its kind. No reader will have the slightest doubt about what is to be studied. Even though relatively long and complex in structure, it reads smoothly. Removing the phrase "from traditional education" might tighten it a bit, but the author may have had reason to remind readers that informal, non-school education had continued for these women. The word "meaning" can be troublesome for many readers, but the rhetorical questions that follow leave little doubt about what is intended.
>
> The first paragraph is longer than the ideal opener. In the art of gentle introduction, anything longer than 10 lines runs the risk of daunting the wary reader. The paragraph might be divided by detaching the closing sentence, which introduces the concept of equity, and combining it with the opening sentence of the next paragraph. With a few added words to connect the theme of equity with the previous questions about personal meaning, the two paragraphs thus organized would yield a slightly more inviting format for the first page.

Because of the importance to women today of issues of self-definition, independence, power, and opportunity, or racism, classism, and ageism (as well as sexism), equity [1] is a central concept among perspectives from which the results of this study will be viewed. The literature of the following disciplines will be examined for their contribution to understanding further these issues as they are related to the problem of older women seeking education in the community college: (1) demographics—of aging, gender, and education; (2) history—of women's movement, and of the community college; (3) life-span developmental psychology; (4) feminist sociological research.

Assuming the first paragraph is left intact, note how the theme of equity forms a bridge between the last sentence of the first paragraph and the opening sentence of the second paragraph. The closer and more evident such ties are made, the easier it is to read and understand any document. Each paragraph must have its own independent, major thought, but the more these thoughts can be made to flow in an apparent sequence of logic, the more clearly the reader can apprehend the writer's reasoning. Whenever the context permits you to do so, it is desirable to end each paragraph by pointing forward to the next thought, and to start the next paragraph with a glance back at the previous thought.

The reference to note 1 leads to a Note section at the end of the main text. This particular note provides a brief definition and discussion of the word "equity" (and associated terms such as equality and equal opportunity) for readers who might not be familiar with the specialized term. As adequate treatment would require a full page of double-spaced text, and as no Definitions section is used in this proposal, placing the discussion in a note is the appropriate choice. Those who need help have it available, and those who do not can ignore the superscript.

The qualitative research process will be used to investigate the experience of returning women in community colleges. In this study the primary methods used will be analyses of transcripts of in-depth, phenomenological interviews of a sample of returning women at community colleges in three states. Selection of participants will be based on fairness to the population of returning women students in their colleges: the interview sample will include a range of ages, ethnicities, class backgrounds, work experience, family histories, and college program choices (liberal arts and vocational programs), in colleges that are urban, suburban, and rural.

The word "fairness" is troublesome here. Usually it is intended to suggest that the selection will be done so as to produce a representative sample. The substantial demands of in-depth interviewing, the size of the data mass produced, and the complexity of any analysis likely to be used all suggest that achieving a truly representative sample would be singularly difficult for a doctoral candidate. It seems more likely that the author intends only to be sure that some important variables are represented among the selected participants. In which case, approximation of the true population of returning women is moot, and the whole matter of fairness is better left unmentioned. What the reader will really want to know is *how* subjects with the desired characteristics will be selected. A few words on that topic would mean more here than any promise about fair sampling.

In the following sections of this proposal the rationale for, and the plan for conducting this study will be outlined more fully. Sections will include: (1) importance of the study; (2) extent of the study; (3) methodology (bias, assumptions and epistemological support, selection of participants, the interview process, interpretation and analysis, profile construction); (4) conclusions and implications; (5) appendices (forms, tables, notes, bibliography).

Advisors vary considerably in their enthusiasm for such brief overviews of organization (and any previewing of content that may be included). Some find it appropriate only here, at the close of the introduction. Others like to find such previews at the end of every major section. Certainly, with an adequate table of contents and the correct use of headings and subheadings, these are a convenience and not a necessity. The use here seems appropriate and may have some of the same utility as an advance organizer in any instructional process.

IMPORTANCE OF THE STUDY

This study is important today because of (1) demographic factors that influence school populations at all educational levels; (2) the confluence of two historic movements: the struggle of oppressed groups (including women) for "equal rights," and the widening stream of offerings in higher education (most apparent in the community college); (3) the potential conflict situation in the community college: wide-open doors and concomitant pressures to close them—the tension between "come-one-come-all" and having "standards," between growth and taxes; and (4) the paucity of studies which look at the story of the woman who goes through those doors.

The above paragraph is anything but elegant. Yet it transmits a great deal of information to the reader in a short space. Some sympathy for the task of reading, however, would lead to a search for ways to simplifying things. At the least we could remove the quotes from around "equal rights" (which probably were there for reasons which could be appreciated only by specialists in the area). The third item could be rewritten so as to merge some of the clauses (as for example, "wide open doors welcoming everyone, and concomitant pressure to close the doors so as to maintain academic standards . . ."). Finally, the conflict between expansion of higher education and growth in the tax burden appears to dangle at the end of item 3. It would be easier for the reader to find it numbered as a separate item.

What is missing from the opening paragraphs of this section is some preliminary indication, however brief, of the unique contribution that a successfully completed qualitative study might provide. It *is* helpful to list all of the converging factors that make problematic the return of older women to higher education. That, however, argues more for the importance of the question than for the study itself. Thirty pages later, at the close of the proposal, the author points out the great utility to community college administrators, faculty, and counselors, of the results that should emerge from this study. That is the point that seems most directly appropriate to a discussion under the heading "Importance of the Study."

The author next proceeds to present supporting evidence for each area identified as bearing on the importance of the study. Facts, statistics, and significant reference sources are woven into a running commentary that argues for the meaningfulness of the topic. We have omitted most of that discussion (about 5 pages) and pick up the text as the author finishes comments about the growing tensions that surround the purposes and operation of community colleges.

These continuing tensions have deeply affected the work and morale of community college faculty (Seidman, 1983). How do they affect the education of returning women students? Considering the numbers of older women returning to colleges of all kinds, but particularly to community colleges, and considering the astonishing growth of community colleges, it is surprising that more studies are not in existence in which these phenomena are examined from the point of view of the woman student. There is indeed a large promotional and critical literature about women students in the community college which consists mainly of descriptions of and recommendations for programs. Among topics addressed are women's centers and access to occupational education. The general tone of these reports may be described by the titles of some of them: *Community College Women: A Golden Opportunity* (Eliason, 1977); *Second Wind: Program for Returning Women Students* (Carter, 1978); "Serving New Populations" (Walsh, 1979). (See also Brawer, 1977; Dibner, 1976; Eaton, 1981; Mezirow et al., 1978; O'Neill, 1977.)

There is, however, little research on this subject in which interviewing is an important element of the methodology. Two useful studies which include interviews, and which demonstrate the need for further research of this kind, are Tittle and Denker's *Returning Women Students in Higher Education* (1980) and the Project on the Status and Education of Women series (1981, 1982). Data in these studies indicate that older women who turn to the community college may do so because it is usually closer to home, less forbidding than the four-year college or university, immediately helpful and welcoming, and less expensive (sometimes free). It offers programs that appear to lead quickly to higher earnings, and special counseling and women's centers are advertised and available. In addition, two years seem more manageable than four when a family must be nurtured. Community colleges also require minimal admissions red tape or entrance requirements (except high school graduation or high school equivalency). Some barriers to re-entry reported by women are: financial need; image of college as only for white middle-class women, the elite, the privileged; concern for the college's relevance to them; fear of being the "only one"; lack of home and community support; needs for child care and transportation. Tittle and Denker's (1980) "vignettes" of ten students are based on a strict interview schedule derived from Levinson's (1978) theory of male adult development, although half of the students were women. Problems for returning women are briefly summarized as anxiety about ability, indecision about careers, conflicts related to school and home, paucity of needed information, the "alien language of academe," and unsatisfactory counseling services. The crucial questions were: Am I intelligent enough? How will I compare with eighteen-year-olds? Will my husband be resentful? Will my children suffer? Do I have the right to make demands for my self-improvement?

A paragraph of this length (over 30 lines in the original) is unreasonable. A comfortable break could have been made at the point where the topic shifts from reasons for selecting community college, to the subject of barriers to re-entry.

Note how the author merges results from three documents under four topical headings: choice of college, barriers, problems, and questions. This avoids the cumbersome task of treating each publication as a separate source, and adds a useful conceptual framework for thinking about the research topic. This kind of writing can make a review of the literature both readable and truly useful.

The sentence dealing with the subjects used in Tittle and Denker's study seems out of place in this otherwise exemplary summary. It might have been placed at the front adjacent to the introduction of the sources, or might have been omitted as not contributing anything essential to the reader's understanding.

Much important information about the returning woman in the environment of the community college is available in the studies cited. Significant and useful as this information is, a sense of the concrete day-to-day life of the students as they go about their work is absent; and absent too is a sense of the inner life of women as they choose their classes and interact with faculty and with other students; a sense of how their college life affects, and is affected by, their work outside the college and their family life, and what these interactions mean to them as women, as workers, as human beings, in this institution which promises them so much. The value of in-depth interview studies of aspects of women's experience—women's work, motherhood, being middle-aged—is demonstrated in British and American feminist research (McGrindle & Rowbotham, 1977; Oakley, 1976; Rivers et al., 1979; Rubin, 1979). A similar approach could be important for illuminating educational experience.

More detail on the methodology of the in-depth phenomenological interview which I propose to use in this study will be discussed in the section on methodology below. I should like to turn first to what I consider the necessary extent or spread of this investigation and to defining its limits.

The author acknowledges the importance of work previously done in the area, but makes clear what is missing. This accomplished, the next step is to argue for the utility of the proposed methodology in providing what has been missed. Notice how smoothly each of those steps is accomplished in the penultimate paragraph.

In the final paragraph the use of "I" rather than the familiar convention of third person ("the investigator") commonly used in quantitative studies seems unsurprising and comfortable in this context. As explained in Chapter 4, the person of the investigator is a proper and necessary part of the inquiry process in the qualitative paradigm. Any attempt to seem distanced from method would sound out of place.

At the close, the author acknowledges the growing need of the reader to learn more about the proposed method. By making this point explicit, the reader is encouraged to remain engaged through the additional step of establishing the limits of the study. That kind of sensitivity of the reader's experience helps to sustain a bond of joint enterprise with the writer.

EXTENT OF THE STUDY

Though the central focus of this study will be the investigation of the experience of returning women students in the community college, certain broad questions about women and education must remain as framework and backdrop. A brief overview in this proposal will replace an in-depth discussion, in the dissertation, of the literature of five related areas of inquiry: (1) demographics of aging, gender, and education; (2) the history of the community college as "open-door" institution; (3) life-span developmental psychology of women; (4) history of the women's movement; and (5) feminist sociological research.

A decision has been made to include in the dissertation report a substantial section of discussion which provides a framework for interpretation of the data. This will differ from the usual "Review of the Literature" which supports definition of the question and justifies the choice of methods and mode of analysis. As indicated in Chapter 3, the functions of the latter must be served in the proposal, and use of the literature tightly restricted to those purposes. The review which is previewed here will serve a different function, one particular to this type of study.

At this point, the reader already will suspect that the center heading above is something of a misnomer. The extent of the study as a whole will not be the subject here. The degree to which the study report will be expanded to include an extensive discussion designed to frame the analysis and presentation of data is the true target. A heading that more accurately reflects that fact would prevent any misunderstanding by the reader.

The first and second of these "backdrop" areas—demographics and the community college—already have been provided sufficient coverage in the rationale above (Importance of the Study). The last three areas are closely interconnected, but are separated here for purposes of a brief discussion.

In order to enrich the essential background for this study—the psychological, social, historical, and political aspects of women's education—I have undertaken the task of examining certain literature by and about women. The necessary minimum for this task appears to include an exploration of what is known about the life-span development of women in relation to learning and schooling; what the record says about the history of women's struggle for equity in education; how and why feminist research has developed, particularly in sociology, and the extent of its effect on individual women who attempt to continue their schooling and work.

The middle years are a "largely unexplored phase of the life cycle," say Brim and Abeles (1975). For the purposes of this study of women students, most of whom are in their "middle years" (30 to 50) some exploration into what is known about this phase of the human life cycle is called for. When the mean age of students in the community college is 27, with the range broadened to include 80-year-olds (Chickering, 1980), our learnings from the study of child and adolescent development no longer serve.

As a result of influence exerted by such factors as the women's movement and the higher proportion of older persons in western countries, a new literature has become available. Though in no way approaching the richness of research and writing on early human development, work on later life development has expanded greatly in recent years (Baltes, 1978; Birren & Woodruff, 1973; Eisdorfer & Lawton, 1973; Erikson, 1980; Jarvik, 1978; Lowenthal, 1975; Mass & Kuyper, 1974; Neugarten, 1968).

In this new literature there clearly is more research on the aging process in general than on the aging of women. The life-span development of men has had more attention in the past than that of women (Kohlberg, 1969; Levinson, 1978); recent studies have concentrated on women (Barnett & Baruch, 1979; Fuller & Martin, 1980; Rubin, 1979; Wetzel, 1982). Other studies reveal differences between men and women at different life stages in their responses to issues of morality, justice, and life choices (Erikson, 1980; Gilligan, 1982). Important differences seem to exist in the way chronological age defines stages in women's and men's lives (Barnett & Baruch, 1978).

Problems such as this are related to the subject of equity and returning women students in some important ways. This is particularly true of the relationship between aging and learning (Baltes, 1978; Botwinick, 1978; Diamond, 1978). Though most longitudinal studies show no loss in intellectual capacity with age, and in some cases a continual rise even through the eighth decade, the returning woman student often has a sense of uncertainty about diminished capacities. Experiences described in interviews of women (McGrindle & Rowbotham, 1977; Seidman, 1983; Tittle and Denker, 1980) demonstrate how their school lives are often affected negatively by cultural stereotypes that become assimilated in their own self-images. Women who are both female and old are victims of a "double standard of aging" (Bell, 1975; Sontag, 1980).

The study of aging and of life-span development is relatively new in the history of the social sciences, but the struggle for recognition of women as persons other than wives or mothers has gone on for a much longer time. With regard to the classic works I shall not discuss here, it is sufficient to say that it is impossible to understand what is happening for women today without a comprehensive reading of the women's studies literature, from Wollstonecraft (1792), Mill (1869), Gilman (1915), Woolf (1929, 1938), and Klein (1949) to the newest wave which began with Simone de Beauvoir's *Second Sex* (first published in 1952), continued with Friedan's *Feminine Mystique* (1963), and gained momentum with the work of many women writers—poets, novelists, social scientists, journalists: Ellman (1968); Firestone (1970); Flexner (1970); Rossi (1973, 1976); Lerner (1977); Olsen (1978); Morgan (1982)—to name only a very few. A passage from Tillie Olsen's *Silences* (1978) captures the meaning behind much of the women's movement literature:

Linked with the old, resurrected classics on women, this movement in three years has accumulated a vast new mass of testimony, of new comprehensions, as to what it is to be female. Inequities, restrictions, penalties, denials, leechings, have been painstakingly and painfully documented; damaging differences in circumstances and treatment from that of males attested to; and limitations, harms, a sense of wrong voiced.

—from *Silences* (One Out of Twelve)
Tillie Olsen, 1978, p. 41

Later in this same work, Olsen describes "the differing past of women that should be part of every human consciousness." Among these pasts, she writes, are the imposed conditions of unclean, taboo; being, not doing; bound feet; corsets; powerlessness; fear of aging; fear of expressing capacities; marriage, slavery, dissembling, manipulating, appeasing—"the vices of slaves."

The discussion at this point has become slightly more polemical than is appropriate in a research proposal. To say that "it is impossible to understand what is happening for women today without a comprehensive reading of the women's study literature" may be true in the abstract, but may leave the reader feeling a bit beleaguered. The point is to reassure the reader that the author *will* make this body of literature understandable and through that will make accessible some sense of what is happening to women today. The purpose of a proposal is to explain and justify a plan for investigation, not to convert or overwhelm the uninitiated.

Much women's literature has concentrated on the problem of equity in education for women. Some authors have traced the tortured story of women's gradual progress from being—some of them—the "daughters of educated men" (Woolf, 1938) to being admitted with reluctance into the select company within institutions of higher education (Deem, 1978; Greene et al., 1983; Sexton, 1976; Spender & Sarah, 1980).

Though we have seen that the *numbers* of women in college have finally come close to being equal to men—and in community colleges surpassing them—the question of equity in schooling is still murky: are women actually being treated fairly and equitably, with all that implies, as students? An example of a problematic area is that of relative numbers of female faculty compared with those of male faculty. Is the question of equity for the older woman student related to the problem of equity for women faculty in community colleges, as well as in other colleges?

Reports by women academics over the last twenty-five years indicate the slow progress that has been made in the establishment of women's positions in colleges and universities, both as faculty members and in administration (Bernard, 1964; Newcomer, 1959; Price, 1981). The combination of rapidly increasing numbers of women students and the very slow increase of women faculty is a theme which has been referred to in the work of Seidman (1983). Faculty are often aware, students less so, of the contradictions inherent in the fact of a minority of women faculty serving as models and mentors for a student body that is becoming more female than male—largely due to the increasing numbers of older women students.

Feminist research is already a source of new ideas on equity in academic institutions. Although theoretical work on women, and usually by women, as originators of a different style of observing the world—psychological and sociological research from a woman's point of view—appears to be still in its infancy, women social scientists in England and the United States have begun to develop their own research styles in the investigation of social and psychological questions and to attempt to free themselves from the patterns and constraints of what they now see as flawed research based on assumptions of the dominant male culture (Bunch & Pollack, 1983; Gilligan, 1982; Lerner, 1980; Oakley, 1972; Roberts, 1983).

I propose to continue the search for the feminist scholar's approach in literature that is related to women and aging, learning and schooling. With the rapid changes and shifting factions in the widening women's movement, and the spreading interchange among women researchers in several countries (Roberts, 1981), it will be important to follow closely the "literature" of news stories and current journals, as well as publications of organizations like the Feminist Press and its counterparts in Great Britain, France, and elsewhere. Though this study is limited to returning women students in this country, it is clear that the press for equity among women is not limited to one institution in one country. How and why this movement has come about is one of the basic questions underlying this research.

Here the author is writing about a personal commitment that extends beyond the proposed study. The reader may well begin to feel put upon. A graduate student's dispositions about future scholarship are of vital interest to mentors, but are not the proper subject of discussion in the proposal. Remember the purpose of the document and stick to it.

One difficulty with the qualitative method of research is identifying and maintaining limits, when in some ways there appear to be none. It is true that to examine *all* the literature in the fields I have suggested are relevant is an impossibility, considering constraints of time and energy, as well as appropriateness. I have set certain boundaries, but may pull the edges in even closer; for example, limiting my review of life-span development material to that related to women and learning in the middle years; limiting attention to women's movement history to the most notable writings of the last fifteen years; and examining only recent feminist sociological work which pertains to education of women—rather than the whole gamut of feminist research. The literature on community colleges is extensive but not all applicable to this study; and the demographics of aging, gender, and education are well-defined and manageable.

The tentativeness here would be disturbing to some advisors. If these are reasonable limitations, why not make them a stipulated part of the contract? The practical answer to that question may be that much of this reading has yet to be done. That is perfectly reasonable at this stage, but a firmer hand in setting limits would be helpful. Reasonable changes usually can be negotiated if it is discovered that they are required.

The limits of qualitative versus quantitative studies—and vice-versa—are well known (Smith, 1983). In this study I am giving up the possible advantages of the clean simplicity of an experimental study which cannot be appropriate for what I want to know (see *Methodology,* below). In exchange, I am plunging into research which will present me with a "vast matrix of interlocking message material" (Bateson, 1979) which must be transcribed, studied, coded, translated, interpreted, and analyzed, with the methods of the field researcher (Johnson, 1975; Lofland, 1971; Rubin, 1979). Anthropologist Jules Henry (1965) has said that "science is the relentless examination of the commonplace." The self-reports of the commonplace, everyday life of women "of a certain age," in this period of ferment searching for equity through education, and of their reflections on their experience, is the material for my search. The next section on the methodology I have chosen will further clarify and define the limits of this inquiry.

Although intended here as a transition pointing toward the section to follow, the paragraph above presents the reader with a jarring shift. The topic of contrasting qualitative and quantitative paradigms is important and complex, but is inappropriate at the conclusion of this section. It deserves a better introduction, and certainly one that does not use the "as everybody knows" ploy. Here the author loses some of that fine, gentle touch that to this point has made the reader feel a collaborator rather than a target. In addition, the author reveals considerable naiveté in describing experimental methods as automatically "clean and simple." Reminding the reader of the purpose served by the section just completed, perhaps indicating appreciation for the rather lengthy deferral of questions about methodology, might make a happier transition.

METHODOLOGY

In this section I shall describe briefly: the epistemological basis for choosing in-depth interviewing as the instrument for investigation of the experience of another person; the selection of participants to be interviewed; the interview process; "profile" composing; and options for interpretation and analysis of the material. As a first step, I should like to make a statement concerning bias, in the form of a short history of the development of my interests and values as they are related to the subject of this research.

Point of View

My mind is not indeed a blank slate on the research questions of this proposal. In fact, my interests, values and close acquaintance with the research problem are the source of motivation of this study.

As noted in Chapter 4, in qualitative research it is customary to confront the issue of objectivity and personal bias in a direct manner. In the pages that follow the author describes those aspects of personal background that would bear on how the research problem is viewed, and that might be expected to influence interpretation of the data. The purpose is not to divest sources of bias, but to clarify them for both author and reader.

In addition to personal and educational background, the author discusses interest in feminism and equity problems as relevant prior involvements. Particular attention is paid to what was learned from a previous National Institute of Education financed study of the work of community college teachers. This material has been omitted here and we pick up the text with the paragraph that closes the section.

I start this study, then, with a recognition of a "vested interest" in its outcome. Not for the outcome to take one direction or another—to demonstrate, for example, that there is or is not an equitable situation for returning women in the community college—but with an energy developed from the concerns of my own experience that will sustain the minutiae of the exploration, and with the recognition that all scientific investigation begins with the observer's "biased" curiosity and continues on its way bolstered and nourished by those values. It is not, of course, possible to keep one's research pure, "objective," and untarnished by one's interests or values or presence (Bateson, 1979; Glazer, 1972; Heisenberg, 1958; James, 1912; Johnson, 1975; Matson, 1966; Myrdal, 1969). It is possible and preferable to search for, recognize, and state such bias (Myrdal, 1969); and to be aware, as William James points out, of ideas that seem especially important to us, that "desire introduces them; interest holds them; fitness fixes their order and connection" (James, 1912).

Epistemological Bases for Choosing In-Depth Interviewing

For investigation of the problem I propose here, I find that a quantitative experimental study cannot tell me what I want to know: the realities of the experience of another human being and how that person thinks and feels about that experience. Knowing that I can never "know"—in the same sense that I "know" my own thoughts and feelings—what another person's experience is "really" like, I want nevertheless to get as close to that knowing as possible. I have, therefore, chosen the in-depth interview as my research instrument. The following is a brief exposition of my assumptions and the philosophic positions which undergird the qualitative approach to this study.

The distinction between "facts" and "values," or between objectivity and subjectivity, cannot be taken for granted, and the observer cannot be conveniently eliminated. William James (1912) makes a strong case for the inseparability of "subject" and "object." If the observer affects, or contributes to, what is observed, there cannot be such an entity as a pure, objective "scientific fact." Social scientist Gregory Bateson goes further: "There is no objective experience; all experience is subjective." The social scientist looks for "the pattern which connects" and "the notion of context, of pattern through time." Describing the data of naturalistic or field research, he says that "what has to be investigated is a vast network or matrix of interlocking message material" (Bateson, 1979). Among other philosophers and scientists whose work have provided pieces of the theoretical structure underlying the methodology of my research are: Mannheim (1936), Polanyi (1962), Rawls (1971), and Sartre (1968).

> The last sentence here seems to be tacked on as an afterthought. Following the powerful case created by artful use of quotes from James and Bateson, it is a shame to spoil the flow of ideas that lead so nicely into the next paragraph. These things happen sometimes when the novice panics and, in attempting to cover every possible base at the last minute, inserts references wholesale. If the references really matter, then they should have been included in a way that displays their significance. If in doubt, leave them out.

A significant part of this study on returning women is based on the assumption that it is possible to discover motives and meanings of other persons through our connections with them, through their words as they communicate with us, and through our knowledge of our own words and actions as we see them reflected in others. As we find verification through our own experience and through hearing the repeated experience of others, we come as close as possible to knowledge about other human beings.

Alfred Schutz, in *The Phenomenology of the Social World* (1967) explores these concepts in depth. An assumption of my research that follows especially from my reading of Schutz, and that is basic to this methodology, is: if women talk to me about their lives as students, and about what led to their decision to return to school, and about what the decision and process mean to them in their lives, I shall then know more than I do now about the interconnections of women's experience in this country and at this time with what it is like to be a student in American schools—particularly, in this case, in the latest version of "post-secondary" education—and I shall perhaps then understand more clearly how the returning woman student is situated in the midst of political, social, and economic changes affecting her schooling and indeed affecting her choices, though she may be unaware of these issues.

Above is a perfect example of a sentence that has gone berserk. Thirteen lines long (in the original), it is impossible to read aloud without several pauses for deep breathing, and it is impossible to understand as "an assumption about methodology." Such monsters are best trapped (and then eliminated) by the simple strategy of reading the text aloud to someone else. If you turn blue before wading through the subordinate clauses, or observe that the eyes of the listener glaze over in utter confusion—something must be wrong. Edit, edit, edit, and then edit some more.

Selection of Participants

For the purposes of this study, the returning woman is 25 to 70 years old; her education has been interrupted for a period of at least several years—perhaps three or four but more often ten to thirty, sometimes more—and she has returned to continue her education in a community college. Eighteen to twenty-two participants will be chosen from community colleges in three states, California, Massachusetts, and New York. The choice of states was made on the basis of per capita expenditures for community colleges in different states: California was strongly supported (third in the United States in per capita expenditure by the state); Massachusetts was 48th, and New York was in the middle—25th (Chambers, 1979). The choice of these three states also offers a wide variety of community colleges in terms of both size and surrounding environment.

Given that most readers will not be disposed to argue the question of exact sample size in a study of this kind, leaving that matter unsettled has all the logic of waving a red flag before a bull. Unless there is some compelling reason, such details should be settled before submitting a proposal. The final number will be arbitrary in any case, and certainly should be open to subsequent negotiation as the events of the study unfold.

As a random sample of the population of returning women community college students, twenty participants is too small a number; moreover, the sample cannot be truly random in an interview study when the subject must consent to be interviewed. Other precautions, then, must be taken in this kind of qualitative study, in which the aim is exploration in depth. In the selection of participants, I have considered a range of ages, ethnicities, class backgrounds, marital and family statuses, children, and fields of study in order to represent fully the population of returning women enrolled in community colleges and to maximize the possibility of looking at a wide spectrum of experience.

In this paragraph the author attempts to explain the selection of participants. The opening sentence is intended to help the reader understand why any expectation for random selection is inappropriate. Whatever the intention may have been in this, there is a serious potential here for misunderstanding. The use of system language words normally associated with quantitative research seems out of place. More to the point, the whole discussion really is not required.

Even well-prepared graduate students display occasional symptoms of defensiveness about qualitative research, lapsing into defensive explanations of why it is not like other forms of inquiry. That may or may not have been the case here, but it would have been far better to go directly to the point—*participants will be selected so as to ensure inclusion of persons with characteristics that seem important in the context of the study.* Arguments about random selection and representative samples are irrelevant to the matter. Given how subjects will be selected, the phrase "represent fully" now is seen as inaccurate, while "maximizing the possibility of looking at a wide spectrum of experience" is precisely the point to be made.

Because the issue of equity is central to this proposed research, and because race, gender, and class are significant elements in the unequal distribution of educational resources, I believe that it is important to cast as large a net as possible in the search for participants of diverse backgrounds. I intend to supplement the nine interviews from a pilot study (Seidman, 1983) with nine to thirteen more. (For table of participant characteristics, see Appendix A. Limited space precludes the inclusion in this table of designations of class and family description, but these characteristics are assessed in the original record.) I am also considering at this time the possibility of adding a small number of interviews of older returning men students, as a frame and additional context for the understanding of the position of women who may have a different view of their imperatives from that of men. (I have interviewed four returning men students as part of a previous study. This group could be a start on this sample.)

The plot thickens. In addition to the problem of an indeterminate number of subjects, the reader now learns that data from a previous study will be merged with material from new interviews conducted after the approval of the proposal. This makes the exact nature of the pilot study a matter of some concern. To complicate things further, in the same paragraph, the possibility of adding a male subsample is raised.

The best advice here is to take things slowly, one at at time—especially things that are likely to attract immediate concern from the reader. Although usually undesirable, merging pilot data with results from a proposed study is not impossible. At the least, questions about the equivalence of method (Will the interview procedures be identical?) must be addressed. As the pilot study appears to have reached publication, the absence of extensive explanation may make some sense. Perhaps it could be assumed that all reviewers had read the report of the earlier study. Whatever the case may have been for this study, in your own proposal be sure to introduce one at a time any points that are likely to be problematic, and resolve each before proceeding. The place to settle questions about possible subsamples is in discussion with the advisor(s), not in a proposal document.

How shall participants be located? Seidman (1983) found that location of participants was most successfully accomplished through informal channels, and wherever possible through peers rather than superiors. The uncertainties about motives of teachers and administrators (students, for example, possibly feeling that their success in school might be connected to consent for the interview) could affect the relationship between interviewer and participant, and thus affect the interview material. In my pilot interviews (Seidman, 1983), students were located through other students in student affairs offices, through counselors and friends of friends not connected with the college hierarchy, through relatives, and through other sources which I believed would least obligate the students to any mode of behavior, or prejudice their attitude toward the interviewing process before meeting with the interviewer. In some cases, an interested women's center coordinator was a useful source.

This process naturally produced many more prospects than were actually selected, thus allowing for final selection to be made according to the categories described above and in the table (Appendix A). The process also cannot guarantee "representation" of every category of returning women students; it also will result in including a larger *proportion* of "minority" women than actually attend community colleges. I prefer to err in this direction as my investigation is concerned with equity for all women. To fill in the last empty cells (see spaces for names in the table), I plan to continue the selection through a process similar to that described above. As will be apparent on observation of the table, some of these prospective participants have already been approached, with an eye to locating women whose age, ethnicity, and field of study match the remaining requirements for diversity.

The first nine students were interviewed in California, Massachusetts, and New York State. I shall select the next nine to thirteen students from the same states, keeping in mind types and sizes of colleges and cities. The distribution so far, of the nine students, is: California, 3; Massachusetts, 2; New York, 4. Final distribution will include at least six from each state.

At this point the reader will suspect that the issues raised by a plan that requires merging data from a prior pilot study with data from a proposed study, is going to receive no further attention. There are a number of supporting arguments that might be made here, some having to do with the nature of qualitative research, and perhaps others made on the grounds of method and circumstance. Given what has been provided in the document to this point, however, our best guess is that few dissertation committees would be satisfied. Whether the rationale offered turns out to be simple or complex, the issue would have to be confronted head-on.

Interview Process

The process of the in-depth phenomenological interview to be used in this study will follow closely the methodology developed by Seidman (1983) and Sullivan (1982). The process can be described generally as open but focused. I shall not use an "interview schedule" but neither will the interview be as casual as a conversation or open to indefinite length. The procedure is for the participant to review the constitutive factors of her life before coming to the community college, and the details of her community college experience; and lastly, to reflect on her past life and present experience, and talk about the meaning that this educational experience has for her.

The purpose for this method of research is *meaning-making*. My task will be to listen as the student reflects aloud on past and present experiences and considers them in relation to significance in her life as an older student, woman, family member, worker, and learner.

Each participant will be interviewed three times, each time for the length of a ninety-minute tape. (All interviews are audiotaped. I generally use a small inconspicuous tape recorder without a microphone and fitted with batteries in case of difficulty with electrical connections.) Interviews will be spaced at least two days apart to allow time for reflection, and if possible no longer than a week apart.

The interviews will be held in a place mutually agreeable to participant and interviewer. With the permission of the college library staff, a small room used for audiovisual materials usually provides privacy and reliable electricity. At least one of the three interviews will be held at the participant's home if possible. The important consideration here is equity—reciprocity and sensitivity to the other person's time constraints. I find this aspect of interviewing attested to in feminist research especially: McGrindle and Rowbotham (1977); Oakley (1976); Roberts (1976); Rubin (1979).

Previous to the first visit, contact will be made by phone, with confirmation by letter, and a date set for the first meeting. I have found it more satisfactory to allow for this initial contact visit before the interview series begins. During this shorter visit, the purpose and nature of the research is explained, the prospective participant fills out a brief information form (see Appendix B) which includes data on age, program, etc., and makes a decision about whether she is willing to be interviewed. If so, dates are set for the next three meetings. At the first of these, participant and interviewer discuss the written consent form (required for university-based research, but also essential for clarity, prevention of misunderstandings, and simple courtesy) and both sign, indicating mutual agreement (see Appendix C for copy of this form). This process allows time for any final uncertainties to be resolved.

Procedures for such matters as incomplete interviews and subject attrition should be established here. For example, if the third meeting proves impossible for an otherwise valuable interview sequence, what happens to the data? It is best to anticipate such events in advance when the investigator and advisors can agree on appropriate decisions.

Each of the three interviews opens with a focusing question from the interviewer: (1) Could you tell me about your life before you came to the community college? (2) What is it like to be a student at this college? (3) What does this experience mean to you in your life? These questions may be flexible as to wording and may be rephrased when the meaning of the question seems unclear to the participant. After the interview has begun, I ask questions rarely, and then usually for clarification. I may comment occasionally to move the talk to another level, or to check on my understanding. But mainly the words will be those of the participant. Almost always, I have found that participants say, "I can *never* talk for an hour and a half!" And almost always they want to continue when the tape is ended. (The rationale for this interview methodology is explained in greater detail in *The Work of Community College Faculty,* Seidman, 1983).

Interviews will be transcribed verbatim (I shall share the task with a typist) resulting in manuscripts of sixty to ninety single-spaced pages for each participant. Because of the volume of this work, it is possible that some compromise with the totally verbatim transcript might be made: for example, abbreviating interviewer statements (Rubin, 1979) and omitting management details that are unrelated or unimportant to the focus of the interview. I hesitate to do this, however, because of the possible research value of having the total record.

It may be impossible to know the magnitude of the transcription task in advance, but it is not impossible to indicate on what basis a decision to abbreviate will be made. A reader can appreciate the problems of data processing, reduction, and display in a qualitative study, but the indecisiveness displayed in the last sentence is inappropriate to a proposal. For any anticipated problem, tell the reader how you will decide what to do. Given that, the reader often will be perfectly happy to leave the difficult details of in-process decisions to the investigator.

Profiles

The interviews (in transcript form) which are strong in all three sections (each section will represent a taped session), complete in the sense of not missing significant material (so that there are no puzzling omissions in the story), compelling in the story-telling and meaning-making, will be selected for "profiles." A profile, as developed by Seidman (1983), is composed from the transcript of an interview series. The words of the interviewer are omitted and the participant's story stands alone. The words are entirely those of the participant unless it is necessary, for reasons of clarity, to add a word or phrase, which will then appear in brackets. A team process may be used for constructing the profile. The major steps include:

(1) Share the process with at least one other person familiar with community colleges and with the research material and method. Each person reads the transcript individually, underlining the sections, words, or phrases which he or she feels strongly should not be omitted from the final story.

(2) Retype, or cut and paste, the manuscript, which should now be reduced by one half or one third of the original.

(3) One person, taking responsibility for the final version of the profile, edits, punctuates, paragraphs, rearranges if necessary for coherence and flow of the story, coding and otherwise disguising identifiable material and proper names, omitting repetitive passages and awkward expressions that might do damage to the dignity of the participant, or that add nothing to the story.

(4) The second person reviews the edited version, checking for unclear passages; suggests revisions or omissions for sense and strength of final version.

(5) Final version of profile is completed by the person who has assumed the main responsibility for this profile.

A similar procedure can, of course, be followed by one person only. I may find it necessary to complete most profiles without assistance. But a team approach has several advantages which are important: a fresh, unbiased (or differently biased) view of the material; a check on the choice of most meaningful material; another ear and eye for language and editing.

As indicated in Chapter 4, the nature of qualitative research often requires that certain aspects of the data analysis be left open-ended. It is impossible to predict the exact form the data will take, or what aspects of the data will present themselves as worthy of attention. Nevertheless, as the author has already accumulated considerable experience with analysis in the pilot study, the reader might expect more decisiveness here. If, for example, profiles for one-third of the pilot subjects were developed through use of a team, then why not set that as a target for the next sample? Finally, having so carefully confronted the problems of bias presented by her own background and personal dispositions, it is puzzling to find that the author mentions no plan to prepare a similar section for the second reader.

The total process is both an intellectual and aesthetic one; the words "construct" and "compose" are both needed in a description of the profile-making process. The important thing to remember is that it is the participant's words we are hearing. The process is something like cutting a diamond to the shape that brings out its best qualities. Profiles thus composed and constructed are compelling communications; they may be compared with the interview work of Terkel (1972) or Coles (1978).

Options for Interpretation and Analysis

The mechanics of working with the material may require more than one copy of each transcript. In addition to, and along with, the profile-making, the analytic process will continue: identifying themes, marking transcript margins, collecting and filing theme material so that it may be easily retrieved.

Here we learn, from an almost offhand comment ("the analytic process will continue . . ."), that in addition to profile construction, the data will be subject to another operation. While it is easy to guess that this will consist of extracting themes, a commonly employed technique in qualitative studies, the matter is inadequately introduced and left almost as an afterthought to the profiling process. At the least, reviewers will want a listing of procedural steps and several illustrations. All this might have been negotiated more gracefully by inserting a short paragraph surveying the several methods (or levels) or analysis before launching into the section on profiles.

No interview process guarantees that the protocols will be full of references to, or insights on, the basic topics of primary interest to the researcher, though the in-depth interview makes this more likely. A question such as, for example, "Were you treated fairly as an older women student?" might elicit only a brief convergent response (Lofland, 1981; Schumann, 1982). But the in-depth interview can provide enough time, an atmosphere of trust, and a setting which encourages the free flow of reminiscence and reflection so that opportunity is provided for a full story to emerge and for reflective meaning-making to take place. That story, in its full and concrete detail, when transcribed becomes the data (material) for analysis and interpretation, which is an ongoing and "continuing process of recording, refining, and reformulating" (Rubin, 1979).

Before all the data are collected, it is not possible to say exactly what final form the analysis shall take. But the process of analysis begins in part with the first field experience and builds gradually as the material is collected (Lofland, 1971). One possibility for the form of the analysis is based on a question of perspective: for example, are the community college's older returning women students finding their educational experience equitable? A model of analysis might be based on the following organization: (1)

grouping of participant interview material according to what was expected or wanted by the student; (2) analysis of the concrete details of the college experience—what was actually found; and (3), given (1) and (2), as well as the participant's reflections on both, how does the educational experience in the community college relate to the issue of equity?

Here the author attempts to anticipate a possible basis for analysis. At this point the reader needs both to sense the broad form that analysis will assume, and to evaluate the author's capacity to establish potentially fruitful formats for reducing the data and extracting meaning. Given the availability of pilot data, the reader might reasonably expect much more here by way of explanation and illustration.

As well as I can now construct a scaffold for unknown conclusions, I see this analytic and interpretive process as a combination of the meaning that the participant makes of her experience and the meaning that I, as researcher, find in the words of the participant, seen through assisting lenses of other observers and writers in related inquiries. Whatever the final form of the analysis, presentation of results will be, in part, in the words of the participant interviewees (profiles) and in part through interpretation of the thematic material that emerges from the collection of transcripts during the ongoing process of field research and analysis (Johnson, 1975; Lofland, 1971; Rubin, 1979; Seidman, 1983).

PLANNED PRESENTATION OF RESULTS

Results of the study will be summarized in a final chapter of the dissertation. This commentary also will include an assessment of the usefulness and effectiveness of the methodology, implications for educational policy change, and indications for further research.

What the author intends by proposing to assess the "usefulness and effectiveness of the methodology" probably is some thoughtful reflection on how fully the actual events of the study matched the intentions of the proposal, and how difficult certain procedures proved in actual execution, as well as how fruitful the results seem in terms of implications for the world of professional practice. The caution to be raised here, for this and any other proposal, is that the question of whether or not the proposed method is an effective means for addressing the question should have been convincingly settled in this document. To promise retrospective evaluation of method is reasonable, but this is not the place to appear to flinch on the choices you have made. Both you and the reader should be convinced that, given the nature of the question and the constraints of your circumstance, this is the best possible study that could be proposed.

Results from this study will illuminate the realities of everyday life in the community college for one fast-growing group in the nontraditional student population. Implications for the future of women in community colleges, and for the future of educational policies for nontraditional student populations, may be revealed through the words of older women students as they talk about their experience. More important, perhaps, will be the possibility for new connections, insights, and understandings for women who are considering a return to school and for those who are already there; for faculty and counselors whose work brings them into everyday contact with re-entry women; and for administrators to whom the returning woman may be just a statistic, albeit a comforting one when enrollments are down and money is scarce. Better understanding of problems of equity in educational institutions—and in the society of which the institution is a reflection—is the ultimate goal of this research.

It is typical to find an author at this point feeling rather optimistic and expansive about the implications of the proposed study. If restrained to only a few paragraphs, most readers will wink at a modest excess of enthusiasm here, even if they suspect that some painful lessons about the limits of inquiry remain to be learned by the novice.

The honest hopes expressed here are what drive the machinery of inquiry. The human need to better understand our world, ourselves, and our institutions, and the human desire to act in more humane and effective ways, are the beginning and end for all research.

NOTE

1. Equity, equality, and equal opportunity: Equal educational opportunity is one of the "rights" sought by women, as by other oppressed groups. I see the movement of women back to college as part of the larger struggle for equal rights of many different groups throughout recorded history. The importance of this movement as part of the women's movement may be fundamental to and primary to other struggles (Engels, 1942; Olsen; 1983). *Equity* is different from *equality* in that it conveys the idea of equal *treatment*. *Equal* means the *same*, or "just like." *Equal rights* says that the *rights* are the same for everyone involved, and that no one shall be deprived of those rights (the equal rights amendment). *Equity* if strictly used is a legal term and has some other meanings somewhat different from the way I use it here. To be treated equitably is to be treated fairly and justly; to be given the rights of all human beings (Rawls, 1971). Fairly and justly do not imply identical treatments, but they do imply a way of thinking that assumes that no human being has greater or more rights than another. Fair and just, or equitable, treatment may require more than equal opportunity. But there must be equal opportunity to permit an equitable situation to occur. The word *equity* is being used more frequently, in titles such as *The Women's Educational Equity Act, The Women's Equity Projects*, and the *Women's Equity Action League*.

APPENDIX A
Expected Distribution by Stage, Age, College, City, Program (liberal arts or career), Ethnicity, Part- or Full-Time
(initials indicate interviews completed)

California		Age	College	City	Program	Ethnicity	PT-FT	Interviewer
1	PM	59	A	J	LA	B	PT	MBS
2	LW	50	A	J	LA	W	FT	MBS
3	MMW	38	A	J	C	H	FT	MBS
4		35	B	K	LA	W	FT	MBS
5		30	B	K	LA	W	FT	DA
6		33	C	L	C	A	PT	MM

Massachusetts		Age	College	City	Program	Ethnicity	PT-FT	Interviewer
1	KB	30	D	M	C	W	FT	MBS
2	LM	70	D	M	LA	W	PT	MBS
3		48	E	N	C	CV	PT	MBS
4		42	E	N	C	W	FT	MBS
5		27	E	N	C	W	FT	MBS
6		30	F	O	C	B	FT	MBS

New York		Age	College	City	Program	Ethnicity	PT-FT	Interviewer
1	LP	25	G	P	LA	W	FT	MBS
2	SL	49	G	P	C	W	FT	MBS
3	HK	49	G	P	C	W	FT	MBS
4	RS	35	H	Q	C	B	FT	MBS
5		28	I	R	LA	A	FT	MBS
6		31	I	R	C	B	FT	MBS

NOTE: Age range = 25-70. Initials under state names are of woman students interviewed in Seidman (1983) study. Other figures are for possible participants; initial contacts have been made. The above is minimum; more interviews are likely.

The table in Appendix A violates the first rule of acceptable construction—it cannot stand alone. It is full of undecipherable material. Further, it is more cluttered than should be necessary. Information about the city, for example, seems nonessential so long as distribution among colleges is provided. Instead of subject initials for interviews already obtained, why not a single word (such as "completed")? The question of how many subjects will be interviewed should be addressed in the text, not at the foot of a table in the Appendix.

APPENDIX B

PARTICIPANT INFORMATION FORM

NAME _____ DATE _____

ADDRESS _____

TELEPHONE (HOME) _____ (WORK, COLLEGE, ETC.) _____

NAME OF COLLEGE _____

COLLEGE ADDRESS _____

PLEASE CHECK WHERE APPLICABLE: LIBERAL ARTS? _____ TRANSFER? _____

    VOCATIONAL OR OCCUPATIONAL PROGRAM? _____ SPECIAL PROGRAM? _____

    OTHER? _____ (PLEASE DESCRIBE) _____

    _____

WHAT IS THE GOAL OF YOUR PRESENT STUDY? _____

_____

PREVIOUS EDUCATIONAL ATTAINMENT (NUMBER OF YEARS IN SCHOOL, LAST

YEAR IN SCHOOL, DIPLOMA, DEGREE, GED, ETC.) _____

_____

_____

PREVIOUS WORK EXPERIENCE _____

_____

_____

_____

BIRTH DATE _____

A CONTACT WHERE YOU COULD BE REACHED IN CASE OF CHANGE OF ADDRESS

OR TELEPHONE _____

_____

This clearly is only a mock-up of the form actually to be filled in by participants. It is possible that the investigator intends to fill this out on the basis of questions asked during the interview. In either case, advisors usually prefer to see any record form in final draft, not as a sketch.

APPENDIX C
WRITTEN CONSENT FORM

Returning Women Students in the Community College

To participants in this study:

I am a graduate student at the University of Massachusetts at Amherst. The subject of my doctoral research is: "Returning Women Students in the Community College." I am interviewing women in California, Massachusetts, and New York State, and possibly in some other states, who have returned to study at a community college after an interruption in their education for any one of a number of reasons. You are one of approximately twenty participants.

As a part of this study, you are being asked to participate in three in-depth interviews. The first interview will be focused on your experience before you came to the college, the second on what it is like to be a student in the college, and the third will be concerned with what it means to you to be back in school—as you reflect on your earlier experience and look ahead to the future. As the interviews proceed, I may ask an occasional question for clarification or for further understanding, but mainly my part will be to listen as you recreate your experience within the structure and focus of the three interviews: your previous life, the college experience, and the meaning of that college experience.

My goal is to analyze the materials from your interviews in order to understand better your experience and that of other women who re-enter schools and colleges for their own various reasons. I am interested in the concrete details of your life story, in what led up to your decision to return to school, in what your everyday experience is like now, and what it means to you. As part of the dissertation, I may compose the materials from your interviews as a "profile" in your own words. I may also wish to use some of the interview material for journal articles or presentations to interested groups, or for instructional purposes in my teaching. I may wish to write a book based on the dissertation.

Each interview will be audiotaped and later transcribed by me or by a typist (who will not be connected with your college and who will be committed, as I am, to confidentiality). In all written materials and oral presentations in which I might use materials from your interview, I will not use your name, names of people close to you, or the name of your college or city. Transcripts will be typed with initials for names, and in final form the interview material will use pseudonyms.

You may at any time withdraw from the interview process. You may withdraw your consent to have specific excerpts used, if you notify me at the end of the interview series. If I were to want to use any materials in any way not consistent with what is stated above, I would ask for your additional written consent.

In signing this form, you are also assuring me that you will make no financial claims for the use of the material in your interviews; you are also stating that no medical treatment will be required by you from the University of Massachusetts should any physical injury result from participating in these interviews.

I, _____ have read the above statement and agree to participate as an interviewee under the conditions stated above.

_____
Signature of participant

_____   _____
Signature of interviewer   Date

Note that the informed consent letter does *not* promise anonymity for the participant. Instead it indicates a commitment to maintain confidentiality, and provides details concerning the steps that will be taken toward that end. That subtle point does not mean the researcher will be any less diligent in protecting the privacy of the participant. It simply reflects the wisdom of not promising something that is not directly under your own control. Note also that while the right to withdraw from the study during the interviews, and to deny use of specific excerpts, are explicitly established, the right to withdraw entirely after a final draft has been reviewed is *not* specified. In this there is an attempt not only to protect the rights of the participant, but also to maintain some reasonable balance with the concerns of the investigator. It might have been wise to include a statement that clearly establishes ownership and proposed disposition procedures for the audiotape and transcript document.

BIBLIOGRAPHY

Note: The following is a working list of literature I have investigated which is related in some important way to the study of the experience of returning women students in the community college. Subject areas include life-span development, the education of women, the community college as institution, feminist research, and aspects of qualitative research methodologies.

Achenbaum, W. Andrew. *Old Age in the New Land.* Baltimore: Johns Hopkins University Press, 1978.

Adam, Barry D. *The Survival of Domination: Inferiorization and Everyday Life.* New York: Elsevier, 1978.

Agonito, Rosemary. *History of Ideas on Woman: A Source Book.* New York: G. P. Putman's Sons, 1977.

American Association of Community and Junior Colleges. *Assessing the Educationally Related Needs of Adults.* Washington, D.C.: The Center for Community Education, 1979.

American Association of University Women. *But We Will Persist.* Washington, D.C.: Author, 1978.

American Educator's Newspaper of Record. *Demographic Predictions for Next Twenty Years.* Vol. 1, No. 29, April 14, 1982.

Andreas, Carol. *Sex and Caste in America.* Englewood Cliffs, NJ: Prentice-Hall, 1971.

Aptheker, Bettina. *Women's Legacy: Essays on Race, Sex, and Class in American History.* Amherst, MA: University of Massachusetts Press, 1982.

Arlin, P. K. "Cognitive Development in Adulthood: A Fifth Stage?" *Developmental Psychology,* 1975, 11: 602-606.

The remainder of the bibliography is not presented here.

Merging a "working list" of background literature with the actual list of references cited in the proposal document would not be acceptable in many graduate schools, and should never be done in the case of a grant proposal. Readers may wish to locate a full citation quickly, without sorting through pages of unused items. Some reviewers make it a regular practice to cross-check the reference list against the citations in the text for exact congruence. That would be most difficult with a merged bibliography. A list of references should consist only of items named in the text of the proposal.

A bibliography of other important documents used by the author is perfectly appropriate as an item in the appendices to the proposal. A list of such background literature may serve the purpose of indicating the sophistication and care with which the author has prepared. If lengthy, such a bibliography may be divided into topical areas as suggested by the author's lead note. Should the author be particularly anxious to draw the attention of readers to the bibliography, a note indicating its location and content may be placed in the introductory section of the proposal.

PROPOSAL 3:
QUASI-EXPERIMENTAL DESIGN

Teaching Children to Question
What They Read:
An Attempt to Improve Reading
Comprehension Through Training in a
Cognitive Learning Strategy

This is a particularly interesting proposal as it involves a quasi-experimental treatment in a topic area, the acquisition of reading skills, that is not often studied in such fashion. The strength of the introduction is that it immediately convinces the reader of the seriousness of the topic—the need to be able to read in our society.

INTRODUCTION

One of the main tasks assigned to schools is that of training students to be linguistically competent. In an industrialized society and national political culture such as the United States, this requires competence in the written as well as the spoken word. It is, for example, very difficult to administer secret ballots except in writing. In the workplace instructions to workers, including safety precautions, are in printed form. Reading is a means to gain control over one's life, whether one is reading

This proposal was prepared by John David MacDonald as part of the dissertation research requirement in the Department of Educational Psychology at the University of Texas at Austin. The dissertation was supervised by Beeman N. Phillips and Clair E. Weinstein. The completed dissertation received the Outstanding Dissertation Award by the Southwest Educational Research Association. Dr. MacDonald currently is a faculty member in the Department of Psychology at Eastern Kentucky University.

about an upcoming election or one is choosing where to shop for food economically.

While reading may be a necessity for everyday living, evidence is ample that many people never acquire the skills necessary for reading. Several years ago, Gibson and Levin (1975) suggested that as many as 25% of all school children are more than one year "below grade level" in reading. In some inner-city schools in New York City, the proportion may be as high as 85% (Fuentes, 1980).

Here the author reveals the purpose of the study. As you will note, later in the proposal a problem and question also are stated.

The purpose of the proposed study, therefore, is to assess the effectiveness of a proposed reading intervention technique, a technique which appears conceptually to be consistent with the recent developments in cognitive learning. Not learning to read has, of course, more than social and economic costs. It has personal costs as well. Never to know the intricacies of John Le Carre's plots, or Joseph Conrad's evocative descriptions, or even the self-awareness that comes from reading about one's own condition, is to be isolated from the national culture, and to some degree, to be a person without a past or a present. Calling the over-60 age group the single largest cohort of functional illiterates, the White House Conference on the Aging (Kasom, 1981) suggested that this population is more at risk for mental health problems due to the isolation, poverty, and boredom that result from being illiterate. But personal satisfaction and participation in national culture are not the only costs of illiteracy.

In the paragraph below, the author makes the critical point that reading is the underpinning for success in all school subjects. This provides a strong rationale for a study in which the major purpose was to identify an effective method with which to improve reading skills. So that the reader will not miss this important rationale, the author both coins and underscores an important word, *keystone,* to describe the construct.

Reading may serve as a "keystone" for other curricular skills, that is, certain skills may be prerequisite to curricular skills in science, social studies, literature, etc. While some authors complain, perhaps correctly, that the reason for "scientific illiteracy" is the emphasis on basic skills or reading instruction for its own sake, it is difficult to imagine a student obtaining a scientific education while not reading. Because of this *keystone quality,* a lack of reading skills may result in low achievement and premature school dropouts. Curtis, Doss, MacDonald, and Davis (Note 1) found that the best predictor of late dropouts was below average scholastic grade-point average (GPA), and many of the dropouts who were interviewed reported chronic reading and other achievement problems and reported that they withdrew because they believed these problems were insurmountable.

Here the author shows that the need for reducing school dropout rates by improving reading performance is relevant to the city in which the study is to be conducted. Thus the problem of developing reading skills in not an abstraction. It is specific to the locale and new information will have potential for immediate consequences, a point that will not be lost on the university committee or the public officials who must approve the execution of the study in the school system.

Withdrawal from school can have dire economic consequences: in this city, 48% of non-high school graduate males aged 16-21 were unemployed, but only 18.4% of the same age high school graduates were unemployed (Bureau of the Census, 1973). It is not inconceivable that illiteracy is related to unemployment.

The section below is an excellent example of demonstrating the need for the study. It directly answers the query we posed in Chapter 1, "why bother with the question?" Sometimes the answer to this is woven into the rationale, as shown below. An alternative, which is sometimes required by committees or funding agencies, is to separate the "need for the study" section from the section on rationale. If this were the case, the earlier discussion of the personal costs of not knowing how to read, the potential for mental health risk, and the likelihood of employers shunning nonreaders could be shortened and combined into an effective section on "need for the study."

Employers seem reluctant to hire illiterate workers because they view them as more likely to injure themselves and their fellow workers, and because they view them as more likely to cost the company large sums of money for misreading instructions (Lauterborn, 1981). Of 800 companies Lauterborn (1981) surveyed, 35% thought it necessary to supplement their employees' education with basic English and business writing. The increasing sophistication of modern weaponry and support equipment along with the failure of the armed services to attract more highly educated recruits has led the Army to invest $37,000,000 over a four-year period in the research and development of instructional systems in basic skills, English as a second language, life coping skills, and cognitive learning strategies (Begland, 1981). Thus good reading skills are of more than personal benefit for the reader; they are related to the economic and defense interests of the nation.

While the reading skills of the nation's school children may be viewed by many as distressing, there are some encouraging indications that reading performance is improving and that poor reading is less of a problem for fewer children. The National Assessment of Educational Progress (Burton & Jones, 1982; National Assessment of Educational Progress, 1976a, 1976b) has reported improving performance on both literal and inferential comprehension items for nine-year-olds, and improvements have surfaced in literal comprehension among 13 and 17 year olds. Differences in reading scores between whites and blacks have declined from a 17 point difference in inferential comprehension in 1970 to a less than 10 point difference in 1980 (Burton & Jones, 1982).

Below is a section that does not speak directly to the question at hand. The volume of specific detail breaks the flow of the introduction. The reader will be struck by the observation that the style of writing is not parallel with the rest of the introduction. It seems clear that the introduction would not suffer if this section were located elsewhere.

In the 1972 assessment, the National Assessment of Educational Progress sponsored a special survey of students' attitudes towards reading and literature. These results are encouraging, if one accepts the validity of student responses to adult interviewers. Of the thirteen-year-olds interviewed, 43% strongly agreed that it is important to study literature, while an additional 34% somewhat agreed with the statement. In the inner-city schools, 58% strongly agreed with the statement. The majority of seventeen-year-olds (90%) believed literature should be taught in every school. A majority of the nine-year-olds (84%) and thirteen-year-olds (78%) reported they read for their own pleasure at least once a week, with 54% of the nine-year-olds and 44% of the thirteen-year-olds reporting they read for pleasure every day. When asked if they had read a particular type of literature on their own (e.g., short story, novel, poetry, etc.) 98% of the thirteen-year-olds replied they had read at least one of the types, and 86% gave verifiable titles when asked. For an adult sample, 89% replied they had read at least one genre, while 76% gave verifiable titles (NAEP, 1973).

In general terms, the outlook is hopeful. However, there remain substantial numbers of children and adults for whom reading is troublesome. Unless they receive effective interventions, their economic prospects are grim, they are disenfranchised from the political process and much of the world's cultural heritage bypasses them. For the 78% of the 1973 thirteen-year-olds who reported reading at least once a week, there were 6% who reported never having read for pleasure. In the 1980-81 school year, some 5% to 6% of the students in the city Independent School District's average daily enrollment had reading problems so severe they required classification for special education services under the category of Learning Disabilities (Bass, Note 2). Knowing what to do for these students to help them improve their reading is troublesome for teachers, learning disability specialists and school principals. Yet, these individuals are legally mandated with providing an appropriate education for these students, that is, charged with improving these students' reading (McClain, 1981).

Despite a large number of research studies of reading instruction, little is presently known about the relative effectiveness of different methods of teaching reading (Maxwell, 1972; Pflaum, Walberg, Karegiones, & Rasher, 1980). Most children arrive in kindergarten not knowing how to read, and most leave high school as fairly competent readers; thus, although we know little about effective reading instruction, most children do learn how to read while in school. It is likely that few students who do not attend school will attain the same reading competence as they would if they attended twelve years of school, although this interpretation of descriptive studies of school non-attendance suffers from selection factors.

Here the author begins establishing a background for the particular approach to be used in this study, that is the identification and measurement of behaviors specific to reading competence.

It seems likely that acquisition of reading competence is directly related to teacher and student behaviors, although at this stage in reading research it is difficult to state precisely what these behaviors are. The attempt to define what these behaviors which facilitate the acquisition of reading comprehension are and to validate their effectiveness as mediators in the acquisition of reading competence should contribute to "cracking the problem of what happens to reading achievement after the second or third grade" (Glaser, 1979, p. 8), that is, after decoding sound-symbol relationships is acquired. Identification of these behaviors may then contribute to a system of intervention practices with regard to reading problems.

The following discussion provides a historical framework through which to understand the significance of the study to be proposed. New techniques to determine teacher and student behaviors relevant to reading acquisition makes possible acquisition of heretofore inaccessible information.

The field of reading diagnosis and intervention has been plagued by systems of non-experimentally-validated constructs regarding the processes involved in reading, resulting in assessment instruments with unacceptably low levels of reliability, and the use of poor assessment instruments has contributed to ineffective intervention procedures (Arter & Jenkins, 1979; Hammil & Larsen, 1974a, 1974b; Hammill, Goodman, & Wiederholt, 1974; Larsen & Hammill, 1975; Minskoff, 1975). However three developments have improved the likelihood of identifying those teacher and student behaviors involved in the acquisition of competent reading. The first development is the identification of a series of learner behaviors which are directed at constructing meaning from text (Bransford, Barclay, & Franks, 1972; Perfetti & Lesgold, 1977; Rumelhart, 1975), behaviors which are directed at understanding and recall (DiSibio, 1982; Weinstein, 1978; Weinstein, 1982; Weinstein & Underwood, 1983; Wittrock, 1979; Wittrock, Note 3) and the discovery that these behaviors can be learned and can be brought within the cognitive control of the learner (Rothkopf, 1970; Weinstein, Cubberly, Wicker, Underwood, Roney, & Duty, 1981).

The second development is in the application of task analysis to the acquisition of curricular knowledge (Chi & Glaser, 1980; Gagne & Briggs, 1974; Glaser, 1976; Resnick, Wang, & Kaplan, 1973). It is now possible to model complex hypothesized reading and knowledge acquisition strategies through the use of task analysis. Thirdly, the development of methodologies for determining causal relations (Blalock, 1971; Duncan, 1975; Wolfe, 1980; Wright, 1971) and of methodologies for evaluating aptitude treatment interactions (Cronbach & Snow, 1977) have been called, along with the developments in cognitive learning (Wittrock, Note 3), "the most significant developments of the past 5 to 10 years, developments that may have significant if not greater influence on educational research during the 1980's" (Kerlinger, 1982, p. 120). The study of causal relations are now being applied to the experimental validation of task-analytic models of curricular skill acquisition (Bergan, 1980; Hill & McGaw, 1981). These developments are of great importance for the assessment of learning problems and for the design and implementation of interventions for learning problems.

At this point the author included an extensive review of the literature. A variety of topics were covered including reading comprehension, individual differences, methodology, and analysis. Since we have suggested a shorter, concise review focusing specifically on decisions for the proposed study (see Chapter 3) we have chosen not to include the review of the literature here.

Statement of the Problem

A small number of children do not attain functional reading skills and suffer economically, socially, and politically. The consequences for these children necessitates that effective reading remediation strategies be developed and implemented. Remediation strategies need to be derived from theories of what it is that good readers do that enables them to be competent readers. Although such theories are in their infancy, they are now specific enough in their implications that specific intervention strategies may be developed and evaluated.

The author now has identified a problematic area (some students do not attain functional reading skills), but only later on does he actually state the question for the study. The paragraph below is intended both to introduce and support the treatment to be examined. For the reader, it would have been helpful to undertake the two communication tasks, separately, and in sequential paragraphs.

One such strategy that has been recommended to reading teachers is having students generate their own questions of the content of the reading material and then having students seek the answers to these questions. This recommendation has appeared in teacher preparation texts (Durkin, 1978), in journals directed to reading teachers (Alexander & Fuller, 1973; Dillworth, 1980; Eeds, 1980; Hopkins, 1979; Olmio, 1975; Seifert, 1980), in journals directed to learning disabilities specialists (Wong, 1979), and in publications directed at psychologists (Comprehension is the key, 1981). Without exception, these authors have presented the technique in a favorable, noncritical light, but little data have been presented in these articles to support this position.

Here the case is made that, although the technique of having children generate their own questions about reading material facilitates reading skills, children must be trained to generate these questions. Here, the proposed study is seen to be firmly grounded in the current understanding of how children learn to read. By identifying the limitations of previous research, the author positions himself to argue for the design features of the proposed study.

Experimental evaluations of this technique have recently appeared (e.g., Andre & Anderson, 1979; Dreher & Gambrell, Note 5; Frase & Schwartz, 1975; Weiner, 1978) which suggest that at least one qualification be made to the recommendations for the use of this technique. This qualification is that children may need to be trained how to generate questions which are targeted on important ideas in order for the technique to be effective.

Unfortunately, previous studies of the efficacy of training students how to use this technique have serious flaws. While the finding that students who generate good questions show greater benefit from the use of this technique than do students who generate poor questions is a well-established one, these authors (with the exception of those of one study) have failed to demonstrate that improvements in question-asking lead to improvements in reading comprehension and reading recall when using the technique (Ander & Anderson, 1979; Dreher & Gambrell, Note 5; Frase & Schwartz, 1975). This failure appears to have been the result of too brief or inappropriate instructional activities.

The statements below argue the need for an intervention of longer duration with a wider range of student abilities. Again, this establishes the grounds for selecting a particular research format.

The author of the one study in which significant improvements in reading recall following training were shown, used a more extensive training program than did other investigations (Weiner, 1978). Weiner's subjects had above-average reading skills, however, as did the subjects in the other training studies. Thus, although the recommendation to use this technique has been directed at teachers of below-average readers, the efficacy of training these students to use this technique has never been tested.

Differential treatment response by reading level groups will be an important variable in the proposed study. The following discussion introduces this concept so that the reader will later understand why an analysis by skill level is proposed.

This technique appears promising, based on the theoretical rationale underpinning its design. Empirical trials of the use of the technique indicate that its implementation is problematic, however. Recently some progress has been made in preparing average and good readers for its use, but the critical question is how poor readers might be best prepared to benefit from the technique. If the technique cannot be made accessible to poor readers, then teachers attempting to use it may have a detrimental effect on their students' reading skills, if only because time spent learning and implementing the technique may be time spent off task. Understanding how to make the technique accessible to poor readers is thus of critical importance before further recommendations for the technique can be made.

> Below is the actual statement of the question. It expresses two questions succinctly. It could have been stated much earlier.

Specific hypotheses appear on the following pages, but this study will be directed at answering the following questions: Can students with adequate vocabulary skills for the material they will be reading be trained to generate good questions, and if so, will the improvement in question-asking result in improved reading comprehension and reading recall when students are told to use the technique?

Hypotheses

In this study the following hypotheses will be tested:

(1) A group of junior-high-school students who are below average in reading and who receive training in generating good questions will ask better questions than will a group of similar students receiving a control training program (when posttest question quality is controlled for pretest question quality).

(2) A group of junior-high-school students who are below average in reading and who receive training in generating good questions will perform better on a task of reading recall than will a group of similar students receiving a control training program (when posttest free recall quality is controlled for pretest free recall quality).

(3) The amount of improvement (pre to post) in free recall will be directly related to the amount of improvement (pre to post) in question quality.

Method

> An overview of the research design would have been helpful at the start of this section. This is a complex study in which many measurements will be utilized. A flowchart or brief outline (see our suggestions

in Chapter 1) would assist the reader in understanding how each type of measurement contributes to the overall purpose of the study.

The first paragraph in this section provides information about the subjects. Inasmuch as the author has suggested earlier that failure to control for grade and reading ability has been an important confounding factor in previous research involving the proposed treatment, it is especially important to provide details about these factors.

Subjects

Students in reading classes in a rural central Texas school district will serve as subjects in this study. About half will be students in seventh-grade required reading classes who demonstrate a wide range of reading ability. The other subjects will be students in eighth-grade remedial reading classes; these students represent about the lower third of the district's eighth-graders in terms of reading comprehension scores on the Science Research Associates (SRA) Achievement Series (Thorpe, Lefever, & Naslund, 1973). Subjects will range in age from 12 years to 15 years.

This next section gives details about the specific tests to be used in the study. Six tests will be used; four that were previously available and two that were designed for this study. The author provides details on the purpose and reliability of each test. Note that reliability for the first test has been reported elsewhere. Accordingly, the author provides just the reliability coefficient and a citation. Interested readers can obtain the reference and the proposal is not cluttered with unnecessary detail. The description of why this subtest was selected is excellent. Readers may wonder, however, why the subtest was administered at exactly 6 months prior to treatment and not some other time. The timing of test applications is a particularly important factor and should be justified with care.

Instrumentation

SRA Achievement Series (Thorpe, Lefever, & Naslund, 1973). This test yields both reading comprehension and reading vocabulary subtest scores. Confounding of these subtests occurs, however, because the vocabulary subtest uses the same materials as the comprehension subtest (Fry, 1965; Guthrie, 1972) therefore only the comprehension subtest (SRA-C) will be used in this research, while another test will be used to assess pretest vocabulary skills. The SRA-C subtest requires students to answer questions concerning main ideas, supporting details, and inferences from a series of reading passages. It has been reported to have an alternate-form stability coefficient of $r = .83$ (Guthrie, 1972) after a one-year test-retest interval. The SRA-C subtest will be administered to the subjects six months prior to the training program.

Three other tests were presented in a similar fashion: (1) Test of Reading Comprehension-General Vocabulary (TORCGV); (2) Test of Reading Comprehension-Paragraph (TORCPR); and (3) Test of Reading Comprehension-Syntactic Similarities (TORCSS). The fifth test, Question Quality Rating, was created by the author. Since no reference is available for this test, greater detail is provided. The author alerts the reader to why the content was chosen and particular procedures devised for administering the test. Note, however, that the actual test is included in an appendix.

Question Quality Rating. This task was created for use in this research, and it will be used as both a pretest and a posttest measure. The reading passages and instructions to subjects are contained in Appendix A. Two reading passages (A and B) were selected from sixth grade social studies texts which had not been in previous use in the district. Passage A, 984 words long, is a discussion of the economies of the British North American colonies (Jones, Young, & Boutwell, 1971, pp. 38-43). Passage B, 695 words long, is a narrative about the struggles to control Mexico from colonial times until the twentieth century (Chapin, McHugh, & Gross, 1971, pp. 62-66). These passages were chosen because students were likely to be somewhat familiar with the content (although much of the content would be new), because the style and readability of the passages are similar to text materials from which students are and will be required to learn from in their school program, and because the passages are complete and long enough to be sensitive to the use of efficient reading strategies while being short enough to allow testing during a single class period.

Subjects read either Passage A or Passage B on the pretest, and the other passage on the posttest; subjects will be randomly assigned to passages. They will be instructed to write down, while reading, "the best questions about the story that [they could] think of . . . questions which [they] could ask someone else [in order to] find out if they had read the story too." Fifteen minutes will be given to complete this task, and they cannot get help from each other. They can request help from the experimenter if they do not understand a specific word; the experimenter will then define the word for all subjects.

The questions which the subjects will generate will be rated on a 1 to 5 equal appearing interval scale with "1" representing a poor question and "5" representing an excellent question. Raters will receive training and practice materials before rating and will be told to base the rating of question quality on the degree to which the question targets important information in the passage and on the degree to which answering the question requires the reader to organize the content of the text. If these two qualities are present to a high degree, raters also are to consider the amount of elaboration required by the question, and the degree to which answering the question taps the higher levels of Bloom's taxonomy, i.e., understanding, application, analysis, synthesis, and evaluation. If raters do not understand the question, it will be rated "1" or poor.

In the paragraph above, the author provides detail on how the raters will score this test. Below he provides a careful description of the raters. In this study the raters serve as a form of instrumentation, and since a good proposal requires that all instrumentation be described fully, the paragraph is needed.

The ten raters are either graduate students in educational psychology ($N = 5$) at the university, or advanced undergraduate education students who have completed a course in Tests and Measurements and have been recommended by their instructor as being skilled at evaluating test items. All raters have had courses in Tests and Measurements, five have had courses in Psychometric Theory, and one has taught Tests and Measurements courses. Seven raters were experienced teachers at either the elementary or secondary level with a median of 4.0 years of experience. The questions generated by students and the instructions and training materials given to raters are contained in Appendix B.

In the paragraph below the author presents the reliability for each of the passages that were a part of the test. Since individual questions were rated, but means used in the analysis, the author provides reliability estimates for both.

To determine reliability of the test, pre- and posttest questions for the same passage were combined and question order was randomized. Five raters (similar to those used in the study) rated all questions for Passage A and five rated all questions for Passage B. The mean of the five ratings for a question was used as the estimate of the quality of that question. Interrater agreement by the Spearman-Brown formula (Winer, 1971, pp. 283-287) was estimated to be $r = .84$ for Passage A questions and $r = .73$ for Passage B. Subjects generated between 0 and 9 questions. The quality estimates for all the questions a subject asked were combined and the mean of these was taken to be the estimate of that student's question-asking skills. Reliability of this estimate by the Spearman-Brown formula was estimated to be $r = .96$ for Passage A and $r = .92$ for Passage B.

Throughout the rest of this proposal, the estimates of student questioning skills are referred to by the mnemonics PREQUES and POSQUES, for pretest and posttest question ratings, respectively.

A second test, Free Recall Quality Rating, also was created for this study. The author presented it in much the same way as the test above and that material has been omitted here. A final item of data will be collected by interviewing students and that step is presented here. Note that the experimenter will debrief the subjects as a part of the final process of data collection.

Other measures. In addition to the previous measures, the *number of questions asked* on both the pretest (PRENUM) and on the posttest (POSNUM) will be included in the analyses. After the posttest, subjects will be asked if they have *used the strategy* they had learned about if they were in the experimental training and will be told to write down their answers on experimenter supplied paper without writing their names. The experimenter will then explain to the subjects that he or she did not know whether this strategy would work, but in order to find out if it did their help was needed because they were the only ones to know if they had really tried to use the strategy.

The procedure for collecting pretest and posttest data is presented in the next section. The level of heading (not separate from the paragraph) should be changed so that it is the same as "Subjects" and "Instrumentation." Note that the author plans for the contingency that some students may not return the parent permission slip. Since it is unlikely that all students will get permission or remember to bring back the letter, it is wise to address this in the proposal.

Procedure. During the second week of the fall semester the subjects' regular reading instructor will explain to them the nature of the research project and distribute parent permission forms to be reviewed and signed if desired by the subjects' parents. This form is contained in Appendix C. If any students are not permitted by their parents to participate, these students will work on individual assignments during assessment sessions and participate in the control group training because the control training is part of the regular instructional program.

The paragraph below performs the function of an overview paragraph. Notice how a simple diagram, as suggested in Chapter 1, would help in grasping the overall pattern of the study.

Subjects next will be administered the Test of Reading Comprehension-General Vocabulary (TORCGV) subtest, the Pretest Question-Asking task (PREQUES) and the Pretest Free Recall task (PRE-CALL). SRA Reading test scores are available for subjects who had been present the previous spring. Following pretesting, subjects will be randomly assigned to control and experimental groups.

The author provides a concise depiction of the treatment group. Details of the specific instructional objectives for the treatment are presented in Figure 1. The figure is logical and easy to read. By presenting this information separately from the text the reader is given the option of reading it for greater detail.

Experimental group. What occurs during the experimental group training is critical to testing the main hypotheses of this

Problem Solving	Questioning Skills	Text Structure	Applications
1.1 Students will be able to identify a situation as problematic and the reason why it is a problem.	2.1 Given a word or phrase from text, students will be able to identify attributes of that word or phrase.	3.1 Students will be able to identify similarities between reading to learn information and problem-solving.	4.1 When given a text, the topic and first paragraph, students will be able to generate explicit statements of information they want to obtain from the text.
1.2 Students will be able to list the six steps for solving problems.	2.2 Given a word or phrase from text, students will be able to state implied attributes of that word or phrase (e.g., "postpone" implies an event, a person controlling its occurrence, a previous time for the event and a new time).	3.2 Given a short passage of discourse, students will be able to identify the probable intent of the author.	4.2 When given a text, students will generate questions about the text and will search for answers in the passage.
1.3 Given either an example of a school (intellectual) problem or a general social problem, students will be able to identify the steps they will follow in seeking a solution.	2.3 Given a word or phrase from text, students will be able to state what information is missing about implied attributes.	3.3 Given a passage of discourse, students will be able to identify the main ideas and their supporting details, and will be able to outline the passage without omitting, adding, or distorting main ideas.	
	2.4 Students will list several types of strategies aimed at obtaining information and will be able to identify several types of questions and the type of information they elicit.	3.4 When given a passage of text and a set of questions about the passage, students will identify where the answers to the questions are likely to be found and will successfully find answers to these questions.	
	2.5 Students will demonstrate improved skills in asking constraint-seeking questions by reducing the number of questions necessary to win the "twenty questions" game.		

(continued)

Figure 1

FIGURE 1—Continued

Problem Solving	Questioning Skills	Text Structure	Applications
	2.6 Students will demonstrate improved skills in domain-seeking questions by reducing the number of questions necessary before a correct subordinate class is identified in the "twenty questions" game.		
	2.7 Given a problem to solve, students will be able to rank a series of informative facts as to their value in solving the problem.		
	2.8 Given a problem to solve, students will be able to make a statement about a possible solution and will be able to test the truth value of the statement by obtaining and interpreting appropriate information.		

study. The training the students will receive involves four components: (a) instruction and practice in problem solving (as a prerequisite to presenting reading comprehension as a problem solving task), (b) instruction and practice in question asking, (c) instruction and practice in recognizing text structure, and (d) practice in asking questions while reading. In Figure 1 more details are contained about specific instructional objectives of these four components. The instructional manual for this experimental training is contained in Appendix D.

The experimental training will be conducted by the experimenter, and all experimental sessions will take place in the subjects' regular classroom. The experimental training will last nine sessions for a total of 7.5 hours of allotted instructional time. All students must attend seven or more sessions to be included in the final data analysis.

The last sentence above establishes the minimum participation standard required for each subject. Those who do field research, particularly in school settings, are aware of the fact that it is *very* unlikely that all subjects will be present for the entire treatment. As we indicated in Chapter 3, it is better to anticipate and resolve such problems before collecting data than to be faced with difficult decisions after the data have been collected and disagreements between student and committee become potentially disastrous.

Below, the author provides concise information on the control group and posttests. Note that students were debriefed after the posttest and that each student then received the alternative treatment, even though further data were not collected for the study. The reversing of treatments ensures that all of the subjects have the chance to experience the primary intervention. If in fact the treatment provides significant benefits, the control group has equal access to them, *after* all data essential to the study have been collected.

Control group. The control group will receive instruction and practice in using a dictionary, a thesaurus, and the library. The instruction will be done by the regular reading teacher and will take place either in the library or in an alcove adjacent to the regular classroom. Precautions will be taken to ensure that the control group cannot hear teaching which occurs with the experimental group.

Posttesting. One day after the last training session, and three weeks after pretesting, the subjects will be administered the TORCPR, the TORCSS, the Posttest Questioning task (POSQUES), and the Posttest Free Recall task (POSCALL). After posttesting, all subjects in the experimental group will be asked if they had used the strategy, about advantages and disadvantages of the technique, and about whether or not they would use the technique again. The nature of the research will again be explained to the subjects and any questions they have about the study will be answered to the best of the experimenter's ability at that time. The following week, treatment conditions will be reversed, with the control group receiving the experimental training, and vice versa.

In the final section of the body of the proposal the focus is on data analysis. The author reports all the techniques to be used for each part of the analysis. More detail would help many readers. It would be particularly helpful if the author had discussed the analysis in light of each hypothesis stated earlier. Including sample tables for the analyses to be performed is a good idea for all studies, particularly when there are as many variables as in this study. An illustration of the path analytic model to be tested should be included here so the model to be tested is apparent.

Data analysis. Reliability estimates for PREQUES, POSQUES, PRECALL, and POSCALL were calculated using a hand calculator with programmable statistics functions. These estimates were doublechecked by the experimenter. All other analyses will be performed using the Statistical Package for the Social Sciences (SPSS) statistics package (Nie, Hull, Jenkins, Steinbrenner, & Bent, 1975) edition 8.3, on the CDC 6000/Cyber 700 computers at the university. Data checking activities will include running subprogram FREQUENCIES to check on variance distributions and plotting distributions on probability paper. Subprograms FREQUENCIES and CROSSTABS will be used to generate the characteristics of treatment groups. Subprograms REGRESSION and PLOT will be used to run preliminary path analyses and to check that regression assumptions have been met, and subprogram REGRESSION will be used to run the final, restricted model path analysis. Subprogram PLOT will be used to generate figures which illustrate significant aptitude-treatment interactions.

PROPOSAL 4: FUNDED GRANT

A Field Test of a Health-Based Educational Intervention to Increase Adolescent Fertility Control

OVERVIEW AND OBJECTIVES

Adolescent premarital pregnancy is a major social and mental health problem in the U.S. and in Texas. More than one-half of all teenagers 15-19 years of age and almost one-quarter of those under 15 are sexually active. Significantly, the age at first intercourse continues to decline; younger adolescents (under 15) are less likely to use effective contraception and wait substantially longer to begin contraceptive usage initially than do older adolescents. As a result of the preceding factors and the larger proportion of teenagers (19 and under) presently in the general population, Texas has the *second* highest number in the nation of pregnancies among women under 15 and the *fifth* highest pregnancy rate (pregnancies per 1000 women in this age group) among 15-19 year olds. In most cases, these pregnancies create serious negative consequences for the adolescents, their families and babies (if they deliver).

The author begins by immediately establishing that the topic of the proposed research is not only of importance, but that it is of particular importance to the state in which the funding foundation resides. That

---

The original of this proposal was prepared by Marvin Eisen, Ph.D., formerly of the University of Texas at Austin, who is currently a Research Psychologist with Sociometrics Corporation of Palo Alto, California. The project was cooperatively funded for the first year by a number of sources, including two regional foundations, an agency of the state government, and two campus research institutes. The second and third years have been approved for funding by an agency of the federal government.

the problem is one of considerable regional significance is highlighted by the effective use of national rankings. The opening paragraph is easy to read, devoid of social science jargon, and sustains the reader's interest.

The foundation to which this proposal was submitted has as its major goal the funding of research devoted to mental health. Thus the author spends the next paragraph showing how the problem to be addressed by the research has direct implications for the mental health of the principals of the study and all others directly or indirectly involved with the problem. Words in the next paragraph such as health risks, clinical depression, suicide, stress, and mental health are guaranteed to catch the eye of members of the board of directors.

The negative consequences involve physical and mental health problems as well as economic and financial burdens for their families and communities. Prenatal, neonatal and maternal mortality rates are higher than those of older mothers. Young teenage mothers are more likely to suffer from medical complications of pregnancy and childbirth. Low maternal age is associated with a higher incidence of anemia, toxemia, surgical delivery, prematurity, low birth weight, birth defects and neurosurgical deficits. Poor nutrition, inadequate or late prenatal care and physical immaturity contribute to the health risks for young teenaged mothers and their children. In addition, teenage mothers are more than twice as likely to be suffering from clinical depression and seven to ten times more likely to attempt suicide than older mothers. Adolescent mothers may be more stressed by caring for their infants, especially if those infants were born prematurely or with developmental delays, as is more likely to occur with teenagers than older mothers. This increased stress and the young mother's general lack of maturity often leads to child abuse and neglect. Overall, both adolescent mothers and their offspring are at greater risk for physical and mental health related problems than older mothers and their children.

The demonstration project proposed is intended to field test preventive services on a community basis for adolescents (13-16 years) who are likely to be at risk for premarital sexual activity and pregnancy. In the initial twelve months of the demonstration we developed and pilot tested an educational intervention program designed to strengthen teenagers' beliefs about the value of individual sexual responsibility and to enhance their motivation for self-discipline and fertility control. The content of the intervention was drawn from the *Health Belief Model* (HBM), a conceptual framework used successfully to predict and understand individual decisions to seek and use preventive health services. The intervention successfully modified teenagers' beliefs about their own *susceptibility* to pregnancy, the *seriousness* of a personal premarital pregnancy and reduced perceived *barriers* to personal abstinence or fertility control.

In the foregoing overview, note particularly the third paragraph, in which the author does two critical things. He introduces the crux of the intervention (the HBM), and he does so by showing that it was used successfully in previously completed research. Readers now have reason to believe that the intervention technique proposed will work, and that the author is well qualified because he already has completed work in this area. This introduction is immediately followed in the next paragraph by a concise description of the proposed project.

In the controlled field test phase presently proposed, experimental educational services will be organized and coordinated by a number of family planning services providers located throughout the State. These agencies will be selected in collaboration with the Texas Department of Human Resources (TDHR) to reflect a statewide mix of provider types and characteristics of interest. During several six-month cycles of the three-year experimental phase of the intervention, groups of unmarried male and female teens will be randomly assigned to the HBM intervention or a "control" educational program by the provider agency that recruited their participation. The impact of the educational interventions on beliefs, motivation, and sexual and fertility control behaviors will be compared twice over a 12-month follow-up period for each provider agency's clients by the University's project staff.

The actual intervention sessions will be delivered by specially trained volunteer health professionals and graduate students who will be recruited from among persons working or training in each specific community or area. The volunteers will present the HBM materials in a series of small group discussions covering approximately 12-15 hours. As suggested by our pilot work, this mode of delivery should address the inconsistent levels of cognitive development and abstract thinking that characterize adolescents in this age range.

Once again, the author reminds the reviewers that pilot work has been completed on this subject, which reinforces the reader's impression that the proposed project will be successful.

The objectives of this controlled field test of the preventive services demonstration project are:

(1) To apply the Health Belief Model (HBM) to the problems associated with prevention and reduction of premarital sexuality and pregnancy among adolescents;
(2) To apply an educational intervention based on HBM concepts and components both to the training of adolescents who are not (yet) sexually active and to those who are (already) sexually active;

Three more objectives, relating to impact of the study, replication plans, and the value of this approach were included in the proposal but have been deleted here. This section on the objectives of the study comes early in the document and alerts the reader to the purposes of the study. The reviewer now has been provided with all of the information needed to read and appreciate the review of literature contained in the expanded Introduction below. This following section artfully combines aspects of the introduction, rationale, and literature review. Notice that it moves from general aspects of pregnancy in teenagers to more specific information important for the proposed study.

INTRODUCTION

Incidence of Adolescent Pregnancy

National and State of Texas projections indicate that approximately 50 percent of older adolescents (ages 15 to 19) are sexually active, and that about 10 to 15 percent of younger adolescents (aged 14 and under) are sexually active (Guttmacher Institute, 1980, 1981; TDHR, 1982). When these estimates are applied to the Texas adolescent population, the figures suggest that about 650,000 older adolescents and 120,000 to 180,000 younger adolescents engage in sexual activity.

Because regular contraceptive use is not common among sexually active adolescents (Zelnik, Kantner, & Ford, 1981), the fertility rate is rather high and is increasing relative to other segments of the sexually active population. In Texas, about one in nine females aged 15 to 19 became pregnant in 1980 (TDH, 1982). This pregnancy rate (about 133 per 1,000 females aged 15 to 19) was the fifth highest in the nation. Of the 92,300 pregnancies of older adolescents in 1980, about one-third (approximately 31,000) occurred to unmarried women (Guttmacher Institute, 1981).

More than half of the pregnancies to older adolescents resulted in live births. These approximately 49,000 births resulted in a fertility rate in this age group of 70.5 per 1,000. Approximately 38 percent (about 1,000) of the pregnancies to younger adolescents resulted in live births, producing a fertility rate of 2.3 per 1,000. Out-of-wedlock births comprised about one-third of the births to older adolescents and nearly three-fourths of the births to younger adolescents (up 10 and 2 percent, respectively, for older and younger teenagers between 1970 and 1980). Combining data from both age groups, it is estimated that teenagers represent about 18 percent of the sexually active women in Texas who are capable of becoming pregnant, but account for almost one-half (46 percent) of all out-of-wedlock births (TDH, 1982).

These figures suggest strongly that the problem of adolescent sexual activity, pregnancy, and birth is even more severe in Texas than in the nation as a whole. When regional and ethnic trends are examined within the State, it can be seen that the problem is especially acute in certain cases. For example, older Hispanic and Black adolescents each account for a disproportional number of out-of-wedlock births in Texas (TDH, 1982). However, if national trends can be applied to Texas, such births have increased disproportionally for Anglo teens during the 1970's.

When fertility rates for older adolescents are examined on a regional basis within Texas, considerable variation is found. This variability is related in a rather complex manner with differences in the ethnic composition of the various regions. In Table 1, for each of the 12 health service regions in the State, (a) proportions of older adolescents falling into the three major ethnic groups, (b) the fertility rates for each ethnic group, and (c) the overall fertility

TABLE 1

Texas Fertility Rates[a] (age 15-19) by Health Service Area and Ethnicity/Race (1980)[b]

Health Service Areas	ANGLO		BLACK		HISPANIC		OVERALL
	% of Population	Fertility Rate	% of Population	Fertility Rate	% of Population	Fertility Rate	Regional Fertility Rate
1. Panhandle Amarillo	80.7	66.0	4.0	129.0	15.0	157.0	82.0
2. South Plains Lubbock	64.0	45.0	6.8	177.0	29.0	152.0	85.0
3. West Texas El Paso	29.5	52.0	3.6	86.0	66.9	62.0	59.6
4. Tri-Region Abilene	79.8	61.0	5.3	129.0	14.8	145.0	77.0
5. Area 5 Irving	75.0	49.0	15.0	135.0	9.6	122.0	69.4
6. Central Texas Austin	70.0	45.0	14.0	118.0	15.0	109.0	65.0
7. Northeast Texas Marshall	76.0	55.0	21.0	111.0	2.5	162.0	69.5
8. South Texas Kingsville	29.0	53.0	2.4	97.0	68.5	84.0	75.0
9. Camino Real San Antonio	42.6	42.0	5.8	82.0	51.7	86.0	66.9
10. Greater East Texas Beaumont	73.0	56.0	23.0	108.0	3.9	108.0	70.0
11. Houston - Galveston	62.9	47.0	19.9	105.0	17.0	110.0	69.3
12. Permian Basin	66.0	65.0	5.0	137.0	29.0	140.0	90.7

a - Live births/1,000 females 15-19
b - Source: Texas Department of Health (1982)

rate for each region are presented. It can be seen from this table that the regional fertility rates range from a low of almost 60 live births per 1,000 in Region 3 to a high of about 91 per 1,000 in Region 12.

While ethnic composition may be partially responsible for this variation, there is considerable region-to-region variation even within ethnic groups. For example, among Black adolescents, the fertility rate ranges from a low of 82 in Region 9 to a high of 177 in Region 2. This latter figure is about 2.5 times higher than the statewide fertility rate of older adolescents. Figures such as those presented in Table 1 may be useful for identifying target client groups or populations and specific regions for educational services in the proposed demonstration project (see Appendix A for a more detailed discussion of the adolescent pregnancy difference by regions).

Inclusion of Table 1 at this point allows the reviewer to continue reading without having minute detail that clutters the text. The table is comprehensive and makes a number of important points that are intended to convince the reviewer of the magnitude of the problem. This type of information is more effectively presented as a table than summarized in a paragraph. The author does go on, however, to focus the reviewer's attention on particular data in the table that have special relevance to the proposed project. Supplemental information on adolescent pregnancy is appropriately placed in an appendix.

Existing Preventive Services

Publicly funded family planning services are provided to adolescents in Texas through Titles X, XIX, and XX. These funds are used to provide both outreach and educational services, as well as contraceptive services.

Deleted here, this section continues, giving details of funding over the years and the numbers of teenagers receiving various forms of service.

Unmet Needs

The Alan Guttmacher Institute (1980) estimates that in 1979 about 315,570 Texas females aged 15-19 were in need of family planning services. The best estimates of the number of adolescents receiving family planning services in Texas indicate that only about one-fourth of those in need are currently being served.

Deleted here, this section continues, providing detailed statistics supporting the fact that a large number of females at the project's target age are not receiving family planning services.

The General and the Specific Research Problem

The general research (and practical) problem is how to get teenagers who are sexually active to use effective contraception consistently and those who are not yet active to see the potential value of contracepting effectively, so that both groups will take action to reduce substantially their risk of having unintended premarital pregnancies. The specific problem addressed by this project is to field test an educational intervention mechanism that will help promote personal responsibility for each participant's sexual behavior and will enhance motivation for effective and consistent contraceptive usage by demonstrating that it produces significantly greater contraceptive usage and leads to less premarital pregnancy than presently used "control" educational services to 13-16 year-olds of both genders and various racial or ethnic groups throughout Texas.

This section is effective in presenting both the general problem and the specific focus of this research. Where the author discusses the "specific problem" the term is used synonymous with "purpose" as used in Chapter 2.

A Public Health Approach to the Problem

We believe that a preventive public health approach to the problems associated with adolescent sexuality and pregnancy that is fashioned within a salient theoretical framework has the best prospects for significant impact. Our approach, based on the Health Belief Model (HBM), seems particularly appropriate because it has been used with good success in various preventive programs for predicting both the initiation and continuing compliance of older children and adolescents; because it has been used to understand fertility control decision making and to predict completed family size for married women; and because it suggests salient intervention points and modes to modify prevention-related motivations, beliefs, and behavior pertaining to fertility control through contraceptive usage (see Appendix B for a detailed review of these studies).

This is a complex, but exceptionally powerful review paragraph. Following a clear statement of commitment, the several situations are recalled in which the intervention plan (HBM) has been shown to work. In addition, the reader is given the choice of reading not only more detailed information about these situations, but critical reviews of research using the HBM. Reviewers will be impressed with the care with which the author has studied the relevant literature, and with the thorough, but thoughtful strategy of providing as much supporting material as possible without interrupting the flow of major ideas in the proposal.

The Model asserts that the probability that an individual will undertake a particular health measure is linked to a number of *personal* perceptions, including his/her *perceived susceptibility* to the disease or condition, the *perceived seriousness* of contracting the disease or developing the condition, and the *cost-benefit ratio* of available preventive health actions (see Figure 1 and Nathanson & Becker, 1983).

The paragraph above repeats information already provided, but serves to introduce Figure 1, which is an elegant demonstration of how the theoretical model (HBM) will be applied to this particular health problem. In the section below, the reviewer is provided with more detail about the evolution of the HBM model.

Development of a Health-Based Educational Intervention Model

Because the HBM-based approach to combatting adolescent sexuality and pregnancy was a new and novel one, the actual intervention content and structure required some development and shaping through pilot work and testing prior to the proposed large scale field testing around the State. The pilot phase took place in the Austin area during the first year of the project. The

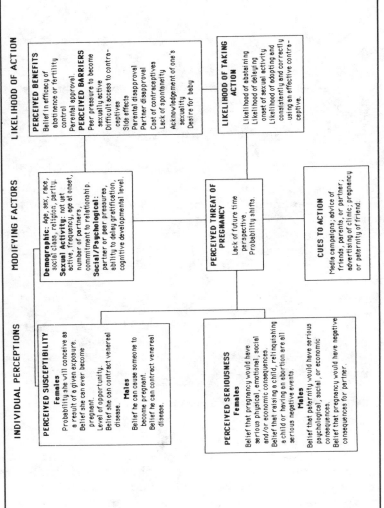

INDIVIDUAL PERCEPTIONS

MODIFYING FACTORS

LIKELIHOOD OF ACTION

PERCEIVED SUSCEPTIBILITY

Females
Probability she will conceive as a result of a given exposure.
Belief she can ever become pregnant.
Level of opportunity.
Belief she can contract venereal disease.

Males
Belief he can cause someone to become pregnant.
Belief he can contract venereal disease.

PERCEIVED SERIOUSNESS

Females
Belief that pregnancy would have serious physical, emotional, social and/or economic consequences.
Belief that raising a child, relinquishing a child or having an abortion are all serious negative events.

Males
Belief that paternity would have serious psychological, social, or economic consequences.
Belief that pregnancy would have negative consequences for partner.

Demographic: Age, sex, race, social class, religion, parity.
Sexual Activity: not yet active, frequency, age at onset, number of partners, commitment to relationship.
Social/Psychological: partner or peer pressures, ability to delay gratification, cognitive developmental level.

PERCEIVED THREAT OF PREGNANCY
Lack of future time perspective.
Probability shifts.

CUES TO ACTION
Media campaigns, advice of friends, parents, or partner; advertising of clinic, pregnancy or paternity of friend.

PERCEIVED BENEFITS
Belief in efficacy of abstinence or fertility control
Parental approval.
PERCEIVED BARRIERS
Peer pressure to become sexually active
Difficult access to contraceptives
Side effects
Parental disapproval
Partner disapproval
Cost of contraceptives
Lack of spontaneity
Acknowledgement of one's sexuality
Desire for baby

LIKELIHOOD OF TAKING ACTION
Likelihood of abstaining
Likelihood of delaying onset of sexual activity
Likelihood of adopting and consistently and correctly using an effective contraceptive.

Figure 1

232

HBM conceptual framework and components to guide and focus the structure and content of the educational intervention stemmed from components of the HBM.

Deleted here, this section continues to explain the development of the HBM model, with frequent reference to specific components in Figure 1. The author guides the reader through the figure, so that the use of HBM in this particular project will be perfectly clear. The next sections explain in general terms the basis for evaluating the intervention and the relationship between that formative process and the planned statewide dissemination of the model. Although details of evaluation methodology are provided later in the section dealing with field testing, the matter of evaluation is touched on immediately after description of the proposed project. This serves to reassure reviewers about provisions for this critical feature.

Evaluation of the Proposed Experimental Intervention Model

The HBM-based preventive services project will be evaluated and its impact compared with each agency's regular program in terms of its *ability to develop, maintain, or increase individual sexual responsibility and fertility control* (i.e., self-discipline, abstinence, or consistent and effective contraceptive usage behavior patterns). Across provider agencies these comparisons will focus upon intervention effects for a wide range of client population subgroups: younger and older adolescents of both genders; all racial or ethnic groups represented in the State; adolescents differing in socio-economic status, income, and family characteristics; and those differing in preintervention sexual and reproductive knowledge, health beliefs, and sexual experience. The Department of Human Resources evaluation staff and The University of Texas at Austin staff will carry out the evaluation plan.

Dissemination of the Intervention Model

Over the projected three-year demonstration period modification and improvements will be made in the intervention and procedures on the basis of formal and informal evaluations. Thus on an iterative basis, the prevention model will be assessed in a variety of settings, with a wide range of client populations, and against a reasonably representative cross-section of preventive services approaches employed by family planning service agencies around the State. If the HBM proves to meet the stated objective more effectively and/or more efficiently than other programs tested, it's our hope that it will be implemented on a programmatic basis statewide following the demonstration period.

Granting agencies are interested in how the proposed project is innovative or unique. It is important to include this as a separate section within the proposal so that reviewers do not have to infer the uniqueness of the study from other parts of the introduction. This proposal has a very strong section that stands out nicely and impresses the reader that here indeed is a fresh approach to a serious health problem. We have included below only the opening descriptive sentence of the first three innovative features described in this section.

Innovative Features of the Demonstration Project

The demonstration project has several innovative features:

- The educational services approach is built upon a well-developed conceptual framework about preventive health beliefs and behavior.
- The HBM approach is combined with a service delivery mechanism—small group discussions—that is especially suitable for use with adolescent audiences.
- The HBM framework allows focus on adolescents who are not (yet) sexually active, as well as those who are.

Expected Results and Benefits of the Field Test Phase of the Project

It is probably premature to generate a large number of specific hypotheses pertaining to empirical results in the Field Test Phase of the study. However, a set of working hypotheses regarding the results and benefits to be expected are:

Here the author presents several hypotheses which, due to the nature of this project, were not written as testable hypotheses. We have not included them because, as noted in Chapter 1, we believe that in most cases it is preferable to write hypotheses in a form that can be directly accepted or rejected.

In the section that follows the author describes the various groups of subjects that will participate in the study. Since a number of types of subjects are needed, it was important to describe each. As examples, we have included here only two of the populations described in the proposal.

PROCEDURE

Participants in the Controlled Field Test

Family planning services providers. We propose that in collaboration with TDHC we select and then contract with various family planning services providers around the state who receive Title XIX and XX funds for participant recruitment, coordination, and selection of community facilities for the intervention sessions. Major selection criteria include:

(1) receipt of Title XIX and/or XX funds;
(2) representation of an important family planning service provider segment and contribution to the overall provider mix being established;
(3) having some type of educational services program in place at the time the study commences;
(4) having in place or being able to start-up easily a community outreach/recruitment campaign aimed at adolescents between 13 and 16 years of age; and
(5) relatively close proximity to relevant professional health organizations and graduate and professional training programs so that community and student volunteers who will be serving as the actual HBM instructors and discussion leaders can be recruited relatively easily.

Health professionals and discussion group leaders. Delivery of services to adolescents through family planning agency auspices will be provided on a volunteer basis by community professionals and by graduate students to fulfill course, experience, or internship requirements in their training or graduate programs. We propose that volunteers be recruited by the TDHR's Office of

Volunteer Services personnel in each region in association with the individual family planning service agencies with whom they ultimately work. These volunteers should include physicians, nurses, clinical and community psychologists, social workers, health educators, as well as graduate or professional students in these disciplines. Every effort should be made to match volunteer ethnic and cultural characteristics with their clients' characteristics when possible. These volunteer trainers and discussion leaders will be specially trained in the HBM approach and appropriate small group discussion techniques by The University of Texas at Austin project staff.

A lengthy section, not reproduced here, was next used to describe the adolescent client populations. In this section the author again employed lists of population characteristics followed by discussion designed to help the reader identify how the proposed project matched the nature of the clients.

As indicated in Chapter 3 it often is beneficial to use instruments that previously have been shown to be reliable and valid. At the beginning of the next section the author integrates already validated measures into the proposed project.

Educational Materials and Research Instruments

The general orientation to designing education materials and research instruments for this project has been to use those previously developed and readily available whenever possible. Therefore, most of the material and models relating to biological, reproductive, and birth control facts and information were selected from existing programs or research projects geared to adolescents of similar ages, backgrounds, and cultures as those being served in this project. Some materials relating to the use of small group methods to address adolescent sexuality and pregnancy issues were selected from available materials developed in other research projects and were modified to meet particular needs and project goals.

Much of the instructional material to train the small group discussion leaders and to distribute to adolescents during the intervention was developed by project consultants and staff to meet specific requirements and objectives. Thus, the materials described below continually will be developed and produced for eventual dissemination to family planning agencies within the State (and perhaps in other areas):

In the full proposal, each of the following items was now presented with a short description of the material's intended use.

(1) Training designs and syllabus guides
(2) Discussion guides for small group leaders
(3) Materials to be provided to the discussion participants
(4) Materials to be provided to the discussion leaders

In the next paragraph, the author presents information on data collection instruments that had been developed in pilot studies. Since much of this material was still in development, draft copies were placed in appendices.

Data collection and research instruments were selected or developed over the course of an earlier pilot study. These instruments assessed areas such as the following: sexual and birth control knowledge, pregnancy and contraception health beliefs and perceptions, sexual activity and contraceptive history, Health Locus of Control, sociodemographic variables, and social relationships (see Appendix D and E for draft materials).

Content of the Educational Intervention

The anticipated content and the general format/structure for the HBM-based educational intervention program is discussed in detail in Appendix F.

In the deleted section above, the author gave a short description of the educational intervention and then referred the reader to an appendix where more detail could be found. The section below summarizes the time frame for the study. Much of the data collection was scheduled to take place over an extended period of time. The use of tables makes it easy to follow which measures will be employed at which points in the field test.

Procedure for the Field Test Phase

Following participant recruitment within each agency, we expect adolescents to be *randomly assigned* to that agency's

HBM-based educational program or to their regular (ongoing) educational services program. Once the teenagers have completed the preventive services intervention (HBM or regular), they will be followed over at least a 12-month period with process and outcome data collected one week after intervention, and six months and 12 months post-intervention by paid student project interviewers who are coordinated by each agency participating in the study. More specifically, the procedure will involve four data collection points during a 12-month period: a pretest session and group educational (or control) small group discussion to be conducted over 12-15 hours, (Time 1); a posttest follow-up one week after the interventions (which will be individually scheduled, Time 2); a follow-up to collect dependent variables at six months post-intervention (individually scheduled, Time 3); and a 12-month follow-up to collect dependent variable data and debrief the participants (individually scheduled, Time 4). (See Tables 2 and 3 for more details.)

A second paragraph, omitted here, contained a short overview of Tables 2 and 3. The variables were introduced in a manner that allows a reader to follow the text without having to spend a substantial amount of time discovering how to use the tables.

Note that on Table 3, a new variable (#1—"Pregnant or not") is added to the sequence of dependent variables in columns 2 and 3. It might help the reader to leave a blank space in the first column where "Consistent use of contraceptives in reporting period" is and move numbers 1 through 7 down so each variable is aligned across the page. If the reviewers are likely to be unfamiliar with how each variable will be measured, a short note after the variable name (e.g., "yes" or "no" after "Contraceptives used at last intercourse") would help to clarify that point.

In the first part of this next section the author reminds the reviewer of the study goals. This excellent strategy serves to emphasize the relationship between the purpose of the study and the data analysis.

PLAN OF DATA ANALYSIS

Overview

The analyses are designed to answer the following two evaluation questions:

TABLE 2
Experimental Design for the Proposed Study

	Time 1	Time 2 (1 week)	Time 3 (6 months)	Time 4 (12 months)
Experimental Groups	1) Pretest: Sex Knowledge Contraceptive Knowledge Health Beliefs Personality Scales Sociodemographic Data Sex and Contraception History 2) Intervention	1) Posttest: Sex Knowledge Contraceptive Knowledge Health Beliefs Manipulation Checks 2) Posttest (same as above)	1) Health Beliefs Dependent Variables	1) Health Beliefs 2) Sex and Contraception
Control Groups	1) Pretest (same as above) 2) Control Discussion	1) Posttest (same as above) 2) No Sex and Contraception Dependent Variables	(same as above)	(same as above)

239

TABLE 3
Dependent Variables for the Proposed Study

Time 2 (1 week post)	Time 3 (6 months post)	Time 4 (12 months post)
1) Consistent use of contraceptives in reporting period	1) Pregnant or not (Male: responsible for pregnancy)	1) Pregnant or not (Male: responsible for pregnancy)
2) Contraceptives used at last intercourse	2) Consistent use of contraceptives in reporting period	2) Consistent use of contraceptives in reporting period
3) Family planning advice sought or fertility control program enrollment	3) Contraceptives used at last intercourse	3) Contraceptives used at last intercourse
4) More information on sex and contraception sought	4) Family planning advice sought or fertility control program enrollment	4) Family planning advice sought or fertility control program enrollment
5) Ceased or reduced level of sexual activity	5) More information on sex and contraception sought	5) More information on sex and contraception sought
6) Became sexually active for first time; use of contraception	6) Ceased or reduced level of sexual activity	6) Ceased or reduced level of sexual activity
7) Consistent abstinence	7) Became sexually active for first time; use of contraception	7) Became sexually active for first time; use of contraception
	8) Consistent abstinence	8) Consistent abstinence

(1) As a result of the HBM intervention, do subjects in the experimental groups exhibit more positive sexual behaviors on follow-up than subjects in the control groups?

(2) Did the intervention have a more positive effect on sexual behaviors for subjects with specific characteristics in the experimental groups (i.e., subjects of certain ages, genders, sexual experience, ethnic groups, personality types)?

These questions seek to determine whether the intervention produced "more positive sexual and fertility control behaviors," where more positive sexual behaviors are defined as:

(1) Lower rates of pregnancy (for males: responsible for fewer pregnancies);

(2) Higher rates of reported contraceptive use;

(3) Greater consistency of reported contraceptive use (contraceptives used for a higher proportion of instances of intercourse);

(4) Higher rates of reported contraceptive use at most recent intercourse;

(5) Higher rates of enrollment in family planning programs;

(6) Advice on sex and contraception sought more often (e.g., from family planning service providers and other sources);

(7) Lower rates of reported sexual activity; and

(8) Longer delays before first intercourse (among those who were previously not sexually active).

The evaluation plan is designed to determine, for each of these outcomes, whether the intervention was effective and for which groups of subjects it was most effective.

In many instances information on study design and sample size would have been presented much earlier in the proposal. In this instance, the delay seems justified by the other important tasks that took logical precedence. As illustrated here, study design and statistical analysis techniques often are closely related. Grouping the two sections together, as below, may improve continuity in some proposals.

In the section on sample size, results from pilot work again are used to support the decisions made. As indicated in Chapter 3, every proposal should provide a rationale for the number of subjects selected. Pilot data are particularly useful in establishing the number of subjects required to obtain the desired inferential power. The author also uses the pilot data on subject attrition to justify the cost of the project. This is an excellent way to convince the foundation that the projected costs for paying subjects are legitimate and needed.

Design

Subjects, recruited by family planning services providers through outreach programs, will be randomly assigned to experimental HBM and control groups. Groups will be further segregated according to age: younger teenagers (13 to 14 years of age) and older teenagers (15 to 16 years of age). Thus, subjects will be assigned to groups according to a two-by-two design in which one between-groups factor is treatment (Experimental vs. Control) and the second is age (Younger vs. Older), for a total of four cells or groups.

Half of the subjects will be randomly assigned to experimental groups, while the other half will be assigned to control groups. Because subjects will be assigned to age-dependent groups according to their age ranges, the sample sizes of these groups will reflect the proportions with which younger and older teens are recruited. It is anticipated that approximately two-thirds of the teens will be older (15 to 16 years of age).

Subjects assigned to the experimental treatment will be placed in HBM-based discussion groups. Control subjects will received the educational programs currently offered by providers. The HBM-based discussion groups will meet over a three-week period. Data will be collected from these subjects before the first discussion session (the pretest) as well as after the last session (the one week posttest). Thus, it should be possible to process one cohort of experimental subjects through the pretest, the discussion groups, and the posttest within a month.

Sample Size

Discussions with Austin area family planning service providers indicate that a provider of average size should be able to process approximately 50 subjects per month. If each provider processes 50 participants per month for six months, it will process about 300 subjects in a six-month period. Four providers delivering the intervention during each six-month period, will result in a total of

1,200 subjects receiving services (2,400/year). Half of these (600) will receive the experimental treatment and half (600) will receive the control treatment. Within each of these treatments, about two-thirds will be older teens and one-third young teens. Thus, among older teens, there will be about 400 experimental and 400 control subjects. Among younger teens there will be about 200 experimental subjects and 200 control subjects per six-month period.

Based on our pilot study attrition data for paid six-month participants, it is conservatively estimated that about half of the unpaid subjects will be available for data collection by the time of the second follow-up (one year). It does not seem unreasonable to anticipate this level of cooperation in a study that deals with a mobile population, depends upon voluntary cooperation, and seeks to collect sensitive information without monetary compensation.

If this estimate is correct, about half of the 2,400 subjects served will be available for follow-up. These 1,200 subjects per 12 months will be sufficient for the data analyses planned. It is considered sufficient to obtain complete data from about 1,200 subjects (300 subjects from each of the four cells in the two-by-two) each 12 months.

Thus, only a sample of the population served will receive testing. Testing a sample, rather than the entire population, has the salutary effect of reducing the scope and expense of the data collection effort. A sample of the size described above will provide quite adequate statistical power for the analyses planned. In order to ensure a sufficient number of subjects with complete data, data will be collected from a larger number during the earlier data collection periods. These sample sizes will be determined while taking into account the expected rate of attrition and the number of subjects served at each site. Subjects will be selected for testing using a proportional selection procedure, so that equal proportions of subjects served will be selected from each provider site.

The data analysis portion of the proposal is subdivided into two categories: major and supporting data analyses. Here the author reacquaints the reader with the purposes and independent variables for the study. In addition, where a little known technique is used (logistical regression), the author adds a few sentences to help the reader understand why the technique is appropriate. The author does not, however, overwhelm the reader with unneeded statistical jargon.

Major Data Analyses

Independent variables will be of two types. The first type consists of between-group variables, namely treatment (Experimental vs. Control) and age (Young Teens vs. Older Teens). The second type of independent variable will be individual differences variables such ethnicity, amount of previous sexual experience, pretest health beliefs, and various personality variables. These individual differences variables are characteristics of the subjects that will vary within groups (e.g., a particular discussion group may have subjects of various ethnic groups). However, the groups will be pure with regard to the between-groups variables (e.g., all subjects in a particular discussion group may be young teens receiving the experimental treatment).

Data will be analyzed with two goals in mind (corresponding to the two evaluation questions discussed previously). First, it will be determined whether the experimental subjects have more successful outcomes than control subjects. Second, it will be determined whether the experimental treatment was more successful for certain groups or types of subjects than for others.

Analysis-of-variance (ANOVA) is the most powerful statistical procedure available for this type of analysis and will be used when appropriate. In terms of ANOVA, the first goal involves testing for a main effect for the treatment variable, while the second goal involves testing for interactions between the treatment variable and the other between-group and within-group (individual differences) variables. In practice, these tests are performed and interpreted simultaneously.

Where the dependent variable is continuous (e.g., amount of sexual activity), a repeated-measures ANOVA can be used, employing the follow-up periods as repeated measures. It may prove useful to include certain pretest measures or personality measures as covariates (i.e., to hold these individual differences constant) in these analyses or to construct linear regression (i.e., multivariate) models to control for potential individual difference variables while testing the necessary main effects and interactions.

However, several of the dependent variables will be binary variables (pregnant vs. not pregnant, used contraception vs. did not use contraception, etc.). Such binary dependent variables make the use of ANOVA or linear regression inappropriate. For the analysis of these variables, logistic regression will be used. Logistic regression is a multivariate technique analogous to ordinary linear regression but is designed for the analysis of a binary dependent variable when the independent variables are categorical (e.g., Anglo, Black, Hispanic) and/or continuous (e.g., scores on personality measure). This method involves estimating the probability of "success" (e.g., no pregnancy, used contraception, etc.) for each combination of the predictor variables.

Thus, for the dependent variables, which are binary in nature, logistical regression will be used in a manner analogous to linear regression to assess the main effects and interactions described above. A computer program to perform logistical regression is available in the Statistical Analysis System (SAS) statistical package. This package is available on the IBM computer operated by The University of Texas at Austin.

In summary, ANOVA, linear regression, and logistical regression will be used, as appropriate, to test the effectiveness of the treatment and to determine whether it is more effective for certain types of subjects (subjects of certain ages, ethnicity, sexual experience, personality types, etc.).

In the paragraph above, the author summarizes and reminds the reader of the techniques that will be used. The use of a summary at the end of an extensive section involving technical details helps the reader pick out and retain the essential elements.

In the next section, the supporting data analyses are presented. Note that in the second paragraph the author describes plans for analyzing the effect of attrition on the study outcome. This type of analysis often is included in social scientific research because it allows the author to know if attrition within and among the groups might have changed the results of the study.

Supporting Data Analyses

The major data analyses are designed to answer the evaluation questions. However, the data collected in this study will be used for several additional purposes: (1) to assess the effects of attrition, (2) to determine the degree to which the treatment was implemented as intended, and (3) to test certain hypotheses concerning the relationship between the HBM and sexual knowledge, beliefs, and behavior.

It is expected that a number of subjects will be lost through attrition. Some subjects who begin the group discussions will not complete them, and others will not be available for the first or second follow-up. In an investigation of this type, it is important to determine the attrition rates for the groups of interest and to determine the impact of attrition on the outcome variables. This is necessary to avoid attributing outcome effects to treatment variables when they are actually a result of differential attrition. Analyses of the attrition rates for the various treatment groups will, therefore, be conducted to detect differential rates of attrition. Comparisons will also be made on the pretest measures between those who completed and did not complete the treatment in order to determine whether systematic differences exist between these two groups.

Several omitted paragraphs dealt here with a discussion of variables that might have changed from pretest to posttest. In addition, the author identified the correlations that would be of primary interest.

The next section presents some limitations of the study. It always is valuable to confront the limitations in any study design, and to describe the ways in which you will try to lessen their effects. The treatment of the first limitation, attrition, is a model for how this can be accomplished.

Limitations

Four limitations inherent in the sample and in the longitudinal design of the demonstration project may reduce the power of statistical analyses and limit the internal validity and generalizability of the findings. First, attrition of participants is a potential problem because it poses a threat to the power of the statistical analyses for testing experimental hypotheses. Since many of the dependent variables in the study are dichotomous (e.g., yes/no) losing participants directly affects the power of the tests. Moreover, attrition may not be distributed randomly among conditions. Interpretation of differences between experimental and control subjects (at 6 and 12 months) could be confounded by the characteristics of those who drop out versus those who remain. Realistically, it is expected that it will not be possible to collect follow-up data for a relatively large proportion of the subjects. Attempts will be made to determine whether there is differential attrition for certain types of subjects and whether those who drop out differ on various pretest measures from those who do not. However, it will not be possible to correct for these differences, if they occur. Thus, inferences will be generalizable only to those subjects who complete the study.

A number of actions will be taken to reduce the attrition rate:

(1) We will impress upon subjects that this is an important study which depends heavily on the follow-up component.

(2) Appointments for succeeding follow-ups will be made at each interview to underscore the fact that follow-up interviews will occur.

(3) Pretest and follow-up interviews will be on a one-to-one basis, and follow-ups will be scheduled to occur at times and places most convenient for subjects.

(4) Some participants will probably come from TDHR client groups; thus their locations are potentially available for follow-up reminders and phone calls.

(5) Where appropriate, letters will be sent to participants to remind them of their 6 and 12 month follow-up appointments.

(6) Follow-up phone calls will be made as necessary. These and other follow-up procedures will be conducted by the same person who interviewed the subject at Time 1. In this way, subjects may develop a more personal relationship with the interviewer which will reduce the likelihood of attrition.

The author follows by discussing other limitations in a similar fashion. This material has been omitted. Below, in presenting the fourth and final limitation, the author discusses the problem presented by self-reports involving sensitive personal data. This potentially serious source of bias is treated frankly and carefully. Information concerning measurement strategies that appear to have lessened the impact of self-report bias is used to assure reviewers that the author is fully sensitive to this potential limitation.

Finally, the potential underreporting bias in self-reports of sexual and contraceptive behavior is a problem with no really satisfactory solution. The extent of underreporting of sexual activities and contraceptive usage is not known in a general teenage population, or, for that matter, in more selected populations (e.g., family planning clinic users). Typically, efforts to validate these reports depend on validation criteria that in themselves are self-report data (e.g., number of previous pregnancies gathered from a medical history).

Some efforts have been made to employ measurement techniques designed to reduce self-report bias. Zelnik, Kantner and Ford (1981) found that there was little difference in reported incidence of sexual intercourse when interviewers asked the question directly or asked the question within a *randomized response technique* format in their 1976 sample of 15-19 year old females. No data for males are available on this point. Others have examined potential response biases in sex surveys and found little underreporting for either sex among 18-22 year-olds (Delameter, 1974; Delameter and MacCorquodale, 1979).

The self-reporting bias is not necessarily a major problem in the present study unless participants' underreporting of sexual activity or overreporting of contraceptive usage interacts with the experimental intervention. Thus, if participants exposed to the HBM intervention are more likely to underreport sexual activity or to underreport contraceptive usage, the group means will be affected and interpretations of causality could be clouded. Thus, it might not be clear whether the treatment was effective or whether the treatment simply led to a higher level of response bias. Again, pretest (i.e., baseline) data on personality and sociodemographic variables may provide some help in eliminating alternative interpretations of treatment effects.

The use of a timetable for indicating when each part of the study will be completed is valuable for both the reviewers and investigators (Table 4). The format of this table is particularly valuable because it progressively shows each step for completing the study. In the interest of space, only the first eight tasks and activities are presented here as examples. The use of both flow diagrams (Chapter 1) and projected time tables (Chapter 7) have been discussed.

The reference section, which is not presented here, contained the 72 references cited in the text of the proposal. Since a specific format for references was not required by the foundation, references were listed in a

---

TABLE 4

DRAFT WORK PLAN AND TIMETABLE (EXAMPLE: 1ST CYCLE)

EXPERIMENTAL PHASE

Tasks and Activities

1. Recruit and Select First Five Family Planning Provider Organizations Statewide for the Controlled Field Study.

2. Solicit and Recruit Parental Involvement, Community and Private Organization Involvement in Each Area where Study is Undertaken.

3. Recruit and Select Community/ Student Volunteers in First Five Areas to Deliver Educational Program.

4. Train Community/Student Volunteers in First Five Sites.

5. Initiate Outreach and Recruitment Programs Geared to Selected Client Groups by Individual Family Planning Providers in First Five Sites

6. Begin Controlled Field Studies on Education Programs in First Five Sites.

7. Begin Post (1 week) Test Data Collection in First Five Sites

8. Data Analysis (Initial Pre-Post Educational Program Impact) for First Five Sites.

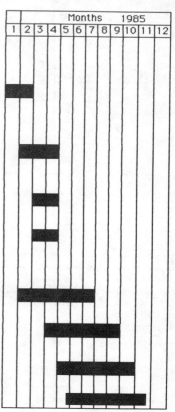

Work Plan Continued Through 24 Tasks and Activities (3 Year Period)

---

format style common to sociological/public health research journals.

The final section of the proposal is the budget. Since this project was funded by a number of different cooperating sources, we have combined and edited the budget for this example. Note that the budget is subdivided by time periods and categories of funding and that each subdivision and category has a separate heading. We have included only the first year of the budget and the summary. The budget for the second and third years has similar categories and format. The author shows in short phrases the method by which he arrived at the dollar figure for each category (see Chapter 7). In the text of the proposal, the author already has discussed the number of subjects needed and other factors that will help reviewers understand the need for particular expenditures before they read the budget.

Note that we have not included actual salary or fringe benefit figures with this proposal. The proposal submitted to funding agencies includes this information in the format of the budget presented here.

BUDGET

YEAR ONE: June 1, 1985-May 31, 1986

SALARIES:

	Salary	Fringe	
Project Director (50% time for 12 months)	$xx,xxx.	$ x,xxx.	
Research Associate (50% time for 12 months)	x,xxx.	x,xxx.	
Programmer I (50% time for 6 months)	x,xxx.	x,xxx.	
Data Entry Operator (100% time for 6 months)	x,xxx.	x,xxx.	
Interviewers (3000 hours × $6.47/hour)	19,410.		
Trainers (Graduate Students)			
($100/day × 3 days × 10 trips)	3,000.		
TOTAL SALARY AND FRINGE BENEFITS:	xx,xxx.	x,xxx.	xx,xxx.

ADMINISTRATIVE FEES:

Agency fee for administrative details		
(10 sites × $1,200/site)	12,000.	
TOTAL ADMINISTRATIVE FEES:		12,000.

TRAVEL:

Training Travel:	
Three people × 3 days × $70/day × 10 trips	6,300.
Three people × $100 travel × 10 trips	3,000.
Total training travel	9,300.

BUDGET——Continued

Project Director Travel:

Ten trips/year, one to each site
One day at $70 per diem × 10 trips	700.
Travel at $100/trip	1,000.
Total Project Director Travel:	1,700
TOTAL PROJECT TRAVEL:	11,000.

OTHER EXPENSES:

Expendable Supplies ($100/month × 12 months)	1,200
Telephone Charges ($150/month × 12 months)	1,800.
Duplication Charges ($50/month × 12 months)	600.
TOTAL OTHER EXPENSES:	3,600.

DATA PROCESSING:

Computer Connect Time (7500 hours × $0.20/hour)	1,500.
Computer CPU Time (5 hours × $230/hour)	1,150
TOTAL DATA PROCESSING:	2,650.
GRAND TOTAL FOR YEAR ONE:	$xxx,xxx.

Omitted here were similar budgets for the second and third year of the study.

SUMMARY BUDGET: June 1, 1985-May 31, 1988

	YEAR 1	YEAR 2	YEAR 3
SALARY AND FRINGE BENEFITS	xx,xxx.	xxx,xxx.	xx,xxx.
ADMINISTRATIVE FEES	12,000.	12,000.	—
TRAVEL	11,000.	11,000.	—
OTHER EXPENSES	3,600.	3,600.	3,600.
DATA PROCESSING	2,650.	4,300.	3,300.
TOTALS:	xxx,xxx.	xxx,xxx.	xx,xxx.

TOTAL DIRECT COSTS FOR THREE YEAR PROJECT: $xxx,xxx.

In the full proposal the budget was followed by a comprehensive justification of each line item. Funding agencies require an explanation of how the investigator plans to use the funding if the proposal is approved. Inasmuch as the request for personnel was a large item in this proposal, the author listed the job responsibilities for each position. It usually is helpful if the investigator has particular personnel in mind for each position, and includes evidence of their experiences and expertise. It is even more impressive if the persons to be appointed already have been working with the pilot project. In that sense, funding the proposal simply would serve to retain previously trained, experienced persons in the proposed project, an obvious advantage to the grantor.

The second area of the budget that merited careful attention was the request for travel funds. Such requests must be given in detail and justified in terms of project demands. Reviewers are alert to detect potential abuses of their resources, and frivolous travel definitely fits that category. The guiding rule to remember when building the budget is that the more carefully the budget is calculated and explained, the more convinced the reviewers will be that the investigator understands what must be done, has been conscientious in planning each step, and not only will accomplish the goals of the study but will do so at minimum cost.

Some General Standards for Judging the Acceptability of a Thesis or Dissertation Proposal

	Desirable	Undesirable
I. Topic		
A. Importance		
1. Basic Research	A clear relationship exists between the topic and existing information in related areas of knowledge. Topic is recognized as substantial by people who are knowledgeable in the area. Topic is articulated to a body of knowledge recognized as broadly relevant to the discipline.	Proposal does not support the importance of the study. Topic seems unrelated to existing facts and theoretical constructs. Proposed study is not inserted into a line of inquiry.
2. Applied Research	Topic is relevant to professional needs, and recognized as substantial by competent individuals engaged in professional practice. There is a clear relation between the topic and existing problems in practice.	Topic seems unrelated to realistic professional concerns and divorced from matters of practice.
B. Scope	The extent of the proposed study is reasonable in terms of the time and resources available to the candidate. A clear indication exists that the student has considered and made provision for each of the demands implicit within the study.	Projected study is grandiose and unreasonable in terms of time and resources. Or, the study is so small or limited in its concern that it may (a) provide little useful information, and (b) involve less than a reasonable exposure to scholarly inquiry for the candidate.

(continued)

APPENDIX A—Continued

	Desirable	Undesirable
C. Advisement	At least one faculty member possessing scholarly competence in the domain of the topic is both interested and available. Resources for developing or obtaining needed technical skills are available and specifically identified.	Faculty members available for advisement lack special competence in the domain of the topic. Needed sources of technical assistance are not identified.
II. Scholarship		
A. Originality	The proposal provides in the definition of the problem, the methodology employed, or the mode of interpretation, some contribution that is different from work previously done and that distinctly is the product of the candidate's own thinking. In replicative studies, special attention is given either to deliberate alteration in method and design or to the unique problems of maintaining equivalent conditions for all critical variables.	Proposed study paraphrases and collects opinions, results, or conclusions of others without criticism, synthesis, or the creative development of an organizing structure. Replicates without intentional and appropriate variation in method or special attention to the problems of creating a satisfactory level of experimental equivalence.
B. Perspective	Student reveals the capacity to relate the topic to a larger framework of knowledge and theory.	Student treats the problem in isolation from previous work, related disciplines, and relevant theoretical structures.
C. Logic	Design of the proposed study is appropriate to the nature of the topic, being no more elaborate than demanded by the question asked. There is congruence among title, problem, hypotheses, procedures and analysis. Student makes explicit the rationale and assumptions that underlie the form of the question and the procedures selected. Alternatives are revealed that might have been followed, and the reasoning supporting the choices made is clear.	Proposed design is more complex than demanded by the question and the present level of knowledge. Design fails to confront important complexities in the topic through the use of methods leading to multivariate analysis. Title does not precisely reflect the central problem. Procedures are not designed to deal with the problem identified as central to the study. Student does not make clear the procedural alternatives that were considered.

(continued)

	Desirable	Undesirable
D. Objectivity	Student clearly delineates the limits, weaknesses, and strengths of the study, and maintains objectivity. Language is restricted to a level made justifiable by previous findings and a conservative appraisal of current knowledge and practice.	Student overgeneralizes from an inadequate body of knowledge or suggests applications that seem unwarranted by the evidence presented. Limitations imposed by selection of the sample or methodology go unnoticed.
E. Depth of Preparation	Student demonstrates familiarity with the major sources of information that relate to the problem, and makes apt and ready application of these to the development of the study. Includes pilot study data, specimen tables and figures, power tests for determining sample size, and relevant sample applications of the methods to be employed. Student clearly has considered the feasibility factors of time, cost and the availability of data. Student indicates how special competencies demanded by the procedures are to be acquired.	Student has not completed a thorough search of relevant literature, or has not assimilated it to the point of understanding the major concepts involved and their application to the problem. Proposal includes no pilot study data or relevant sample applications of methods to be employed. Student fails to recognize the sophisticated scholarship needed for the use of such procedures as sampling, use of demographic data, test and questionnaire construction, interviewing, or the selection and use of psychometric instruments.
III. Presentation		
A. Mechanics	Proposal is well edited, with adequate attention to grammar, sentence structure, spelling, and all matters of mechanical accuracy. The style is terse, with a minimum of unnecessary words and irrelevant commentary.	Obvious failure to proofread as revealed by mechanical errors. Unnecessary use of descriptive words and phrases. Rambling style, introduction of peripheral commentary, and use of trite jargon.

B. Documentation	Citations are limited to and consistently provided for (a) concepts, procedures, or materials (including quoted materials) that are the unique products of particular individuals and fall under the broad canon of "credit due," and (b) positions, interpretations, or methodological alternatives elected by the author that might require the support of further argument and explication as developed in supplementary references.	Inadequate reference to the relevant literature, failure to give credit where due, or failure to indicate sources likely to be needed by the interested and critical reader. Overabundance of documentation in which citations are irrelevant, needlessly repetitious, or refer to matters clearly within the public domain. Extensive use of direct quotations that are not justified by their contribution to the main tasks of the proposal.
C. Organization	Proposal has a logical, easily understandable sequence from initial statement of the problem through the last appendix. Major topics are separated under appropriately devised subheadings. Format tailored to meet demands peculiar to the topic.	Order of topics violates logic and causes reader to skip forward and back to make sense of the presentation. Words are used to indicate systematic meanings, prior to their definition in the text. Arbitrary format followed even when inappropriate to topic.
D. Clarity	Procedures are described in terms of specific operations. Copies of such relevant materials as test instruments, interview schedules, directions to subjects, criteria for selection of experts, and pilot test data are appended to the main proposal document. Given the level of detail contained in the proposal, any appropriately trained researcher could carry out the study with results not differing substantially from those that would be obtained by the author. Explicit, step-by-step sequence of operations is presented.	Report makes vague references to unspecified procedures that are described only in general terms or that are linked together by relationships that leave their purpose unclear. Such important operations as "a structured interview", "an analysis of literature," "an evaluation of materials," or "a test of attitudes" are not presented in explicit forms such as particular test instruments, lists of criteria, procedures for analysis, or experimental operations. Exact temporal sequence of individual parts of the investigation is not made clear.

APPENDIX B

Annotated Bibliography of Supplementary References

Few published documents are available in which the authors have focused specific attention on the preparation of the research proposal. Much of the advice available to the novice will be found in three kinds of sources; in each the authors give primary attention to other tasks. First are textbooks about research, which deal largely with methods of conducting research. Second are books designed to enhance the reader's ability to obtain grants. Many of these deal more extensively with how to locate funding sources and how proposals are evaluated than with the details of preparing the proposal. Third are the instruments developed for use in evaluating the adequacy of reported research. These instruments deal, *ex post facto,* with the products of proposals. For the imaginative reader, publications from each of these classifications may yield important assistance in the proposal writing process.

We have not listed here the many fine books on research method and design. Books such as Borg and Gall's *Educational Research* (1983) and Lincoln and Guba's *Naturalistic Inquiry* (1985); [both are cited in our reference list] are available in many college bookstores. Colleagues, committee advisors, professors in related areas, and library reference specialists can help the novice locate a good research text appropriate to his or her research. This annotated bibliography contains publications that we have found particularly helpful for persons preparing a research proposal.

American Psychological Association. (1982). *Ethical principles in the conduct of research with human participants.* Washington, DC: Author.

In the first few pages of this monograph, a committee of the American Psychological Association presents 11 ethical principles by which to guide the conduct of research with human subjects. The principles make worthwhile reading by themselves. The remaining sections of this booklet provide a detailed discussion of issues that were considered in the development of the principles. This is an essential reference for those conducting research involving human subjects.

American Psychological Association. (1983). *Publication manual of the American Psychological Association* (3rd ed.). Washington, DC: Author.

This paperbound manual contains a comprehensive set of standards for the technical process of scholarly writing. It is a standard reference that is consulted frequently by most graduate students and professors in the social and behavioral sciences. The major topics covered are: (1) content and organization of a manuscript, (2) expression of ideas, (3) editorial style, (4) typing instructions, and (5) submitting a manuscript and proofreading. The book includes thorough illustration of standards for punctuation, construction of tables, and use of citations in the text. The sections on headings, seriation, and nonsexist language will be particularly valuables to novice proposal writers. The suggested format and citation style are now accepted or required by a large number of universities and research journals.

Bauer, D. G. (1984). *The "how to" grants manual.* New York: Macmillan.

Written by a specialist who has conducted seminars for thousands of grant seekers, the manual is aimed at making the proposal preparation process cost-effective. This is the hard-boiled, cost-benefit analysis approach to shaking the money tree. The extensive section on how to monitor government funding sources would be invaluable for a novice researcher without access to support services of the kind normally provided in a large university. Inclusion of detail such as a checklist for what to ask if you visit a public funding official or office, will make the text interesting even for the veteran grant seeker. The manual is intended to be used in conjunction with a companion piece from the same publisher, *The Complete Grants Sourcebook for Higher Education.*

Campbell, D. T., & Stanley, J. C. (1963). *Experimental and quasi-experimental designs for research.* Chicago: Rand McNally.

Although this is ordinarily thought of as a treatise on research design (certainly it is one of the most lucid treatments of design ever produced for a broad readership), the authors of this elegant monograph have so much to say about the broad standards of systematic inquiry that it should be consumed by every graduate student early in his or her research preparation. Building on the format provided by a theoretical model of validity for inquiry, the authors examine 16 different quantitative designs for research and a host of vital issues that touch the preparation of sound proposals.

Cook, T. D., & Campbell, D. T. (1979). *Quasi-experimentation: Design and analysis issues for field settings.* Chicago: Rand McNally.

In this book the work of Campbell and Stanley is extended to the design of quasi-experimental studies in settings outside the laboratory. The first two chapters include an update of the information on validity found in the earlier work, *Experimental and Quasi-Experimental Designs for Research.* Six other chapters include extensive reviews of quasi-experimental designs. For each design, there is a discussion of the trade-offs made when using that format, and the options for completing data analysis. This latter aspect of the book makes it essential reading for anyone using one of the designs. Reading should be completed prior to meeting with a consultant for advice on design or statistical analysis. The book provides much more than a standard research methods text and is a valuable addition to the bookshelf of any aspiring researcher in the social or behavioral sciences.

Davis, G. B., & Parker, C. A. (1979). *Writing the doctoral dissertation: A systematic approach.* Baron's Educational Series.

An inexpensive paperback that provides a view of proposal and dissertation writing from the vantage point of business management. Accordingly, it is no surprise to find performance checklists, schedule projections, procedures for interacting with advisors and committees, instructions for design of computer analysis, and a complete model for dissertation management at the center of this handbook. The chapters on topic selection and proposal development, collectively 40 pages, provide a step-by-step guide, as well as a good deal of sound advice. As with the present text, Davis and Parker link proposal development first to the tasks to be accomplished, and then to the major subsections of the document. The social science designs used for illustration will be comfortable for readers in a wide variety of disciplines. Altogether, the management approach to dissertation writing makes a great deal of sense—particularly for those whose organizational skills might profit from improved planning and greater structure.

Davitz, J. R., & Davitz, L. J. (1977). *Evaluating research proposals in the behavioral sciences* (2nd ed.). New York: Teachers College Press.

This revised and expanded edition of the authors' widely used *A Guide for Evaluating Research Plans in Psychology* is designed for students involved in planning or critically evaluating research studies. The first part of the guide, "Criteria for Evaluating a Research Plan," contains a summary of the essential points to be considered in evaluating research proposals. The discussion of each of these points is preceded by a list of important questions students should ask about research. The second part of the guide, "The Language of Research," defines important terms and concepts employed in behavioral research and illustrates their use with concrete examples and applications.

Day, R. A. (1983). *How to write and publish a scientific paper* (2nd ed.). Philadelphia: ISI Press.

Although the author did not set out to address issues related to the proposal process, he provides an excellent overview of the writing process for young scholars. In a logical sequence, he examines each aspect of writing a paper for publication. Topics in the book include how to prepare a title, list the authors, design a table and submit or present a paper. Chapters in the second half of the book give attention to the mechanics of writing and provide an overview of important concepts in scholarly exposition. While the book is written from the perspective of a scholar in the natural sciences, it requires no specific knowledge of that area. The liberal and effective use of humor throughout the book makes easy reading for both novices and experienced writers.

Kalish, S. E., McCullum, J., Henry, Y., Schoenthaler, A., & Grady, S. (Eds.). (1984). *The proposal writer's swipe file.* Washington, DC: Taft Corporation.

This work contains 15 prototype proposals. All were prepared by experts and all were successfully funded. Only lightly edited, the documents are printed in their original formats. These are not applications for funds to support research, but just about every other type of proposal is represented. Those proposals were prepared to seek support for curriculum projects in higher education include examples in the areas of social, biological, and physical sciences. For anyone who has never seen a real proposal, or wants to review a number of proposals from a variety of areas, this is the perfect resource.

Krathwohl, D. R. (1965). *How to prepare a research proposal.* Syracuse, NY: Syracuse University Bookstore.

In 50 concise pages, Krathwohl examines the considerations that must be confronted during the formulation of a grant proposal. This monograph provides suggestions for writing the main proposal sections: problem statement, related research, objectives, procedures, design, and facilities. It also provides practical information helpful to solving the nettlesome problems of constructing a budget, explaining personnel to be used, and developing a workable time frame for the project. Suggestions even are made for writing an abstract of the proposed study. The table of contents serves the dual purpose of organizing the monograph's content and providing a checklist with which to analyze a proposal's strengths and weaknesses. The book may be obtained from the Syracuse University Bookstore, 303 University Plaza, Syracuse, NY 13201.

Lauffer, A. (1983). *Grantsmanship.* Newbury Park, CA: Sage.

In this easy to read book, a master of grantsmanship and resource development describes in step-by-step detail how to write successful proposals for grants to support social service programs. The author makes clear the distinctions among government, foundation, and business/professional sources of funding. This book does not describe the specific process of developing research proposals, but the imaginative reader will find that many of the suggested procedures travel well from social service to scholarship.

Strategies to use in working with different kinds of funding sources are described in detail. This includes a discussion of how various review processes work, and differences in the review criteria used by various grantors. Also included are excellent exercises designed to develop the analytical skills described in the chapters. Sections on what to do after the proposal has been submitted, how to deal with rejection, and how to swing into action if the proposal is funded make this text a particularly useful guide for the beginner.

Leedy, P. D. (1985). *Practical research: Planning and design* (3rd. ed.). New York: Macmillan.

This large (313 pages) softcover textbook is used widely in introductory-level, undergraduate, research courses. Styled as a "do-it-yourself, understand-it-yourself" manual, the content covers both methods for conducting research and guidelines for writing about research. This is a generic rather than a subject-specific text. Language, illustrations, and reference material have been selected to allow use in a wide range of professional and disciplinary areas. Taken together, chapters dealing with the research problem, the literature review, the research plan, and the research proposal, plus a fully critiqued proposal contained in the appendices, constitute the most extensive coverage of proposal development in any contemporary textbook. The chapter on 'Writing the Proposal," however, provides only 7 pages of general commentary on the specific demands associated with the document itself. The 25-page specimen proposal may be more useful to many beginners, both for its detail and for Professor Leedy's astute commentary. The generic content and survey format will not meet the needs of most graduate students.

Madsen, D. (1982). *Successful dissertations and theses: A guide to graduate student research from proposal to completion.* San Francisco: Jossey-Bass.

This book provides some practical advice for graduate students about to undertake the task of completing the thesis or dissertation requirement. The author discusses the dissertation process from initial preparation for the comprehensive exam to final composition of a journal article based on the completed dissertation. Only one chapter is devoted to the research proposal, and much of the advice is general rather than specific. The section devoted to starting the dissertation may be particularly valuable to those having trouble getting underway.

Smith, R. V. (1984). *Graduate research: A guide for students in the sciences.* Philadelphia: ISI Press.

Although intended for students in the natural and biomedical sciences, this book will be valuable for students in all fields. The author provides an overview of the graduate student experience in research-oriented departments and universities. The book begins with a review of department and university organization, information that may be particularly helpful to graduate students attempting to understand the structure of graduate education. The chapters on "Ethics and the Scientist" and "Research with Human Subjects, Animals, and Biohazards," and an appendix containing advice on preparing consent forms for human subjects, will be especially valuable to novice researchers.

White, V. P. (1975). *Grants: How to find out about them and what to do next.* New York: Plenum Press.

Written in a happier and more affluent time, the optimistic tone of this popular text might be tempered if prepared today. The sections dealing with information sources and government offices have long since been outdated, but the three central chapters dealing with the application process are as sound today as a decade ago. Accompanied by specimen pages, the author begins with "What to Do Before You Apply" and proceeds through detailed specifications for writing the proposal, to end with an insightful chapter on "How Grants Are Awarded." For anyone who has never prepared a projected budget, the advice and illustrations dealing with this subject will be invaluable.

APPENDIX C

Standards for the Use of
Human Subjects and Specimen Forms
for Informed Consent

Most colleges and universities have an Institutional Review Board (IRB) responsible for overseeing and approving research involving human subjects. At some larger universities, departments may have human subject review committees that first act on the proposed research and then report to the IRB. Whether the study proposal is associated with a graduate degree or with a grant application, investigators should obtain the guidelines for human subject review at their institution, and do so early in the preparation process.

An almost universal step in conducting research with human subjects is obtaining the informed consent of each participant. Subjects must have the opportunity to be informed about the study (particularly what they will be required to do, and the risks and benefits of that participation), ask any questions they might have, make a decision as to whether they wish to participate, and sign a letter of informed consent. Chapter 3 contains a detailed discussion of informed consent accompanied by a listing of the primary requirements in that process.

The three informed consent letters presented in this appendix are edited examples from successfully completed research projects. The individual documents reflect the specific demands for informed consent in each research context. The first example is from a laboratory study. The second and third examples are from a field study conducted in a school setting where both teacher and parental consent were required. By changing the details, these letters can be adapted for use in other research settings.

SAMPLE A: LABORATORY STUDY

letterhead of the institution/agency

You are invited to participate in a study in which the response speed of young and older adults is examined in the following tasks: (1) reacting as rapidly as possible to a light stimulus by saying the consonants "ss" and "zz" into a microphone, and (2) reacting as rapidly as possible to a light stimulus by pressing one or two fingers against microswitches.

Data compiled from your performance will be kept in strict confidence at all times. Only the investigator and supervising professor will have access to the information. Following the collection of data your individual identity will be removed from all records. In this manner, information regarding your participation will be kept confidential.

Possible risk factors from your participation are no greater than normal daily activity. However, you cannot expect to be compensated for any discomforts or injury as a result of your participation in the experiment described here. The investigator in this study is L. L. Student. The supervising professor is Dr. X. Bert Supervisor. If you have any questions that we have not answered in person you may contact either of us at 555-1234.

Your signature below indicates that you have decided to participate in this study and that you have read and understood the information in this consent form. Your decision to participate in this study will not prejudice your present or future association with this university. If you decide to participate, you are free to withdraw consent and discontinue participation at any time without prejudice. If you desire a copy of this consent form, one will be provided for you.

Thank you.

Participant's signature _____ Date_____
Principal Investigator_____ Date_____
Signature of witness_____ Date_____

SAMPLE B: FIELD STUDY

letterhead of the institution/agency

I would like to request your cooperation in the conduct of a study of instruction in classes you are teaching this year. The study is titled "A comprehensive investigation of the correlates of instructional effectiveness." We hope to learn more about how teacher and student behaviors are important for learning. This information will contribute to research in education, and may be beneficial to future teachers.

If you should decide to participate, you will be asked to teach a two week unit of instruction wearing a miniature microphone. The class will be videotaped for future coding of teacher and student behaviors. Students will be pretested and posttested. Your students will be asked to maintain the same seating patterns throughout the course of instruction. Should you decide to participate, one thirty minute orientation session will be required prior to beginning the study.

Any information obtained in connection with this study that can be identified with you will remain confidential and will be disclosed only with your permission. Only averages and other descriptive statistics will be reported in any publication. In addition, only three trained coders associated with the university will view the tapes and none will be able to identify you by name. Your decision as to whether or not to participate will not prejudice your relations with the Department of Education or the University. If you decide to participate, you are completely free to withdraw consent and discontinue participation at any time.

If you have any additional questions, please contact me at 555-1234. Thank you.

Sincerely,

A. Professor
Assistant Professor

You may keep the top part of this form.
. . . .

I have decided to participate in a study of learning, to wear a miniature microphone while teaching the unit of instruction, and to allow my class to be pretested, posttested, and videotaped. My signature indicates that I have read the information above and have decided to participate. I realize that I may withdraw without prejudice at any time after signing this form should I decide to do so.

_____   _____

Signature   Date

SAMPLE C: PARENTAL INFORMED CONSENT

letterhead of the institution/agency

Dear Parent:

I am presently involved in the preparation of future teachers at State University. I am interested in the aspects of schooling which relate to how students learn to read. This information is valuable in preparing teachers and can contribute to our knowledge of how to help students improve their reading skills.

I would like permission for your child to participate in a study which will be conducted as a part of his or her regularly scheduled class. The only changes from the normal class will be an initial test of student reading ability and the fact that each class, for a two week period, will be videotaped. Your son or daughter will be identified on the videotape, but at no time will their scores on the tests or their videotapes be available to anyone but researchers involved in this study. Students will not be identified by name at anytime in any reports of this research. If you decide to allow your child to participate you are completely free to withdraw consent and discontinue your child's participation at any time.

As the results of this study are completed, I will provide the principal with a summary which will be available to you upon request. If you have any questions, please contact me at 555-1234.

Please sign and return this form as soon as possible. Thank you very much.

Sincerely,

A. Professor
Assistant Professor

Child's Name _____
Child's Date of Birth _____
Parent Approval (signature) _____
Date _____

Index

About the Authors

LAWRENCE F. LOCKE is Professor of Education and Physical Education, and Chairperson of the Department of Professional Preparation at the University of Massachusetts at Amherst. A native of Connecticut, he received bachelor's and master's degrees from Springfield College and his doctorate from Stanford University. He has been a prolific writer on the production and utilization of research on teaching and teacher education. As a teacher, graduate student advisor, and consultant he has supervised the preparation of many research proposals and taught a wide variety of classes related to the proposal development process.

WANEEN WYRICK SPIRDUSO is Ashbel Smith Professor and Interim Dean of the College of Education at the University of Texas at Austin. She is a native of Austin, and holds bachelor's and doctoral degrees from the University of Texas and a master's degree from the University of North Carolina at Greensburo. Professor Spirduso's research focuses on the effects of aging on the mechanisms of motor control. She has directed students in the proposal process for over two decades and has received numerous research grants from the federal government.

STEPHEN J. SILVERMAN is Assistant Professor in the Department of Physical and Health Education at the University of Texas at Austin. He is a native of Philadelphia, and holds a bachelor's degree from Temple University, a master's degree from Washington State University and a doctoral degree from the University of Massachusetts at Amherst. Professor Silverman's research focuses on teaching and learning in physical education. He currently teaches classes in research methods and statistics.

NOTES